Praise for GIRL SLEUTH

"Through the history of Nancy Drew, Rehak sheds light on perhaps the most successful writing franchise of all time and also the cultural and historic changes through which it passed. Grab your flashlights, girls. The mystery of Carolyn Keene is about to begin."
— Karen Joy Fowler, author of *The Jane Austen Book Club*

"Melanie Rehak chronicles a character who influenced at least two generations of women (and certainly women mystery authors) in a highly readable, exhaustive book designed to give the perky teen her due."
— *The Boston Phoenix*

"Amiable and thorough. Rehak does a terrific job of bringing to life the writers and editors who constituted Carolyn Keene."
— *The New York Times Book Review*

"Melanie Rehak unspools the fascinating story of how Nancy came to be. [An] absorbing and delightful book." — *The Wall Street Journal*

"For longtime Nancy fans who pick up Rehak's book, just one warning: You will not have read more than a chapter or two before you are filled with longing to return to the world of River Heights. Don't begin this book unless you remember where you stashed your own copy of *The Secret of the Old Clock*." — *The Christian Science Monitor*

"Whatever becomes of [Nancy Drew's] future... Rehak has given her past its due in this vivid, unpretentious and sympathetic history."
— *Newsday*

"Grown-up fans can comfort themselves with Melanie Rehak's wonderful *Girl Sleuth*. A fascinating tale." — MSNBC.com

"Rehak's book is such an engrossing read that it made me hungry for some Nancy Drews. Rehak writes with gusto and intelligence about Benson and Adams, their publishing worlds and American women's history. She's a good sport. She does her work with spirit, and she does it well. In the end she solves the mystery of where Nancy Drew came from and how she grew. Nancy would be so proud." — *Chicago Tribune*

"In *Girl Sleuth*, critic Melanie Rehak cracks the case of the [Nancy Drew] series' origins." — *Entertainment Weekly*

GIRL SLEUTH

GIRL SLEUTH

NANCY DREW
AND THE WOMEN
WHO CREATED HER

Melanie Rehak

A Harvest Book
Harcourt, Inc.

Orlando Austin New York San Diego Toronto London

Requests for permission to make copies of any part of the work should be submitted online at
www.harcourt.com/contact or mailed to the following address: Permissions Department,
Harcourt, Inc., 6277 Sea Harbor Drive, Orlando, Florida 32887-6777.

www.HarcourtBooks.com

Letters and memos from the Stratemeyer Syndicate Records (1832–1984)
in the Manuscripts and Archives Division, New York Public Library, Astor, Lenox and
Tilden Foundations, are used in this book by permission of Simon & Schuster, Inc.
All rights reserved. NANCY DREW is a registered trademark of Simon & Schuster, Inc.

NANCY DREW MYSTERY SERIES® NANCY DREW and all related characters and images
from the frontispieces of *The Clue in the Diary, Mystery at the Moss Covered Mansion*, and
Mystery at the Ski Jump, the 1973, 1969, 1946 book covers from *The Mystery of the Tolling Bell*,
and photograph of Harriet S. Adams are © and registered trademarks of Simon & Schuster, Inc.
All rights reserved. The classic hardcover editions of these Nancy Drew titles are available
from Grosset & Dunlap, an imprint of Penguin Books for Young Readers.

Material from the Mildred Augustine Wirt Benson Papers reprinted by permission of the Iowa
Women's Archives, University of Iowa Libraries, Iowa City. Material from Stratemeyer Syndicate
Records reprinted courtesy of Beinecke Rare Book and Manuscripts Library, Yale University.
Material from the Wellesley College Archives reprinted courtesy of the Wellesley College
Archives, Margaret Clapp Library, Wellesley, MA. Material from the *Toledo Blade*
and the *Toledo Times* reprinted by permission of the *Toledo Blade*.

The Library of Congress has cataloged the hardcover edition as follows:
Rehak, Melanie.
Girl sleuth: Nancy Drew and the women who created her/Melanie Rehak.—1st ed.
p. cm.
Includes bibliographical references and index.
1. Wirt, Mildred A. (Mildred Augustine), 1905– Characters—Nancy Drew.
2. Detective and mystery stories, American—History and criticism. 3. Women and literature—
United States—History—20th century. 4. American fiction—Women authors—History and
criticism. 5. Young adult fiction, American—History and criticism. 6. Adams, Harriet
Stratemeyer—Characters—Nancy Drew. 7. Young adult fiction—Publishing—United States.
8. Girls—Books and reading—United States. 9. Keene, Carolyn—Characters—Nancy Drew.
10. Drew, Nancy (Fictitious character). 11. Teenage girls in literature.
12. Stratemeyer Syndicate. I. Title.
PS3545.I774Z874 2005
813'.52—dc22   2005009129
ISBN-13: 978-0-15-101041-7 ISBN-10: 0-15-101041-2
ISBN-13: 978-0-15-603056-4 (pbk.) ISBN-10: 0-15-603056-X (pbk.)

Text set in Electra
Designed by Lydia D'moch

Printed in the United States of America
First Harvest edition 2006
A C E G I K J H F D B

To my family

CONTENTS

INTRODUCTION

GRAB YOUR MAGNIFYING glass, because this is a mystery story. At first glance, its star is a girl detective, a legendary foiler of plots and teen avatar of justice. But, really, the mystery lies beyond the realm of her adventures. It's in the story of how she came to be an American icon and why she's stayed one for decades. It's in the lives of the man who dreamed her up and the women who shepherded her into existence and molded her character. Most of all, it's in the long-buried secret behind the identity of Carolyn Keene, the woman who has kept generations of little girls sneaking a flashlight under the covers after bedtime to finish reading just one more chapter of a Nancy Drew Mystery Story.

For some of us, who had our flashlights summarily removed by mothers and fathers in the know, more creative methods were required. At the age of about ten, I used to pretend I was afraid of the dark so that my parents would leave the light on in the hallway outside my bedroom, then I would flip around in my bed and hang over the bottom edge. Straining to hold my book at such an angle that it would catch the sliver of light from the doorway, I would keep going until the lines literally blurred in front of my eyes. My favorite title, which I must have read and reread dozens of times between the ages of eight and twelve, was *The Mystery of the Tolling Bell*. As always, it featured Nancy—"eighteen and attractive...unusually sensible, clever, and talented," with her trademark red-gold hair, which often blew in the wind to appealing effect; tomboy George, "athletic looking, with short dark hair"; and George's cousin Bess, giggly and slightly plump, as she was in every book. The story concerned a cliff-side sea cavern haunted by a ghost who was said to ring a warning bell just before the tide rushed in and turned the rocky chamber into a watery grave for anyone caught there. It was crammed with Nancy's do-gooder sense of responsibility, loads of French phrases (primarily concerning a subplot involving a phony cosmetics company called Mon Coeur) that Nancy had no trouble translating for her pals, and fascinating information on the history and making of bells. There were also the usual twists and turns, painted with none-too-subtle strokes. Nancy was knocked unconscious—a feature of many books in the series—and there were secret passageways and an evil man named Grumper. At one point, Nancy and George tie up a thief and sit on his chest to make sure he doesn't escape. The teen sleuth, as always, figures it all out in the end, including how the mysterious bell is being rung by the ocean tides and who's behind the phony cosmetics. She pronounces her solution in a speech studded with exclamation points: "'Just as I thought!' Nancy told herself as she hugged the damp wall to keep from being seen. 'This is the interior of the tolling-bell cave! And the ghost can only be one person—Grumper!'"

As was often the case, this revelation was not sufficient to put Nancy out of danger. Instead, it led immediately to her near death in the spooky cave. She was saved, in part, by her boyfriend Ned Nickerson, but she was careful not to rely on him too much. The book's final exchange was a masterful display of the coy deferral that was Nancy's trademark when it came to Ned, which I loved as much as the craggy cave scenes and the road trips in the famous blue car.

"Mysteries!" Ned exclaimed, turning out the lantern. "Haven't you had enough of them?"

Nancy was sure she never would have. Soon an intriguing invitation would involve her in another baffling mystery, *The Clue in the Old Album.*

"Anyway," said Ned, "there's one puzzle I wish you would solve for me."

"What's that?"

"Why you always change the subject when I try to talk to you about something that isn't a bit mysterious!"

Nancy smiled and said, "Ned, someday I promise to listen."

The books I read had been my older sister's. They were hardback, with alluring yellow spines and the cover illustration printed right onto the boards. *The Mystery of the Tolling Bell,* in particular, had numerous chocolaty fingerprints on the pages where the action was tense. I happened to know, though, that there had been other editions before these; my mother had described them to me. Her Nancy Drews were royal blue hardbacks with a shocking orange silhouette of Nancy and her magnifying glass on them, covered in bright dust jackets illustrating a scene from the plot. She had read them with a zeal equal to mine all through the 1940s. These books — or, rather, their absence — had long since attained mythic status in our household. One of the most familiar refrains of my childhood was my mother lamenting the loss of her Nancy Drews, which had been given away by her mother to other gleeful recipients after she grew up. If only she had known, my mother would say, she would have told my grandmother to hang on to them for my sister and me.

But, of course, no one knew. No one knew that the girl detective dreamed up in 1929 by a wildly imaginative children's book author named Edward Stratemeyer would go on to become one of the bestselling characters of all time. Even Stratemeyer himself, who at the time of Nancy Drew's debut was a juvenile publishing legend and millionaire thanks to the success of his earlier series—including the Bobbsey Twins and the Hardy Boys—didn't have an inkling. No one knew that Nancy Drew would be adored by little girls for thirty years, and then, just as it seemed her power was waning, deified by women's libbers who recognized her as one of their own even though she would never have thought of marching for her rights or against a war: "I was such a Nancy Drew fan...and I'd love to know how many of us who are feminists right now in our 30s read those books," the president of the National Organization for Women (NOW) told a newspaper in 1976. No one knew the sleuth would be turned into a movie character in the 1930s and a TV character in the 1970s, and that both ventures would be, instead of the instant hits that were anticipated, total failures. It turned out that regardless of the decade, readers were so loyal to the Nancy they knew that even the slightest change in appearance or tone made them furious.

But what her fans didn't realize was that Nancy Drew had not remained static on the page, either. The books I read as a child in the 1970s were not the ones my mother had read, even when they shared a title. The sleuth had become at once more modern and more genteel in the intervening years, and her adventures had gone from the atmospheric yarns of the early days—lots of rainstorms and scenic descriptions—to more action-packed, streamlined plots that fared better in competition with television and the movies. She had been through two different writers and a host of editors, all of whom tried to imprint her with their own beliefs about who America's preeminent teen detective should be. But even had I been aware of this, it wouldn't have made a difference. My Nancy was the real Nancy as much as my mother's was, and all of these Nancys had long since elevated the character from the pages of cheap serial novels into the pantheon of American culture.

The reason for this exalted progression became clear when I recently read all fifty-six original Nancy Drews. I discovered that the series often relies on formulaic dialogue, totally implausible escapes, and absurd plot twists that Agatha Christie would never have approved of. But I also realized that the stories themselves are secondary. What we remember is Nancy: her bravery, her style, her generosity, and her relentless desire to succeed linger long after the last page has been turned, the villain sent to jail, the trusty car put into the garage. Even though hardly anyone can recall what, exactly, went on in *The Hidden Staircase* or *The Whispering Statue* or *The Quest of the Missing Map*, we know precisely what it was about Nancy that held our rapt attention for so many years. She remains as much a part of the idea of American girlhood as slumber parties, homework, and bubble gum. As one editorial published in the early 1980s asked, perfectly seriously: "If there is a woman who during childhood's hours did not mold a clay dish, bake an Indian pudding, join the Brownies, and carry the high notes of the National Anthem at school, is there one who never read Nancy Drew?"

There was not then, and there is not now. Rarely a year has gone by in the last fifty or so—ever since the first generation of little girls who read the Nancy Drew Mystery Stories got old enough to write newspaper and magazine articles—without someone, somewhere, attesting to the power of the teen sleuth in passionate print. Among the paeans are essays by wives, lawyers, doctors, journalists, and even the occasional father. Feminist mystery writer Sara Paretsky wrote a tribute to her called "Keeping Nancy Drew Alive." Another adoring fan titled her valentine to the teen detective "I Owe It All to Nancy Drew." Novelist Bobbie Ann Mason went so far as to write an entire book about the beloved girl detectives of her childhood, with Nancy as its star. "I'm still a girl sleuth, setting my magnifying glass onto words and images and the great mysteries of life," she writes in the introduction to the new edition (originally published in 1975, the book was reissued in 1995).

By now there are countless examples of Nancy Drew as the very embodiment of all things industrious, intrepid, and truthful in a world where such role models are too few. She's still the one we turn to as a representative of our best interests—even our national ones. Global terrorism? It's not too tough for the girl detective, who, at least in the opinions of some people, might be an improvement over the officials actually in charge of gathering evidence. Writing in the *New York Times* about the intelligence failures before September 11 and then–National Security Advisor Condoleezza Rice's complaints that intelligence reports "don't tell us where, they don't tell us who, and they don't tell us how," Maureen Dowd retorted with a three-word answer: "Paging Nancy Drew." From the moment I began working on this book, it seemed someone, somewhere, was calling me at least once a week to tell me about a Nancy sighting, and newspaper clippings from around the country that mentioned her appeared in my mailbox regularly. The spontaneous gasps of pleasure that her name evoked at first amazed me, and then became routine (though they still pleased me). Her name (or, appropriately less often, Ned Nickerson's) is often the only solution to a crossword clue that frustrated puzzlers can figure out.

All of this attests to the enduring presence of Nancy Drew, but none of it answers the question of *why* she has endured. Certainly she taught all her readers many things that are useful no matter what the era or circumstances. We learned from her how to think for ourselves, how to jump eagerly into adventure and then get out of the scrapes it inevitably involves, how to get to the truth, and, perhaps most importantly, how to spin into action when things are not right. We also learned how to dress properly for the events at hand, to make tea sandwiches and carry on polite conversation, and to be good friends to both those we love and those in need. All of these things remained constant, even when the details surrounding them—the clothes, the location, the slang—shifted with the times.

Nancy's great appeal and strength, we all assumed, flowed directly from her author, the famous Carolyn Keene. Beloved as quickly and completely as the detective she wrote about, she was the woman every little girl imagined as the prototype for Nancy herself, a woman who had not only been as daring and clever as Nancy when she was a child, but had grown up to write about it. From the beginning, readers sent letters to "Miss Keene" by the hundreds, asking her to help them with problems, offering plot suggestions, telling her about their attempts to solve mysteries of their own, and expressing their undying love of both her and Nancy Drew.

There was no Carolyn Keene. She was simply a pen name,

one of many dreamed up by Edward Stratemeyer in his crowded Manhattan office. Nevertheless, we were not wrong in our assumptions about where Nancy got her power—we just didn't realize we were getting two trailblazers rolled into one. Their names were Harriet Stratemeyer Adams and Mildred Wirt Benson.

Along with her sister, Edna, Harriet Adams inherited her father's children's book company, the Stratemeyer Syndicate, at the time of his death in 1930. A graduate of Wellesley College with no business experience and four young children at home, she became that rarity even today, a female CEO, during the early years of the Depression. She thought more of honoring the family name than going against tradition, and she ignored, among other things, the comments of people who thought her children would be ruined by her career. She stood firm against the men in publishing who she felt treated her like a little girl and worried about how to take care of her family while also running a company long before there were any resources for working mothers, or even much sympathy. She also loved to throw a good party and routinely opened her New Jersey farm and summerhouse, Birdhaven, for everything from weddings to office picnics to Easter egg hunts. From the mid-1950s on, Harriet, in addition to being a mother, wife, and businesswoman, was Carolyn Keene, a role she embraced completely, never once dwelling on the inconvenient fact that someone else had filled it before her.

That someone was Mildred Augustine Wirt Benson, Nancy Drew's original author. Benson grew up in a small town in rural Iowa, and, in addition to being a diving champion, was the first woman to get a master's degree in journalism from the University of Iowa. She was a quick, determined reporter both before and after the women's pages—a section for which she refused to write as long as she lived, referring to it with characteristic disdain as "jams and jellies"—became a regular feature of American newspapers. Like so many women, the fictional character she most admired as a young girl was stalwart, intelligent, and slightly obstreperous Jo March of Louisa May Alcott's *Little Women*, whom she found reassuringly "at odds with so many of the day's domestic-type fictional heroines." Though she was just slightly taller than five feet, Benson had such force of character that at the age of ninety-three she was described by a cowed fellow reporter as having "a tangle of white curls and the dismissive air of Robert De Niro."

Like the woman each of us imagined Carolyn Keene to be, Harriet and Mildred were modern—ahead of their times, even. Outwardly very different, they had a fierce determination in common. More than that, though, they were pioneers during periods of both great progress and great regression for women in this country, examples of persistence and strength and a reminder that even at moments in history—the turn of the century, the late 1920s, the 1950s—that we tend to think of as sorry times for women's rights, there were always women who simply refused to be held back. Both Carolyn Keenes were tough when they needed to be, adventurous, and utterly unwilling to bend to the will of others. And while they disagreed with one another on the particulars of Nancy's behavior, both Harriet and Mildred envisioned her as a girl who could do what she wanted in a world that was largely the province of men, just as each of them had done.

In their stories lie not only the details of women's progress in America over the last century, but the secrets behind the character who inspired the pioneers of that progress to keep going forward in the face of adversity. Like Nancy Drew's, Harriet's and Mildred's histories have remained untold until now, but once you've delved into them, you'll never again be able to think of the girl sleuth without thinking of the women behind her. It's as impossible to imagine Nancy without their influence as it is to imagine American women without Nancy's. A role model for millions of girls, she has always been that most elusive, more essential thing as well: a trusted companion. One grateful adult appreciator wrote in the early 1980s: "As a 9-year-old, I felt that Nancy Drew was as much my friend as Ellen Kreloff down the block or Denise Walker around the corner." There is no higher praise, really. Governed as it is by the wild and mysterious inner lives of little girls, the neighborhood club has always been one of the toughest gangs to crack—even for a detective.

1

THE STRATEMEYER CLAN

These suggestions are for a new series for girls verging on novels. 224 pages, to retail at fifty cents. I have called this line the "Stella Strong Stories," but they might also be called "Diana Drew Stories," "Diana Dare Stories," "Nan Nelson Stories," "Nan Drew Stories" or "Helen Hale Stories"...

Stella Strong, a girl of sixteen, is the daughter of a District Attorney of many years standing. He is a widower and often talks over his affairs with Stella and the girl was present during many interviews her father had with noted detectives and at the solving of many intricate mysteries. Then, quite unexpectedly, Stella plunged into some mysteries of her own and found herself wound up in a series of exciting situations. An up-to-date American girl at her best, bright, clever, resourceful and full of energy.

IN SEPTEMBER of 1929 children's book mogul Edward Stratemeyer sent one of his inimitable typed memos to Grosset &

Dunlap, his longtime publisher, describing a new line of books he hoped they would launch the following spring. Though he proved to have an uncharacteristically tin ear when it came to choosing a name for his heroine—any other option on his list of possibilities had a better ring to it than "Stella"—his sense of her life and her intrepid personality were flawless. While they had no way of knowing that Stratemeyer's girl detective would eventually become a celebrity not only in the children's book world but in the world at large, Grosset & Dunlap's editors certainly knew a good thing when they saw it. They accepted Stratemeyer's series on the basis of his memo, which also included brief plotlines for the first five books in the series, and his reputation, which, by the time "Nan Drew" burst on to the scene with her fashionable outfits and boundless intelligence, had been the source of admiration and envy—and a great fortune for Stratemeyer—for several decades. When his latest proposal reached their Manhattan office, he had been writing for children for more than forty years and was so steeped in the idiom of his chosen genre that he had given even the events of his own life—which were rather straightforward and businesslike when it came down to it—the sheen and thrill of a juvenile story.

This transformation had begun at the moment of his first serious publication in a children's story paper in November of 1889. It was a fanciful tale called "Victor Horton's Idea," and it told of a boy who went out into the world to live life—unsuccessfully, it would transpire—like the characters in his favorite dime novels.

> Victor was fifteen years old, naturally bright and lively, and if he had not held so high of an opinion of himself, he would have been a first-rate lad.

Besides being conceited, Victor was dissatisfied with the quietness of country life. He longed to go forth into the great world and achieve fame and fortune.

Now, though this idea is often a very laudable one, it was not so in the present instance. Victor's idea upon the subject had been gathered wholly from the pages of numerous dime novels and disreputable story papers loaned him by his particular crony, Sam Wilson, and was, therefore, of a deceptive and unsubstantial nature, and likely to do more harm than good.

The details of Victor's exploits appeared in installments over five weeks, crammed into the narrow columns of a richly illustrated black-and-white children's broadsheet out of Philadelphia called *Golden Days for Boys and Girls* (subscription price $3 per annum). Alongside them ran informative articles with titles like "How to Make a Guitar" ("Those who have read the articles on 'Violin Making' and have succeeded in making one would, perhaps, like to make a guitar if they knew what a simple matter it is"); interesting trivia; and true stories about heroic rescues of humans by dogs.

Stratemeyer was twenty-six years old, tall, slender, and bespectacled, with a brushy mustache, dark hair combed back off a high forehead, and a preternatural instinct for the arc of a good tale for young people. He had, according to one news report, "a scholarly appearance...and his eyes are a trifle contracted from constant application to his work." Indeed, in person, Stratemeyer betrayed no signs of the flights of fancy that had produced Victor and would go on to invent countless other young scalawags, heroes, and heroines over the next forty years. As one reporter would later describe him, he was "a tranquil-faced man, with kind, good-humored eyes...[and] a curiously deliberate manner of speaking. One doubts if he has ever been hurried into a decision or ever given an answer to a question without earnest consideration." He also had a healthy sense of perspective on his chosen field. By the end of Victor Horton's travails, the young man announces to his hapless friend Sam: "Dime novels are a first-class fraud!"

Nonetheless, they were the field that Stratemeyer aimed to get into. Myth had it that he had written "Victor Horton's Idea" on a sheet of brown package paper during quiet moments while clerking at his brother's tobacco store in Newark, New Jersey. In spite of having recorded very clearly in his own notes that he had written the story at home, Stratemeyer, knowing better than most the value of a good yarn, repeated the entertaining falsehood about its conception whenever he was asked to. As one news feature of the era printed it, complete with the final triumph of will and self-knowledge over discouragement:

> His initial long story—18,000 words—was written on store wrapping paper and later copied onto white paper. The author, who was then twenty-five, was not satisfied with it so he laid it aside. After a year…he revised the manuscript carefully and sent it to *Golden Days*. The check for $75 he received Stratemeyer bore proudly to his father, Henry J. Stratemeyer. "Look at this," he said. The father, who had told him he was wasting his time writing the tale and might be better engaged in a more useful activity, regarded the check, then jerked up his glasses. "Why, it's a check made out to you!" he exclaimed. Stratemeyer explained he had received it for the story the parent had tried to discourage. "Paid you that for writing a story?" his father repeated. "Well, you'd better write a lot more of them."

In addition to his paycheck, Stratemeyer received something even more valuable: some sage—not to mention prophetic—advice from the editor of *Golden Days*. "I think you would become a good serial writer if you were to know just what was required, always remembering that each 'to be continued' must mark a holding point in the story." The young author not only took these words fully to heart, but would incorporate them, practically verbatim, into his own advice to writers for years to come.

Born on October 4, 1862, Edward Stratemeyer was the youngest of six children, three of them half-brothers, and all of them musically or artistically talented. His father, Henry Julius Stratemeyer, had come to the United States from Germany in 1837, along with a wave of German immigrants that only got larger and larger as the nineteenth century progressed. Many of them, including Henry Stratemeyer, headed out to the California coast in search of the shiniest, most tempting American dream of them all: gold. By 1851, though, Henry had mined more fool's gold than the actual metal, and he headed back east to Elizabeth, New Jersey, to visit his brother, George, also an émigré; his brother's wife, Anna, and the couple's three sons. Surrounded by family, Henry decided to stay in Elizabeth and settled into shopkeeping, advertising himself as a "wholesale and retail dealer in tobacco, cigars, snuff and pipes."

Two years after his brother's arrival in New Jersey, George Stratemeyer was stricken during a cholera epidemic. Knowing death was near, he asked Henry to stay in America and look after his family. Henry agreed, and in 1854, not long after George's death, he married his brother's widow, making his three nephews into his stepsons. Henry and Anna went on to have three more children: Louis Charles, born in 1856; Anna, born in 1859; and Edward, born in 1862. The family was well established in the cultured, comfortable merchant circle of Elizabeth and was barely touched by the War Between the States. Neither a military man nor a willing volunteer, the elder Stratemeyer had no trouble staying out of it.

As they grew, the Stratemeyer boys were put to work in their father's thriving tobacco store, in order that he might teach them the basics of commerce and, especially, entrepreneurship. The children also received musical training. Edward's sister, Anna, who would become an accomplished pianist, received her entire schooling at a prominent conservatory in town. Edward, on the other hand, was educated in the public schools of Elizabeth, and though he had an ear for music, too, preferred language. "You ask when I first wanted to become an author," he wrote to an acquaintance in 1919. "I think I must have been about six years old when I attempted to write my first story." He displayed an early interest in publishing, as well, running around his neighborhood with a toy printing press—an accoutrement that was all the rage at the time—turning out items for the pleasure of his friends and family. He would interview local residents about the goings-on in their lives during the week, then print up their answers in a newspaper that he sold back to them, at the price of one cent, on Saturday mornings.

Two chapbooks followed, with the entertaining, inscrutable titles *That Bottle of Vinegar* (1877) and *The Tale of a Lumberman as Told by Himself* (1878). The latter included, in bold black-and-white, the confident statement "E. STRATEMEYER PUBLISHER" on its cover. Stratemeyer was just sixteen years old, but he had grown up reading the books of Oliver Optic (the nom de plume of William T. Adams) and Horatio Alger, the two predominant boys' fiction authors of the period, and the adventure-filled, rags-to-riches stories, as well as their action-packed dime-novel counterparts, left an impression on him that lasted well into his adult years. As he recalled fondly in an interview: "I had quite a library, including many of Optic's and Alger's books. At seven or eight, when I was reading them, I said, 'If only I could write books like that I'd be the happiest person on earth.'"

Stratemeyer graduated from Elizabeth High School, the vale-
dictorian of his class of three. Afterward, as was the norm for even
a middle-class boy—only 1 percent of Americans attended college in the 1870s—he received two years of private tutoring in
rhetoric, composition, and literature. He continued to combine
clerking in a tobacco store—his brother Maurice's this time—
with writing, refining his stories, and selling them to the story
papers that were appearing all over the country, like the *Penny
Magazine* (which paid him $1 for "A Horrible Crime"), the *Ex-
periment*, and the *Boys' Courier*.

The very existence of so many papers for children was a relatively new phenomenon. Most of the early nineteenth-century
children's magazines had been connected to religious orders of
one sort or another—the *Children's Magazine* was Episcopal, the
Encourager was Methodist, and so on—and all of them had a tendency to be didactic and somewhat dull. But by the middle of the
century, secular papers that took as their task merely the amuse-
ment of children were beginning to make their presence felt.
One of them, *Our Young Folks*, printed the work of Longfellow
and Whittier among others, until in 1874 it was subsumed into
what would become one of the most enduring children's magazines in the country, *St. Nicholas*. Just prior to its launch, Mary
Mapes Dodge—*St. Nicholas*'s editor and the author of the international children's bestseller *Hans Brinker; or, The Silver Skates*
(1865)—announced that, in something of a departure, the magazine would contain "no sermonizing...no wearisome spinning
out of facts, nor rattling of the dry bones of history...the ideal
child's magazine is a pleasure ground." Over the course of its run,
she was able to attract to her pages literary luminaries who were
more accustomed to writing for adults, among them Mark Twain,
Rudyard Kipling, Christina Rossetti, and Jack London.

Edward had been publishing his work, for the most part, in magazines that made up the other category of children's papers — the "penny dreadfuls," as they were known in some circles. At last, with the publication of "Victor Horton's Idea" in *Golden Days* in 1889, Edward crossed "the gap between the 'respectable' juveniles and the blood-and-thunder bang-bang-bang type of cheap weekly for boys." He had also formulated the first pseudonym that would go on to become a household name. Though the story was eventually published under his real name, he had originally thought, with his mother's encouragement, to submit "Victor Horton's Idea" under the name "Arthur M. Winfield." She apparently felt that the last name would make him a shoo-in for success — "to win in his field" — and he added the middle initial himself, prompting her to remark: "M is for millions. Perhaps some day you'll sell a million of your books." In 1899 Stratemeyer would recycle the Winfield pseudonym for his first successful series, the Rover Boys. By 1926, when the final volume of the series was published — there were thirty in all — it had sold not one but five million copies. As one hometown newspaper boasted: "NEWARKER WHO WRITES FOR THE MOST CRITICAL OF ALL READERS HAS FAR EXCEEDED STANDARD OF SUCCESS HIS MOTHER SET."

Following the sale of "Victor Horton's Idea," Stratemeyer began to publish more and more, first stories and then dime novels. He also moved from his family's home in Elizabeth to Broad Street in downtown Newark, some six miles away, and bought a stationery store, which he ran with the help of a clerk in order to earn a good living while he continued to write. In the spring of 1891, he married Magdalene Van Camp, or Lenna as he called her, the youngest daughter of a local businessman. She encouraged her husband in his literary pursuits and was by all counts a devoted wife who considered her marriage to Edward "the only great act of her life." A bookkeeper by training, she gave up her job when the couple married.

Lenna had a wicked sense of humor and a lively intellect — she and her husband shared an abiding interest in music and theater — but she was also something of an invalid, a trait she would pass on to her younger daughter, Edna. Though she suffered frequently from migraines and a heart condition, she was nonetheless deeply interested in Edward's work and helped him on occasion with publicizing his books and even editing them. Thanks to Edward's tireless writing and some wise investments, by the time his children were born, the family could afford household help, including a nanny for the girls. Nevertheless, Lenna was an involved parent when it came to decisions about education and how her daughters would be raised. To Edward she was simply "the best wife a man could have." He referred to her frequently and affectionately in letters to his friends and business acquaintances, alluding to the fact that she, like his daughters, was a frequent test audience not only for manuscripts he got in from his writers, but for books being published by rival companies that he thought it best to get a handle on. "Mrs. S has read about half of the 'Gringo' tale and liked it," he wrote to one of his authors, "and my two young daughters, Edna and Harriet, are interested in the other volume not only because of the story but also because you have an Edna and Hattie in it."

Soon after his marriage, Edward began to do freelance work for Street & Smith, a New York–based publishing house that was one of the most prolific sources of both story papers and dime novels. Street & Smith employed writers to produce "formula fiction" — including detective novels, comic novels, adventures, and sports stories — and came down with a heavy hand on anyone they thought deviated too much from their guidelines. Edward, who would later adapt many of their practices when he formed his own company, was no exception. The first story he submitted was criticized as "altogether too much of a burlesque, and it offends in the particular of morals. We believe a rollicking story along humorous lines can be written for juvenile readers without anything that would tend to make the parents frown." But Street & Smith's editors recognized his talent, telling him, "We feel certain that you will be able to please us when you fully appreciate our wants."

Their "wants," it turned out, ran to the true crime—as long as it was tasteful, apparently—or at least to the idea that truth is stranger and more compelling than fiction. As one dazzled reporter for *Publishers Weekly* described the operation:

> [Street & Smith] employs over thirty people, mostly girls and women...It is their duty to read all the daily and weekly periodicals in the land...Any unusual story of city life—mostly the misdoings of the city people—is marked by these girls and turned over to one of three managers. These managers, who are men, select the best of these marked articles, and turn over such as are available to one of a corps of five and transform it to a skeleton or an outline for a story. This shell, if it may be so called, is then referred to the chief manager, who turns to a large address-book and adapts the skeleton to some one of the hundred or more writers on his book.

Young single women—at least those in the lower class—were entering the workforce in significant numbers by this time. In 1890 roughly 60 percent of them were employed in the kind of relatively unskilled jobs Street & Smith offered, and mostly in the large cities of the Midwest and the East. In the decades to come, these veterans of the workplace would be at the forefront of the long fight for women's rights, but for the moment they were simply in great demand, especially at a place like Street & Smith, which was at the apex of its success. Urban dime novels, which had first begun to appear in the 1860s and '70s, exploded into the marketplace in the '90s. The houses that published them, of which Street & Smith was one of the most successful, had a limitless need for copy to fill the pages of these cheap, staple-bound "books" with gaudy cover pictures and promises of lurid detail inside. In keeping with the rapidly changing country, the dime genre, which had once been concerned with the likes of Daniel Boone and Davy Crockett, turned into a refuge for criminals and gangsters and tales of city woe; Edward was happy to supply their exploits. He churned out tales for the Nick Carter Library (*The Gold Brick Swindlers, or, Nick Carter's Great Exposure! The Dalton Gang Wiped Out; or, Nick Carter's Deadly Rifle!* screamed the titles, like so many dramatic headlines) and the New York Five Cent Library, "a brand-new library of thrilling stories written to the very hour," according to Street & Smith. None of this, however, prevented Stratemeyer from focusing on his other work.

The "Literary Account Book of Edward Stratemeyer 1889–1900; Being a complete list of all the original manuscripts written and printed, with the amounts received for the same" shows just how much copy its owner was capable of turning out, as well as how good he was at peddling it:

"True to Himself; Or, Robert Strong's Struggle for Place." Written in my store in Newark, N.J. 427 Broad St. Jan. 1891. Accepted by Frank A. Munsey Apr. 1891 Price $120.00 Printed. Note given. Paid.

"Beyond the Edge of the World, a Pre-Historical Romance." Written at Waterville, N.Y. June & July 1891. First work on the typewriter.

"Mayor Liedenkranz of Hoboken; Or, The Gallant Captain of
the Pretzel Schnetzen Corps" Written at Roricks on order for
Street & Smith, N.Y. Price $50. Printed. Paid For.

"The Monmouth Track Mystery; Or, Dash Dare's Solution for
a Remarkable Case," written at home, June 1 to 10, 1892. Sold
to R.L. Munsey, N.Y. price 60.00. Paid for. Printed.

The list rolled on and on, interrupted only once, late in 1892,
by the record of two occasions even more momentous than
selling a piece of writing. On December 12, 1892, a small hand
drawn in the margin of the notebook pointed, with one weighty
finger, to an entry reading: "Went to work on Street & Smith's
editorial staff at Forty dollars per week." The next line read,
simply: "Baby girl <u>Harriet</u> born Sunday, December 11 1892, at
8:40 A.M. weight 8¾ pounds." In one fell swoop, Edward became
a salaried writer and a father. He was pleased about his professional advancement and exuberant about his daughter. As he
wrote to a friend a few days later: "This week, I sold a book.
Today, unto us was born a baby girl."

"I GREW UP in a story-book house," Harriet Stratemeyer Adams
rhapsodized over and over again in her later years. "My earliest
recollection of my father was when he was playing with my sister
and me — outdoors, indoors; and we had continuous stories — not
just bedtime stories, but all day long...my recollection of him as
a child has more to do I think with his imagination than anything." Edward, just entering the prime of his writing career
when she was a small child, often tried out new story lines on
Harriet and her sister, Edna, two and a half years her junior, before putting them down on paper. The favorite family game was

another version of this; Edward would gather his offspring and spin an instant story around whatever topic they picked for him. He excelled at it, delighting his daughters. At the age of eighty-eight, Harriet was still bragging to reporters: "I was fortunate to have a father who could tell an original story at a moment's notice."

Much like his books, Edward's stories for his daughters often took the form of serials in which the same characters appeared night after night. Harriet's personal favorite characters were two fops named Mr. Bobalincoln and Mr. Whistler, whom Edward must have created for his daughters' pleasure alone as they never appeared in print and he was too shy to invite the neighborhood children in for a listen. He did, however, accept other devotions from the local boys who frequently dropped by to ask him questions about his characters' progress and when his next book would be out. Though he abhorred any kind of organized lecturing, he was always interested in the boys' reactions to his work and considered them far and away his best critics. "I am afraid I shall have to decline your invitation to address your boys' department," he wrote at one point to the head of the Newark YWCA. "I am no public speaker, and have always declined to inflict myself on the public in that way. I am sorry that your committee of boys did not call upon me, for I am always glad to meet the boys, even though I do not feel equal to addressing them publicly. All my 'talking,' so to speak, is done through the medium of my books." Even when newspapers and librarians disparaged his writing, he was content in the knowledge that the only constituency he cared about admired his work ardently and trusted him to be their guide. As he once implored a disagreeable editor: "Don't take the heart out of a fellow when he is straining every nerve to the utmost to make every boy in these United States his warm friend."

The Newark neighborhood of Roseville, where the Stratemeyers lived, was an ideal place for him to come into contact with his fans, for it was filled with children. Boys could be found "on the block" at all times of day, playing baseball and marbles. There was no such thing as a playground, nor any need for one, as the area was still covered by "an endless stretch of vacant lots that seemed to the boyish eye as limitless as the Argentine pampas or the western prairies." Though it was officially a part of the city of Newark, Roseville was fast becoming a tranquil antidote to the crowded, roaring downtown. The city had been purchased by New England Pilgrims from the Hackensack Indians in 1667, for the price of about $700, though no money had exchanged hands. The transaction read like nothing so much as a thrilling scene in a Stratemeyer story, payment having been made in the form of "fifty double hands of powder, one hundred bars of lead, twenty axes, twenty coats, ten guns, twenty pistols, ten kettles, ten swords, four blankets, four barrels of beer, ten pairs of breeches, fifty knives, twenty hoes, eight hundred and fifty fathoms of wampum, twenty ankers of liquors and ten troopers coats."

Since its Indian days, Newark had been transformed into the centerpiece of New Jersey industry. The downtown buzzed with factories that made plastic and forged iron, as well as numerous insurance companies, railroad depots, and thousands of immigrants from Germany, Poland, and Italy, among other places. By 1897, when Harriet was five years old, its population was roughly a quarter million people. But Roseville, just a few miles from the center of town, still showed signs of its recent transformation from farmland, and on its edges working farms remained. "Streets had been cut through lots that still showed ridges where the plow had tilled. Glacial boulders were commonplace. Houses were... few [and] swamps were at hand for exploration."

In spite of this, Roseville was not without a certain flair. One contemporary of Harriet's, recalling the halcyon days of his youth, described how growing up there, one could count "the pleasure of city, suburbs, and country in his common experiences. He grew up with most of the sophistication of the city lad, but he knew cows, horses, farming and the freedom that alone can be found where no concentrated population has safeguarded itself with restrictions." The neighborhood also boasted excellent schools. Roseville was a well-off, white, God-fearing community, a world apart from the working-class, predominantly foreign neighborhoods in other parts of the city.

For upper-class girls like Harriet and Edna — Edward's earnings and investments along with Lenna's private income set the family well above the average — playing in back lots and in the street was less acceptable than it was for the boys they knew. The outdoor pursuits open to girls fell more along the lines of hopscotch, hide-and-seek, hoops, and jacks. Roller-skating was popular, too, though the long skirts in fashion made it treacherous. Girls were allowed outside by themselves, but not after dark and only with at least a bit more supervision than their brothers. Games and recreation were also critical vehicles for imbuing girls with the idea that they were different from boys. They were given dolls by the score in order to teach them how to be mothers, and one child-rearing book published in 1905, when Harriet was thirteen years old, suggested that mothers throw tea parties with their daughters "so they could 'acquire niceties of speech and manner.'" As historian Victoria Bissell Brown notes, girls of the era "adopted the assumption that women were — or should be — more moral, less materialistic, more selfless, and less aggressive than men...Rare was the girl who emerged from this era's upbringing with a secure sense of her own independence or an unbridled eagerness to pursue her own interests."

Nonetheless, Harriet, or Hattie as she was known, was as much of a tomboy as the times and her Victorian-era parents permitted. This was acceptable, but only up to a certain point—as one girl put it in a 1902 interview, "After the age of thirteen, a lady should not climb trees unless to get away from a dog." Dark-haired, with a solid build and a long face, Hattie claimed to be "the best one-handed fence vaulter" in the neighborhood in spite of the high collars, dark stockings, and dresses she wore. Though she was not often found trading books or marbles over fences with neighborhood boys, Harriet couldn't help but come into contact with the opposite sex on a regular basis. A certain amount of interaction with boys was also encouraged, as it provided "the inculcation of respect for and interest in that which was masculine." Among the boys she was acquainted with was a nearby neighbor, Russell Vroom Adams, whose family kept chickens in the backyard. The Stratemeyers bought both chickens and eggs from him, and, as Harriet recalled, "my sister and I used to tease him unmercifully." These encounters, mean-spirited though they may have been, somehow formed the beginning of the solid foundation on which Harriet's marriage to Russell in 1915 would be built.

The mockery that poor young Russell endured was also a sign of the willful streak Hattie developed early on. It flared up in situations when she felt she was being treated unfairly, beginning when she was still a schoolgirl. Her parents, perhaps thinking that as the eldest she could carry on the family name as her middle name after she married, had not given her a middle name at birth. But Harriet would have none of it. When her grandmother gave her the gift of a locket with her initials engraved on it, the intertwined "H" and "S" looked to her like a dollar sign, which she found embarrassing. Determined to change her lot in life, she took Margaret as her middle name and informed her friends that they were to address all mail to her, from then on, as Harriet Margaret Stratemeyer. But she had neglected to tell her father, and he discovered her plan, presumably when one such-addressed letter arrived at the Stratemeyer home. The result was a cutting lecture on the all-important subject of taking pride in her given name, a lesson that Harriet remembered as long as she lived.

She repeated the story of her youthful digression so often it became part of her lore, much as Edward's story about the publication of "Victor Horton's Idea" had become part of his. A mini-drama composed of one part determination and one part bowing to tradition, it was Harriet, through and through. On her eighty-third birthday, the staff of the Stratemeyer Syndicate, which she had been running for forty-five years by then, wrote a song to commemorate the events of her life. It included these lyrics, to be sung to the tune of "Mary, Mary," concerning the infamous incident: "Born without a middle name, / we found out you took one secretly! / For it was Margaret, Margaret— / That's the name I chose for me. I could have chosen Sue or Mary Lou / or Marjorie / But it was Margaret, Margaret— / That's the name I tried to claim. / But Daddy said, 'No dice. / That's just not nice.'"

Some of Harriet's boisterousness was tempered by Lenna's ever-present medical problems, which often dominated the family's lives and necessitated quiet in the house. So, as one might expect of any child expected to avoid creating a disturbance, not to mention the child of a storybook writer, Harriet spent a great deal of time reading. She was enamored in particular of Dickens, whose humor she admired along with his clever uses of the coincidence as a plot twist, and of *Grimm's Fairy Tales*. To a sheltered, privileged child, these stories offered at least secondhand experience of the kind of challenges and thrills she did not encounter in her own world. Harriet's was a gentle, innocent childhood, but in her adult

life she reflected that she had not always been happy to be so protected. She felt a certain kinship to Nancy Drew, she thought, because the girl detective was "what I would have liked to have been
at her age." (Of course, as Nancy Drew, Harriet would have only
had to give up the restrictions on her freedom, not money, nice
clothes, a car, or a devoted relationship with her father.) On one
occasion, when a reporter was present, she couldn't help revealing her regret about the restraints put on her by society and family in her childhood and adolescence. "A couple of hours with
the spritely, curly-haired author...and a visitor realizes that Nancy
Drew leads the kind of life that Adams would like to have lived instead of the more traditional early twentieth-century upper-middle-
class life that was her lot. 'Oh I would have loved to be a teenage
detective and solved all mysteries,' Adams says wistfully."

Still, Harriet developed into a bright, headstrong girl. She attended the public school in Roseville, where she did well but had
a tendency to jump to conclusions. One day in second grade, her
teacher asked the class if anyone knew what a furlough was. Harriet raised her hand immediately, sure she knew the answer. "A
donkey," she said. With a look of consternation, her teacher asked
why she thought this was the right answer. Harriet replied: "I saw
a picture of a soldier riding through the woods. Under it was the
title 'Jim going home on a furlough.'"

———— ❧ ————

WHILE HIS DAUGHTERS were busy growing up, Edward, too, was
maturing. In the years following Harriet's birth, he wrote at a rate
that seems almost unimaginable. Between May of 1892 and November of 1893, he produced forty-two dime novels, and that
same year he published his first book under his own name, with
an apposite subtitle, to say the least. *Richard Dare's Venture; or,*

Striking Out for Himself was originally a serial that had appeared in *Argosy*. A classic tale of a boy who makes good by using his wits and working hard, the book was beloved from its first appearance, leading Stratemeyer to thank his audience in a subsequent edition: "The author had hoped that it would receive some notice; but he was hardly prepared for the warm reception which readers and critics alike all over the country accorded it. For this enthusiasm he is profoundly grateful. The street scenes in New York have been particularly commended; the author would add that these are not fictitious, but are taken from life."

Edward was beginning to discover his love for basing tales of crime and derring-do on solid research. It was a practice he would come to refer to as the "difficult task to collect the material I want, a tedious study of reference books, biographies, works of travel and histories," but that he nonetheless enjoyed and felt he owed his readers. He had held his much-heralded editorial job for only six months before being let go, and was once again writing full-time (Street & Smith had promised to continue using his stories on a regular basis). In 1895, after two years of writing stories, he left Street & Smith behind to become the editor of another short-lived story paper, *Young Sports of America*.

But the depression of the 1890s was in full force, brought on by a slowing of investment in the railroad, the main engine of economic expansion in the 1880s, and exacerbated by an agricultural crisis caused by indebted plains farmers and a long stretch of uncooperative weather conditions. It finally culminated in a stock market plunge in 1893, affecting everything from unemployment, which some estimates place as high as 18 percent by the middle of the decade, to advertising. Staying afloat in business, for Stratemeyer as for everyone else, was almost impossible. As one publisher wrote of his trials:

Of all the deadly schemes for publishing, that of juvenile publishing is the worst. It is hopeless...for as the boys and girls mature they take adult periodicals. It is a question of building new
all the while. Then again, the advertiser has no use for such
mediums. He wants to talk to money-spenders—not depend-
ents—not children.

Before too long, of course, it would be precisely the children
whom advertisers and publishers wanted to reach, but for the time
being, adults still held sole control over household purchases.

Despite the grim business climate and the arrival of his second daughter, who joined her older sister on May 29, 1895, Edward decided in 1896 to bring out his own story paper. As part of
his work for *Good News*, he had become acquainted with his boyhood heroes, William T. Adams and Horatio Alger. Alger, for one,
found him to be "an enterprising man, and his stories are attractive and popular. Under favorable circumstances, I think he will
win a fine reputation." With Alger's support, and some reprints
of his stories to boot, Edward launched his masterpiece, which
he christened with the marvelously optimistic name *Bright Days*.

Alas, even a man of such consistency as Stratemeyer could
not make a success of *Bright Days* in the imperiled market. It
soon became critical to adapt to changing conditions, chief
among them the shift from magazines to books for children.
Stratemeyer began to cast his eye on the emerging children's
book market, for which, with his instinct for both business and
the passions of young people, he proved to have a knack. By the
end of 1897, he had published twelve books in a series called
Bound to Win. Soon thereafter he began what he called "an experiment in historical writing," offering a book based on the Revolutionary War called *The Minute Boys of Lexington* to the very
respectable Boston publishing company Estes & Lauriat. It sold

well, and Edward wrote a second one, *The Minute Boys of Bunker Hill*, after which he abandoned the series.

For in that same year, Stratemeyer struck his first juvenile storybook gold in a manner that would have thrilled his forty-niner father. The Spanish-American War was escalating, making publishers loath to take any risk at all as their sales slumped. As one editor told Stratemeyer in a letter, "The people do not seem to have the time to read anything but the newspapers at present." Not one to be daunted, Stratemeyer decided that if Americans were interested in the news, they would be interested in fiction that was based on it. When Commodore Dewey defeated the Philippine-based Spanish squadron at Manila on May 1, 1898, in one of the United States' great victories of the war, Stratemeyer was ready with the Old Glory Series for Young People.

The first volume was entitled *Under Dewey at Manila; or, The War Fortunes of a Castaway.* Requisitioning the country's top hero of the moment, Dewey's executive officer Charles Gridley — who had let off the first shots of the battle at Dewey's famous command, "You may fire when ready" — the book chronicled the adventures of a boy named Larry Russell who was "lost overboard while on a trip with his folks from Honolulu to Hong Kong. Adrift on a bit of wreckage, he is picked up by the 'Olympia,' Captain Gridley, Commodore Dewey's flagship." A publisher bit, and the book came out, with blinding speed, in August of 1898. Its sale price was $1.25, and it was resplendent with a sailor on the cover waving a brightly colored American flag that was three times his size. As one account embellished the event rather grandly, adding to the Stratemeyer legend: "Almost before the smoke of battle had cleared away, Stratemeyer had produced *Under Dewey at Manila*. And as the popularity of the Little Admiral swelled and soared, so the book sold edition upon edition.

It established Stratemeyer as a writer of juveniles." By Christmas of that year, *Dewey* had sold six thousand copies—no mean feat for a wartime publication.

Not one to waste a smash hit, Stratemeyer immediately sent out a proposal for the series that would become his other early success: The Rover Boys Series for Young Americans—affectionately known, in no time at all, as "the Rovers." The exploits of Dick, the sober eldest brother; Tom, the fun-loving practical joker in the middle; and Sam, the straight man for his brothers, were set at a military school. Their mother was dead and their father was away "exploring in Africa," so the boys were sent off to boarding school, free from meddling adults once and for all. They (and later their doppelgänger sons) would go on to break sales records for clothbound books. At the peak of their success, according to one reporter, "The Rover Boys broke out upon the country like measles." As far as their adventures were concerned: "Motivations were of the essence of simplicity. A face at the window, a missing suitcase or the overheard conversation of the enemy was sufficient to send the Rovers off on stirring trips that lasted for 52,000 words."

It was the first series that bore a resemblance to those that would make Stratemeyer's fortune. In contrast to his historical stories, the Rover Boys were anything but timely; instead, they were ageless, and their "author," Arthur M. Winfield, was, too. They were also middle class. The familiar Alger story had become outdated, and the Rovers, as one critic put it, "were never embarrassed by a lack of funds...they had less to strive for than to protect." Both boys and girls loved the brothers without reserve and hoped they might come alive right off the page. One young man, Luther Danner of Loudonville, Ohio, received the following gentle letdown from Stratemeyer in response to a passionate fan letter: "Although many of the incidents in the stories are taken from life, the Rover boys are not real individuals, and consequently I cannot send you their address."

For the next five years, Stratemeyer turned out series after series. He was by now firmly established, and expectations were that he would stay that way. One critic wrote, "Mr. Stratemeyer thoroughly deserves his popularity, and he drives his typewriter without becoming careless or indolent as a result of the remarkable success he has attained."

Proving the point, in 1904 Stratemeyer dreamed up another wildly successful series of stories about a group of well-off children who had adventures all over the world and always remembered their manners. Their names were Bert, Nan, Freddie, and Flossie, otherwise known as the Bobbsey Twins. Stratemeyer wrote the first book himself, under the pen name Laura Lee Hope (he later assigned the series to Howard Garis, one of his first "employees" and the author of the Uncle Wiggily books). Their first adventure, *The Bobbsey Twins; or, Merry Days Indoors and Out*, appeared in the fall of that year. The two sets of twins, aged eight and four (they would later grow up to twelve and eight), were the epitome of simple, cozy stability, right down to their perfectly complementary personalities and physical attributes: "Nan was a tall and slender girl, with a dark face and red cheeks. Her eyes were a deep brown and so were the curls that clustered around her head. Bert was indeed a twin, not only because he was the same age as Nan, but because he looked so very much like her...Freddie and Flossie were just the opposite of their larger brother and sister. Each was short and stout, with a fair, round face, light-blue eyes and fluffy golden hair." With this jolly band, Stratemeyer tapped in to the kind of world that was to become the mainstay of juvenile books for the next fifty years. It was real enough to be recognizable to readers, but everything in it was improved upon. Parents were generous, punishments rare, and everything always seemed to work out in the end.

These were also the first books by Stratemeyer that took into account not only a younger age group, but female readers. It was not yet popularly believed that little girls were worth catering to as an audience, as they had shown themselves to be perfectly happy to borrow books from their brothers to get their adventure fix. As Stratemeyer sized it up, "Almost as many girls write to me as boys and all say they like to read boys' books (but it's pretty hard to get a boy to read a girl's book, I think)."

Furthermore, there was competition for girls once they reached a certain age in a way that there was not for boy readers, and publishers—and Stratemeyer—believed it made the investment of both time and money in too many girls' series unwise. In an interview around this time, Stratemeyer displayed his admirable grasp of both publishing and human nature: "The little girl begins at perhaps 7 years of age to read girls' books written for her. By the time she is 12, she is ready for the [adult] 'best seller' and will have nothing else. A boy will cling to the boys' book till he is 15 or 16, often older."

Still, the success of the Bobbsey Twins could not fail to affect Stratemeyer. He began to expand his winning formula to include the opposite sex, taking into account another, more personal reason for doing so. As he noted in a letter to a successful girls' book author: "I have two little girls growing up fast, so I presume I'll have to wake up on girls' books ere long."

By 1905 Edward was easily the most successful juvenile writer in the country, and he had even more ideas than he could keep up with: As he had confessed in 1903, he had "the plots and outlines of a score of books in [his desk]." He had also begun to recognize that his pseudonymous works, written under the names of Arthur M. Winfield and Laura Lee Hope, were earning him more money than books by Edward Stratemeyer, such as the Old Glory series. The market would never be saturated, he reasoned, as long as he could think up another pen name. As he wrote to one publisher: "A book brought out under another name would, I feel satisfied, do better than another Stratemeyer book. If this was brought out under my own name, the trade on new Stratemeyer books would simply be cut into four parts instead of three." He was also "neck deep in contracts on books" and could barely keep up with himself.

So he decided to act on a consolidation scheme he had been thinking over for some time. He intended to model his new company on the Street & Smith plan, writing outlines for series and handing them out to ghostwriters, who would work under the pen name assigned to each series. This way, no one would ever be the wiser about who was actually doing the writing, and if it became necessary to change authors, there would be no risk of alienating readers. He himself would edit all the manuscripts for consistency, so that even if volumes in the same series were written by more than one person, the final product would be of apiece with the entire series. By controlling all of his characters, pen names, and manuscripts, and more or less renting them out to publishers for royalties, he would be able to sell different books to different houses, thereby grabbing a larger share of the market and putting his many idle story ideas to use. He would pay his ghostwriters, whom he hired from local newspapers and by placing ads in trade publications like the *Editor*, a flat fee for each manuscript, usually ranging from $75 to $150 depending upon their effort and experience. The amount of work done by the ghostwriter versus the amount of work done by Stratemeyer on any given book could not be determined, though Stratemeyer always had the last word. In addition, he required that his authors not tell anyone which books they wrote and under which pen names—they gave up "all right, title and interest" to their stories in every release form they signed and further agreed that they would "not use such pen name in any manner whatsoever"—though they were allowed to say they worked for the Syndicate, and Stratemeyer did not prevent them from writing elsewhere.

The Stratemeyer Syndicate, in essentially the form in which it would remain for the next three decades, had been launched. In 1905, the first year of its existence, Edward Stratemeyer earned $6,757.74, triple his earnings just a few years earlier. The following year, he earned $8,757.18 and paid out $2,267.00 for manuscripts and advertising, leaving him with $6,490.18. It was almost the same amount of money for less work on his part; his business idea had been a sound one. "The syndicate idea is booming, and I am now negotiating for sixteen copyrights of A No. 1 stories," he wrote to Mershon Company, one of his New Jersey publishers. "I think when all is in shape I shall have the best line of juveniles on the market, written by those who know exactly what is wanted." Edward Stratemeyer was on his way to becoming, as one magazine would later anoint him, "the father of…fifty-cent literature."

THANKS TO HER father's wise scheme, by the time Harriet was fifteen, the young, well-to-do Stratemeyer clan had moved to a large, stylish three-story Queen Anne house on North Seventh Street in Roseville. In addition to three bedrooms, the house had a fireplace in the parlor, a small balcony off the second floor, and a laundry room in the basement where their hired help did the wash. The Stratemeyers also employed a cook and a chaffeur for Lenna. The third floor contained Edward's flower-papered private study, where he dreamed up his characters and committed them to the page first by hand, and then by typewriter. His debut as an operator of this technological marvel was thrilling enough to merit mention in his literary account book. In the same way that he reveled in keeping up to the moment with his car purchases and enthusiastically embraced all the newfangled time-saving devices America had to offer, he adapted, with marvelous aplomb, to his new luxury. "Did you ever use a typewriter?" he wrote to a friend. "It took me just a week to get used to it and now I would not work in any other way for the world."

While Edward wrote, his girls were constantly being reminded to keep quiet lest they should disturb their father's great imaginings upstairs. Harriet recalled her father's private aerie as "a sunshiny room, book lined, attractive and warm," and it had the lure of the forbidden for the children, who were not allowed in very often. Far above the street, wearing a three-piece suit even for writing at home, Edward would put in two chapters' worth of work on his typewriter in the morning, come down for lunch with his family, and return for a third chapter in the afternoon. As if to repay them for their indulgence of his mental process—for he was a generous father, if a strict one—Edward never worked in the evenings or on weekends and took his family on long summer vacations to the Jersey Shore, Martha's Vineyard, or other pleasant locales.

When she was not on such a leisure trip, Harriet attended the prestigious public Barringer High School. She had long passed the age at which she could climb trees, and social activities around the turn of the century were restricted mostly to groups. Dating was unheard of unless a boy had serious intentions—and even then he had to work up to seeing his girl unchaperoned — so, like most girls of her social standing, the structure of Harriet's teenage life was built upon school, family, and church. Adolescence was just starting to emerge as a period of life that was set off from what came before and what came after, and as high school enrollment increased dramatically in the early years of the century, school became the organizing principle behind adolescence in a way it had never been before. Teenage girls were not yet in thrall to fashion, consumerism, or pop culture of the kind that would become synonymous with the very idea of adolescence by the twenties, and so Harriet led a fairly quiet life. Thanks to her family's money, she, unlike the majority of teenagers at that time, did not have to work after school either at home or outside of it. Instead, she spent her spare hours with her family and friends and concentrated on her schoolwork.

She did not always study as hard as she could have, though. A pop quiz about Sir Walter Scott's "The Lady of the Lake" near the end of her secondary schooling ended in an episode similar to her elementary school gaffe about the donkey. The story, which opens with a famous scene of a stag hunt in a forest and evolves into an epic tale of love and clan rivalry, intertwines James Douglas, the outlawed uncle of the royal family, his daughter Ellen, and several other characters, two of whom are suitors to Ellen. Amazingly enough, considering her father's line of work and her own interest in books, Harriet had never been taught what a heroine was. The books of her childhood tended to feature rather weak, weepy little girls whose main function was to overcome adversity with good Christian values. Rebecca of Sunnybrook Farm, star of the eponymous book published in 1903, when Harriet was eleven, joined earlier counterparts like the melodramatic Elsie Dinsmore, a deeply pious poor little rich

girl who longs for love from her father and has to contend with
a mean schoolteacher. True heroines were few and far between,
and girls were barely aware that there was any alternative. Even
the ones who sought adventure by turning to boys' books did not
venture very far. As one reading study noted, "The exciting stories mentioned by the girls are very quiet compared to those mentioned by the boys." Harriet had few examples, and her father, for
one, was certainly not in the habit of encouraging his daughter
to be an adventuress, lest it should spoil her for what he considered to be the true calling of all women. "He thought I should
stay home and keep house," she remembered later. As a result,
she believed that the hero was the most important character in
the story, and the heroine the second most important. When
asked to fill in the pop quiz blanks for who occupied each of
these roles in "The Lady of the Lake," she wrote, without hesita-
tion, that the hero was James Douglas and the heroine was the
stag. Poor Ellen was nowhere to be found.

But this overconfident streak also made Harriet determined
from a young age to seek out an education when the majority of
teenage girls did not even consider it. At the turn of the century,
40 percent of college students were women, but that was still
less than 4 percent of women between the ages of eighteen and
twenty-one. Though it was girls of Harriet's class who made up
most of the student bodies at elite eastern colleges — tuition and
fees even at public schools were expensive for a middle-class family, and scholarships were rare — the majority of wealthy girls took
the more traditional path of simply finishing high school and
living at home until they were married. It never took long; the
average marriage age for women in 1910 was twenty-one. Not
Harriet, however. Fully supported by her parents, who, while they
were not exactly progressive, placed great stock in intelligence

and rigorous education and believed that their daughters would be better wives if they had the ability to help their husbands in their professions, Harriet began to ponder her future. So it was that in the winter of 1909, Edward Stratemeyer contacted a select group of colleges on his daughter's behalf. Among them was Wellesley, already at that time a venerable institution with a reputation for having, in the words of one observer, "a strong religious undercurrent and a subtle something, one might call it an upper current, of idealism."

Certainly there was no question that whatever college Harriet attended, it would not be coed, nor would it be too far from home to preclude frequent visits in both directions. In addition to Wellesley, Edward's letter requesting information went out to a group of well-established women's colleges up and down the East Coast: Vassar (founded in 1861), Barnard (1889), Smith (1871), and Bryn Mawr (1885). By the end of 1909, Harriet had settled on Wellesley, saying later that she preferred it because it was more conservative than the other options she reviewed. As was the custom, Harriet's high school diploma and her father's ability to cover her bill were enough to reserve a spot for her in the class of 1914. Edward had offered financial references to prove he could pay the $175 annual tuition, plus the cost of his daughter's room, board, and extra music lessons. Included among these references were not only his bank in New Jersey but also the publishing house of Lothrop, Lee & Shepard, which he no doubt chose for its location in Boston, very close to Wellesley. He often used business meetings with the company as an excuse to go up to the college, beginning with a trip in April of 1910, with Harriet along to inspect the campus.

The visit was a great success. Though Harriet would be required to take entrance exams in everything from Shakespeare to

Chaucer, algebra, Latin, and modern languages to determine her course of study, both she and her father were confident that she would demonstrate enough learning to enter the college without serious handicaps. In addition to making a flurry of arrangements concerning clothes and furnishings for her new rooms, Harriet was taking extra French lessons in preparation for college language courses and, like any teenager about to leave home for the first time, anxious about who her roommate would be. By all accounts, she was looking forward to the new challenge as she attended to various last-minute items, including the mailing of her "Chemical Laboratory Notebook" to Wellesley to prove she had achieved the necessary standards in that subject.

While Harriet was busy dreaming of college, Edward and Lenna had enrolled her sister, Edna, then fifteen, in a private girls' boarding school called the Centenary Collegiate Institute in Hackettstown, New Jersey, about forty-five miles away. She had been taking violin lessons for several years already and was signed up to study "a 'combination' course of violin instruction, art (painting) and literature and languages." No doubt the Stratemeyers had it in mind to ease their younger daughter's path to college — with a private school education, there would be no need for extra language lessons and fretting over the chemistry course as Harriet had. After less than a month at her new school, however, it became clear that Edna was not adjusting. She went home for a visit, and Edward wrote to the headmaster to say that she "appears to like the school so far as the teachers, pupils and studies go, but does not seem to be able to get used to being away from home and her folks." Still, he was optimistic and believed that with his and Lenna's encouragement, their daughter would come to see the value of the kind of independence and intellectual curiosity her sister so cherished.

The episode was a harbinger not only of Edna's future in general, which would be marked by a nervous disposition and poor health, but her relationship to Harriet, whom she eventually came to feel had been given everything in comparison to her paltry share. In late October Edward wrote again to the headmaster, describing the family's fruitless efforts to impress upon Edna the benefits and pleasures of going back to school: "Yesterday Mrs. S and myself tried again to induce her to return but she collapsed so completely that I knew it would be folly to attempt it, that she would be in no condition to study…as soon as I can possibly get away I will be up with her to help her in packing."

The Stratemeyers eventually sent Edna to a local private school called Miss Townsend's, and from then on she stayed at home, content there even as Edward loaded his elder daughter and all her belongings into his new Cadillac in September of 1910 and drove her up to Wellesley in style. Harriet was about to enter into the years she would claim as the most formative of her life in terms of her will to succeed as a wife, mother, and businesswoman. The Wellesley motto, "Non Ministrari Sed Ministrare"—"Not to be ministered unto but to minister to"—became Harriet's motto in all things, and she intoned it on numerous occasions. Eventually, she claimed it for Nancy Drew, too, saying: "Why is Nancy Drew so good? Because of the Wellesley College motto," and telling reporters that she was sure that had Nancy ever gone to college, she would have been a Wellesley girl.

2

MILDRED

IN THE SUMMER of 1905, just a few months after Edward Strate-meyer launched his newly formed literary syndicate into the world, Mrs. Lillian Matteson Augustine, resident of the tiny prairie town of Ladora, Iowa, gave birth to a baby girl. Her name was Mildred. She was delivered at home on July 10, in the scorching heat of summer on the Great Plains, by the town doctor and surgeon—who also happened to be her father, Dr. J. L. Augustine.

Jasper Augustine, like Edward Stratemeyer the son of a forty-niner, was an Iowa native. He had grown up on a farm in the town of Agency, then gone to medical school at the State University of Iowa in Iowa City. Upon graduating in 1893, he moved immedi-ately to Ladora, where he established "a most extensive and suc-cessful practice." Not only was Augustine the local medical authority, known for his devotion to keeping his knowledge of pro-cedures and treatments up to date and for his diagnostic "touch," but he was an officer of the town bank and the president of the Ladora Lumber and Grain company. His stature was such that he merited a profile in the magisterial 1915 tome *History of Iowa County and Its People,* which chronicled the beginnings of the region and its most prominent citizens.

While Augustine was an exceptional man and doctor with, perhaps, more than the average amount of civic pride in his blossoming town, there was another, simpler reason for his high standing in so many institutions: In a settlement of fewer than three hundred people, there were not enough men to fill the official positions created as it expanded. Located in Iowa County, roughly eighty miles from the state capital of Des Moines, Ladora had been founded in 1867 and officially incorporated in 1880. It was a prototypical homesteader town, forged from the open prairie by pioneers in search of a better life. Originally the province of the Sac and Fox Indians, the land had been sowed with cornfields for decades by the time Mildred was born. Ladora was an up-and-coming place, with its own mill, post office, railroad depot, school, churches, and saloons. It even had a town song of sorts, with a refrain that listed the various amenities and institutions that bigger places counted as their own, and then proclaimed, with characteristically stubborn local pride, "The little town of Ladora is good enough for me."

Though some mistook it for being of French origin—La Dora—the town's quirky name was actually the inspiration of a music teacher by the name of Mrs. General Scofield, who suggested using three syllables from the musical scale—"la," "do" and "ra," or "ray"—as the town name. Perhaps for lack of a better one, the idea was met with virtually unanimous approval. It seemed, in any case, wholly appropriate for a town that had its own opera house, its own band, and a thriving cultural life.

Jasper and Lillian Augustine were passionate participants in this life, believing, like many of their fellow Ladorans, that dwelling in a small town should be no obstacle to a refined existence. Lillian, in addition to being her husband's assistant in his practice and running the household—which also included Mildred's older brother, Melville—was an accomplished painter and musician. She played the piano and organ frequently at social gatherings and official town functions, as well as at the Presbyterian church, to which she was devoted. (Her daughter did not share this piety, recalling much later: "My mother was quite a church goer and she tormented me to death going to church. I went as long as I had to and then I never went to church again.") Of the Augustines, she was the more conservative parent—Mildred remembered her mother always encouraging her but also trying to make her "into a traditional person. But I resisted that. I just was born wanting to be myself." The daughter of one of the area's original Vermont pioneer settlers, Lillian Augustine was a stern, loving woman, not much given to shows of affection, who held herself and those around her to high standards. Mildred's salvation came in the form of her more liberal father, who took her on house calls with him along the dusty back roads, first by horse and buggy and later by car. Though he was not musical like his wife, Jasper Augustine had a literary streak, as evidenced by his eager participation in the Chautauqua Literary and Scientific Circle, a group modeled on the legendary program started in 1874 by the Methodist minister John Heyl Vincent on Lake Chautauqua in upstate New York.

Originally a kind of weeklong summer camp for families that specialized in education for Sunday school teachers, reflecting the nation's growing interest in the professionalization of teaching, the nondenominational, though very vaguely Protestant,

Chautauqua assemblies soon grew into gatherings that welcomed anyone interested in "education and uplift" in the form of lectures, plays, music, and readings. By the turn of the century, Chautauqua was known as "a center for rather earnest, but high-minded, activities, that aimed at intellectual and moral self-improvement and civic involvement." In the words of Theodore Roosevelt, it was "typically American, in that it is typical of America at its best." Its adult education courses of study could be followed in one's living room as easily in Iowa as they could in New York, and as graduates of the program went out into the world, spreading the movement's gospel, independent Chautauquas sprung up all over the country, with an especially large number in the Midwest. Geared toward the lower and middle classes, Chautauqua was an emblem of the new American zeal for self-betterment through education. For women, especially, the program was one of the few ways to gain the skills they needed in order to rise above confined roles as farmers' wives or domestic help in the years when very few other opportunities were open to them. "Chautauqua functioned for many lower- and middle-class women much as the elite women's colleges did for upper-class women," according to the group. "They were training grounds from which women could launch 'real' careers." What came to be called Circuit Chautauqua, in which performers traveled around the company and set up temporary shop in towns and settlements, spread nationwide. By the time the movement crested in the mid-1920s, they were appearing in forty-five states around the country and playing to upward of forty million people a year.

It was exactly the kind of program suited to an up-and-coming prairie town settled by intelligent men and women in search of a new life. Ladora's Chautauqua was run and put on by locals, who enlightened their fellow townspeople on everything from politics and psychology to music. On one occasion, at least, Jasper Augustine took advantage of the opportunity to perform and tried his hand at Hamlet's soliloquy. He was a great lover of Shakespeare, a fact that had not always been appreciated by his wife. Instead of presenting her with a diamond ring when asking for her hand in marriage in the late 1890s, the exuberant young suitor had offered a complete leather-bound set of the bard's works. She never let him forget it.

By the time of Mildred's birth, the Augustines had built themselves a large wooden house on Ladora's main street. A sign of Jasper's burgeoning medical practice, it had a huge porch and a bedroom apiece for Mildred and Melville. There was enough money for a bit of help, so there were no chores to be done and Mildred was generally left to amuse herself. Such comfort, however, had to be earned by someone. "There was an awful lot of work in the family," Mildred once said, looking back on her childhood and pondering the roots of her own tireless work ethic. Her mother assisted her father at his practice and, she remembered, "They worked sometimes until 8 or 9 o'clock at the office and those times I ate whatever I could find for food." Relentless prairie pioneer energy ran deeply through the Augustine family.

In 1907, when Mildred was only two years old, Lillian's beloved Ladora Presbyterian Ladies' Aid Society published a pamphlet of "Favorite Quotations." Each church member was asked to choose a motto that had especially inspired him or her, and these various lines were bound together in a pamphlet and handed out to the congregation. The collection testified to the self-sufficient, stoic nature of Ladora Presbyterians, but it also revealed their wide range of reading and their feeling for a philosophical, often lovely, phrase. Like his gift of Shakespeare to his bride, Jasper Augustine's choice belied the image of the man of science who had no time for the more ephemeral things in life. The line from Ruskin that he contributed exemplified his physician's nature, but it was also concerned with a man's soul: "The nobleness of life depends on its consistency, clearness of purpose, quiet and ceaseless energy." His wife's choice, from Episcopal bishop of Massachusetts Phillips Brooks, echoed this idea while casting it in a more feminine, though hardly submissive, light: "Be such a woman, live such a life, that if every woman were such as you, and every life like yours, this earth would be a God's paradise."

Melville, who was seven years older than his little sister and later would go off to join the army, had inherited his parents' sense of industriousness. He chose a simple quotation that embodied the very essence of the American dream, despite having first been uttered by the Roman historian Sallust, who lived from 86 to 34 B.C.: "Every man is the architect of his own fortune."

As for Mildred, she was a toddler, barely capable of speaking full sentences. Nonetheless, her high-minded family bestowed upon her some lines from Milton. The passage they chose was perfectly in keeping with the Augustine ethos, and Mildred, though she surely had no idea at the time that it was hers to aspire to, would live up to its sentiment for the rest of her life: "Truth, that golden key / That opens the palace of eternity."

⸙

LIFE FOR CHILDREN in a small prairie town like Ladora was full of the outdoors, and Mildred and her friends were free to roam anywhere they pleased. Athletically inclined from the start, Mildred had a great deal of freedom and was a frequent sight at coed baseball games played in backyards around town, wearing dresses her mother made for her — she herself despised sewing and left it behind as soon as she could—and stockings, her red-gold hair swinging behind her in a long braid. In the summertime she also jumped rope—her favorite grandfather would hold one end of the rope from his rocking chair and tie the other end to a porch support—and made mud pies, which she sold for a penny apiece. In the deep, frigid winter, she went ice-skating, always alone, on a frozen creek nearby, and in the spring she helped her grandparents tap trees for sap and boil it into maple sugar. Even seven decades later, Mildred still remembered with perfect clarity going out to see Halley's comet with her family when she was six years old. The Augustines stood on the unpaved main street that ran past their door and "watched the firey beast, with long devil's tail, move low across the horizon," she recalled. "The ornery rascal seemed very close and unfriendly."

Mildred learned to read so early that she couldn't even remember it, and got started on the classics straightaway. "I had a little affair with Peter Rabbit when I was just four or five years of age," she remembered ruefully. "And I wanted that book so badly...so I went and copied it by hand." Her parents, though they had the means, didn't realize how desperately their daughter wanted to own the store-bought version of Beatrix Potter's tale, a slight that, while she revered her mother and father, Mildred never forgot. But literary riches, albeit borrowed, were soon to come her way nonetheless. On a summer vacation to Chicago, Mildred discovered an institution that was to be her saving grace, at many times and in many cities: the public library.

The grand building on Chicago's Michigan Avenue, built out of solid stone—the great fire of 1871 had changed that city's construction methods forever—was a product of the same kind of civic sentiment that led to the rise of Chautauqua. In the 1880s and '90s, Americans were just beginning to understand the public library as a means of disseminating information to all people equally, and Mildred was a part of the first generation to benefit from this new ethos. As the movement to provide free books to all Americans grew, it gained many notable champions, including Andrew Carnegie, who eventually spent more than $56 million to build libraries in towns and cities all over the country.

So it was that while Mildred's father brushed up his surgical skills at Cook County Hospital and her mother attended to other matters relating to his practice, their daughter, who had been dropped off alone in the safe sanctuary of the public reading room, spent eight hours a day devouring books. "Coming upon a shelf of fairy stories, I read each wonderful book as fast as I could," she remembered. Back in Ladora, she had to make do with what she could get, which wasn't much. The town was too small to have its own library, and though Carnegie's famed program had came to Mildred's area, it bestowed a library not on Ladora, but on the nearby town of Marengo. The Marengo Public Library was opened just after Mildred's birth in August of 1905, but she never went there. Her father made use of the horse and buggy, and later the family car, for house calls, and no one had time to take Mildred the long seven miles to Marengo.

This was a difficult situation, to say the least, for there was nothing she cherished so much as reading. "I read everything I could get my hands on as a child," she told an interviewer, including the newspaper, in which she followed the far-off events of World War I as it escalated. "I craved to read, but the available literature neither challenged nor satisfied me. Magazines in part filled the void. *St. Nicholas*, a monthly, was my favorite," she remembered. "I devoured every page, but mystery serials by Augusta H. Seaman and a series of career articles devoted to men who accomplished unusual things in the work world especially appealed to me." Even the town's high school library, her one possible resource for books, was a bust, "a single glass case filled mostly with dusty textbooks and a complete set of Dickens, through which I struggled laboriously." On the long, hot summer days, when even the school library was closed, she would sit in a big leather chair in the family's sparsely furnished library and attempt to read her parents' few and lugubrious volumes. "[They] weren't very readable books most of them," she confessed later. So, in order to get her fill—or at least as close to it as was possible—she did the obvious thing, with her usual determination: "I just borrowed them from whoever. I got books wherever I could find them."

This often meant getting books on loan from the town boys, which was fine with Mildred. She was an inveterate doll-hater and much preferred boys' pastimes anyway. After she proved herself, they even allowed her to join their games, provided, she explained, that she played "according to their rules and I couldn't be a sissy." School recess was a far cry from the genteel snack time familiar to later generations. In fact, it was out-and-out warfare: "We had a hut that we built down there on the school yard and we had fights...during recess time...we had organized battles, with sticks, and we'd pound each other [until] they put a stop to that," Mildred recalled. "We could hardly wait to recess to start our fights." She liked boys' books just as much as she liked their battles. Among the volumes she tore through were not only the books that Edward Stratemeyer had loved as a boy, but the ones he had begun to write. "In general, I preferred boys' books to those written for girls," she remembered. "I raced through many of the Horatio Alger books because they were everywhere, the *Rover Boys,* and a few of the popular *Ruth Fielding* stories, never dreaming I would be asked to write this series in later years."

Her mother had somewhat different ideas about Mildred's recreation habits, however. "She was always trying to get me out of the books. She thought I stayed in the house and read too much so she was always trying to get me to go outdoors and play with the other children." Perhaps for this reason, her mother entered her into school early, just before she turned five, so that she could at least have the company of other children for the final month of the school year. This idea seemed a fine one until Mildred learned that because of her age, and because she'd had only a month of schooling, she would not be moving on to the next grade with her classmates. She was highly distressed and, never one to be left behind in any sense of the word, in the coming years twice made up for the repetition, first by going through high school in three years and then by completing college in the three years after that. She graduated from the University of Iowa just a month or so shy of her twenty-first birthday.

Always, there was one thing on Mildred's mind. "I…wanted to be a writer from the time I could walk. I had no other thought except that I would write." In keeping with her lifelong belief that writing was essentially a self-taught skill, she toiled alone on her efforts. Her parents never read what she was working on, even when she was a young girl, but they did provide two very valuable commodities: "My mother always encouraged me to keep writing and my father provided the stamps." As she hung around the post office waiting to see if any of her submissions to magazines would come back with an acceptance attached to them, Mildred used the spare time to compose and mail fan letters to her favorite movie star, Lillian Gish.

Just before her fourteenth birthday, her unshakable faith in herself—not to mention her indiscriminate use of her father's stamps—was rewarded. In the June 1919 issue of her beloved *St. Nicholas* magazine, emblazoned with the Silver Badge Award, appeared a very short story by Mildred Augustine titled "The Courtesy." She had been entering the magazine's contests for several years already, and at last she had been recognized. Though *St. Nicholas* did not award any cash, the venerable magazine gave the young author her first taste of the thrill of publication, much as it had the infamous poet Edna St. Vincent Millay, who as a child had published her first poems in *St. Nicholas* roughly a decade earlier.

The page announcing Mildred's success opened, as usual, with an editor's note that featured an illustration by a child at the top. It showed a graduate and a bride, and had been created by a fifteen-year-old contributor to the magazine. In the note beneath, the anonymous writer extolled it as "a fitting introduction to the month of roses, and weddings, and glad (or tearful) farewells to school or college!" And then came something a bit different. "The Courtesy" was a tiny fable about the merits of good behavior and the golden rule with just a touch of the *Lord of the Flies* about it:

Mrs. Gardner sat gazing out of the window. In her lap lay a letter. The door opened and her daughter Andrea entered the room. Mrs. Gardner, smiling faintly, said, "I have received a letter from Aunt Jane, who will arrive next week to spend the winter with us." For a moment Andrea was too surprised to speak. Then she burst into tears.

A week later Aunt Jane arrived, parrot, umbrella, baggage and all. She was even worse than Andrea had imagined. She breakfasted in bed, grumbled at everything, was courteous to no one, and was, in short, as Andrea declared, "a perfect grouch."

As time passed, matters grew worse. The parrot screeched incessantly, and the house was in a constant uproar.

Several weeks after her arrival, Aunt Jane overheard a conversation that caused her much thought. Coming noiselessly past Andrea's room, she heard Andrea clearly say: "Aunt Jane thinks that we should do nothing but wait on her and show her every courtesy, while she just bosses and grumbles. For my part, I think that courtesy is as much her duty as ours. If only she were pleasant, it would be much easier for us to be courteous to her."

Aunt Jane silently entered her room.

Next morning the Gardners were surprised to find Aunt Jane down for breakfast. Later, she helped wash the dishes without even grumbling.

Weeks passed. Aunt Jane became so helpful and cheerful it was a pleasure to have her around.

When spring came, the Gardners wanted her to remain, but, declining, she announced her intention of traveling, providing Andrea would accompany her. Andrea — not from courtesy, but because she really liked Aunt Jane — accepted.

No one except Aunt Jane knew, and she never told, that it was Andrea who had first shown her the need for true courtesy.

The story clearly had its roots in Mildred's experience of being a smart, impatient child to whom adults did not defer as often as she thought they should. Having exorcised her demons in print in a most satisfactory manner, she was more certain than ever that writing was what she wanted to do with her life.

She began to send short stories incessantly to church magazines and newspapers. Her first big sale came when she was sixteen, to the Nazarene Publishing Company, which bought "Midget" for the grand sum of $3.50. Midget, the title character, was a girl who would reappear regularly in Mildred's writing throughout the next two decades. Like her creator, she was an excellent swimmer, a girl who agonized when her "fancy diving" wasn't up to par, and who, in a later story, would rescue a panicked, drowning swimmer, holding her in a "safe and scientific way" until the swimmer gave in to Midget's experience. She also played basketball, like Mildred. In one episode, she is being relied upon to bring the home team to victory and told that luck is with her as she goes out for the final moments of the game. "Luck was it? Well she guessed it wasn't luck. She would show them what it was." By the end of the tale, having won the game, of course, she is speaking with hard-headed, Mildred-like practicality: "After this, I will never be foolish enough to think that people get things in this world unless they get out and work for what they want. There isn't any such thing as luck."

Midget's assessment of the world closely mirrored a clipping that Mildred had cut from a publication called the *American Magazine* and pasted in her high school memory book. It was titled "Code of a 'Good Sport'" and listed the ten requirements for that honor:

1. Thou shalt not quit.
2. Thou shalt not alibi.
3. Thou shalt not gloat over winning.
4. Thou shalt not be a rotten loser.
5. Thou shalt not take unfair advantage.
6. Thou shalt not ask odds thou art not willing to give.
7. Thou shalt not always be ready to give thine opponents the shade.
8. Thou shalt not overestimate an opponent, nor overestimate thyself.
9. Remember that the game is the thing and that he who thinketh otherwise is a mucker and not a true sportsman.
10. Honor the game thou playest, for who playeth the game straight and hard wins even when he loseth.

Mildred must have cut this out on her birthday, for pasted onto the same page of the book are two horoscope readings for the day that she thought rang true enough to save. The first one ran, "You have a rather stern and rigid disposition, quite vain and self-satisfied. You believe in your way of thinking and doing things, too intolerant of the beliefs of others for your own good...A child born on this day should prove steady and persevering with every chance of rising in life." The other astrological reading added, "A child born on this day is likely to be given to disputes and wrangling, and may be proud and imperious unless carefully trained in early youth."

This, then, was Mildred when she graduated from Ladora High School in 1922, one member of a class of four. She played baseball, volleyball, and basketball, and she had been a "decided hit" as the character of the landlady in the senior class play. She also played the xylophone extremely well, usually as a member of the Ladora Band, for which she also played the slide trombone. On occasion, she played at the town Chautauqua, sometimes accompanied by her mother on the piano. She had done summer school in Iowa City in order to finish high school in three years, and she was ready for more urbane surroundings than the small town of Ladora. "Senior activities were dismal," she recalled of her graduation week, "as four persons couldn't stir up much excitement...no matter how hard we tried...I just wanted to forget about it and move on to better things."

Mildred was assigned to give the class prophecy—a speech imagining the futures of the foursome—"a fantastic document over which [she] labored many weeks." This portion of the graduation proceedings took place in the town's movie house. When Mildred rose to give her address, a "fringe of hang-abouts" outside began to honk their horns so loudly that it obscured all other sounds. Mildred was devastated. "I tried to speak above the honking but couldn't. The tooting kept on without a break and no one inside the theater made any attempt to go after the hoodlums. Not until I finished the reading did the disturbance cease. No one inside heard a word of my speech. Hurt and angry, I tore up the manuscript." Though she claimed later on that the experience had taught her never to take her writing too seriously, in truth, it was the idea that others might not take it as seriously as she did that she grasped for the first time that evening, and it made her furious.

Mildred was headed west to the State University of Iowa in Iowa City, where she enrolled as a freshman in the fall of 1922. The big state colleges had been accepting women with great success for decades by now, and though it was still comparatively rare for girls to attend college, their numbers had doubled between 1910 and 1920. The previous generation of women had used the college campus as a place to organize for suffrage and assert themselves politically. Thanks to their efforts and the victories they had won, Mildred's generation would use it to find themselves in a whole new way.

3

ALMA MATER

"THE HIGHER EDUCATION of Women is one of the great world battle cries for freedom," thundered the founder of Wellesley College in the school's opening sermon in 1875. "I believe that God's hand is in it…that He is calling womanhood to come up higher, to prepare herself for great conflicts, for vast reforms in social life, for noblest usefulness." Henry Fowle Durant was a true New England blue blood, descended from English immigrants who had come over in the 1660s. A lawyer, he had become rich after handling a claim for a rubber company and investing in their product, which he recognized as the future. The land just outside Boston that Wellesley College occupies—five hundred acres of rolling hills and forest, including a lake—was originally intended as a country estate where Durant and his wife, Pauline, planned to build a pleasure palace for their gifted young son. When the child died of diphtheria at the age of eight, Durant and

Pauline, heartbroken, struggled to find meaning in their lives. For Henry Durant, the process included a religious conversion, and while he first thought to found an orphanage in his son's memory, he came to believe that he could best do God's work by educating women. During the recent Civil War, women had proved eager, among other things, to take over teaching duties from their absent men, only to find themselves ill prepared to do so. This was in great part the result of the prevailing attitude that, as one Boston physician put it, "woman's brain was too delicate and fragile a thing to attempt the mastery of Greek and Latin." Durant chose to believe otherwise, and he put his real estate behind his convictions.

In 1875, twelve years after Durant's son's death, Wellesley opened its doors. The idea of higher education for girls was no longer completely foreign, though it was still viewed as inappropriate in many circles. In 1873 Robert Hallowell Richards, a professor of mining engineering at MIT, made a list in his journal of what he believed to be the pros and cons of coed education. He admitted to himself that men and women were "together in the family, why not in the school?" But still, he felt that educating the sexes together would do nothing but create "feelings and interests foreign to the lecture room." As late as 1899, long after the founding of Vassar, Barnard, Smith, Bryn Mawr, and Radcliffe, Charles William Eliot, the president of Harvard, was speaking out against the efficacy of education for women. Amazingly enough, he chose the inauguration of Wellesley's fifth president, Caroline Hazard, to express his views on why educating women was a means to no real end. Though many single young women of the lower classes were employed in unskilled work, he noted that "the so-called learned professions are very imperfectly open to women, and the scientific professions are even less accessible;

and society, as a whole, has not made up its mind in what intellectual fields women may be safely and profitably employed on a large scale." He had personally approved an expansion of Radcliffe, which was soon to become a more integral part of Harvard, but women's colleges, he believed, were still viewed as "luxuries or superfluities which some rather peculiar well-to-do girls desire to avail themselves of." He also thought that these schools should stop pretending to be counterparts to those for men. They should cease the practices of "grades, frequent examinations, prizes, and competitive scholarships" and follow a program that would not injure women's "bodily powers and functions." He finished up by pronouncing, "It would be a wonder, indeed, if the intellectual capacities of women were not at least as unlike those of men as their bodily capacities are." (Wellesley did not, in fact, give women grades until 1912 — prior to this they were simply told whether or not they had passed.)

Nevertheless, by 1880, nearly a third of all college students were women — forty thousand of them in total. Their numbers only grew in the 1890s, when the field of home economics was introduced by none other than the wife of the dubious Robert Hallowell Richards of MIT. Ellen Swallow Richards was not only the first woman admitted to MIT in 1870 — with the understanding that it was not to set a precedent of any kind — but also its first female professor. She, like her fellow home economists, "thought that homemaking was too complex and too important to be left to chance transmission from mother to daughter." Instead, they believed young women should be trained in the domestic arts in the classrooms and labs of the university, so that they could "run their homes according to the most up-to-date scientific knowledge." This included "the application of business and industrial management techniques to the homely tasks of cleaning and cooking."

But even as it offered women new chances in education as both students and professors, the field of home economics also further emphasized the idea that a woman's role was in the home, bringing it out of the old century and into the new one.

For colleges seeking to educate women in the liberal arts, there were other kinds of hurdles, and schools like Wellesley were not exempt from them. In its first year of operation, 314 students were admitted to the college. When it came time for them to take the entrance exams for placement into classes, however, only thirty proved to be qualified to undertake the work expected of them to earn a college degree because of their inferior education in the lower grades and high school. The result was that in its early days Wellesley, like many other women's colleges, accepted many girls into a kind of preparatory program for first-year students.

When Harriet arrived in the fall of 1910 and settled into her closely supervised off-campus house — Wellesley, like all institutions of higher education, had been growing quickly since its opening thirty-five years earlier, so a great number of students, generally the younger ones, had to live in such arrangements — the program had long since fallen by the wayside. In any case, she would not have needed it. "I am glad to report that my daughter Harriet passed her examinations at Wellesley with ease and so goes in without conditions," Edward Stratemeyer wrote to his editor at Lothrop, Lee & Shepard, who had driven the Stratemeyers to the Wellesley campus on one of their visits the year before. "She is nicely located at Mrs. Lawrence's...directly in front of the main gate of the grounds, and likes it very much."

<hr />

HARRIET'S YEARS at Wellesley marked the beginning of a pivotal shift for American women, who were just beginning to muster

the collective strength and numbers that would ultimately propel
them to success in the long battle for woman suffrage. The fight
had begun as far back as 1776, when Abigail Adams, writing to her
future-president husband, challenged him: "In the new code of
laws which I suppose it will be necessary for you to make, I desire
you would remember the ladies, and be more generous and favorable to them than your ancestors...Remember, all men would be
tyrants if they could. If particular care and attention is not paid
to the ladies, we are determined to foment a rebellion, and will
not hold ourselves bound by any laws in which we have no voice
or representation." His answer was the answer women would receive on the subject, in one form or another, for the next 144
years: "As to your extraordinary code of laws, I cannot but laugh."

Adams's attitude prevailed among the creators of the Constitution, and when it was ratified in 1791, it established free white
males as the only Americans eligible to vote. Defeated, activist
women turned instead to the abolitionist movement, working to
eradicate slavery and assuming that by helping black men get the
vote, they would be helping themselves as well. One of the first
indications that this idea might be pure folly came at the 1840
World Anti-Slavery Convention in London. The United States
had sent Lucretia Mott, a leader of the women's abolitionist movement, as its delegate. Upon arriving, she learned that women
would not be allowed to speak.

Nevertheless, the gathering was the beginning of one of the
most important relationships in the history of women and the
vote. There, Mott made the acquaintance of Elizabeth Cady
Stanton, who would soon emerge as one of the guiding lights of
the women's suffrage movement. By 1848 the two had crafted a
plan to hold the first women's rights conference, "to discuss the
social, civil, and religious condition and rights of woman." It at-

tracted some 260 women and about 40 men—not a great number, but still enough to get noticed. But Stanton and Mott's plans were thrown off course by the Civil War, when many women abandoned the cause. When the fighting was over, though, the suffrage movement—strengthened by the organizational skills its women had learned doing war work—scored its first victory. In 1869 Wyoming became the first state in the union to grant the vote to women. Technically it was still a territory, but when Congress tried to object to granting it statehood because of the recent change in voting laws, the intrepid legislature simply said, "We will remain out of the union a hundred years rather than come in without our women."

Then suffragists took the battle national. Susan B. Anthony, another former abolitionist who devoted her life to suffrage, appeared in front of every session of the U.S. Congress from 1869 to 1906 to ask for the passage of a national suffrage amendment, but it was to no avail. Instead, the group took the only approach it could, a state-by-state one. It organized rallies and attempted to cast votes (Anthony herself was arrested for one such attempt in 1872). Finally, in 1870, Utah granted women the right to vote, followed by Colorado in 1893 and Idaho in 1896.

But this initial burst of enthusiasm for bringing women to the polls faltered quickly in a country where the majority of women had no public voice and in most cases were incapable of even imagining themselves in any roles other than the domestic ones they were used to. By the turn of the century, more than fifty years after Elizabeth Cady Stanton and Lucretia Mott had made their Declaration, matters had not progressed. The powerful Women's Christian Temperance Union (WCTU), formed in 1874 in Ohio by women who wanted to close the state's saloons to prevent the "immoral" effect of alcohol on family and community life, had

expanded to advocate for a variety of social programs. Its president, Frances Willard, quickly realized that the WCTU could not
hope to bring about any of the changes it was lobbying for without the power to vote, so she made the enfranchisement of women
the group's main goal. The result was that many women who had
opposed the vote on the grounds that it would distract them from
their roles as homemakers now began to support it. A new generation of suffragettes had also cropped up to run the National
American Woman Suffrage Association (NAWSA), formed under
Cady Stanton's leadership in 1890 when the National Woman
Suffrage Association merged with the more conservative American Woman Suffrage Association.

But neither they nor the WCTU seemed able to reanimate
the movement. Despite their best efforts, no more states granted
women voting rights between 1896 and 1910. At a 1902 Senate
hearing regarding a sixteenth amendment on women suffrage,
the frustrated organizer of the New York State suffrage movement, Harriet May Mills, pointed out how much everything else
for women had changed.

> At the beginning of the nineteenth century no married woman
> could own a cent of property. At the beginning of the twenti-
> eth century women, married or single, may own and often do
> own millions.
>   Then another reason for this large increase in the property
> of women is that they are now allowed to earn their own living
> in almost any business, and there are to-day at least 4,000,000
> of us earning independent incomes. We feel that it is a great
> injustice, gentlemen, when we are such large shareholders in
> the Government, when we are such large participants in busi-
> ness affairs, to be denied any voice in the Government.

It was quite different in the old days, when married women were always under tutelage, and had no rights of their own, when they did not even own the clothes they wore. There might have been a little more justice in giving the votes to the man and denying it to the woman, but certainly it can not be fair to-day.

Some people say that this property is all represented by the men, and that they cast the votes for us. Gentlemen, in my State of New York there are 40,000 more women than men; and is it not a great burden to put upon the men to ask them to represent not only themselves, but 40,000 more women than the double of themselves?

I do not see how it is possible for any man to represent a woman.

It would take until the next decade, when activists finally brought into their ranks the lower-class workers who had been laboring for so long without protection or representation, for the suffrage movement to revive. But this time there was no going back. When Harriet entered Wellesley in the fall of 1910, the signs of impending change were everywhere. The Wellesley Equal Suffrage League was founded that same autumn, and when new president and Wellesley alumna Ellen Fitz Pendleton was inaugurated during the fall of Harriet's sophomore year, she made it clear that the mission of the college—any college, whether for men or women—had been conspicuously updated in anticipation of the changes to come. "I ask you to consider this morning the two-fold function of the college, the training for citizenship and the preparation of the scholar. The exigencies of our mother tongue compel me to use the masculine pronoun, but it will be understood that references are made to college students of both sexes." Preparation for participation in national civic duty was now a part of the curriculum.

As in the nation, however, support for suffrage was not guaranteed on the Wellesley campus. In 1911 California approved giving women the vote even as the National Association Opposed to Woman Suffrage was founded. Opinion was equally divided on campus. Early that year a vote was taken to see how many students approved of giving women the vote, and the majority did not. The *Wellesley College News* thought it was because of "lack of knowledge and indifference" on the part of anti-suffragists on campus, though in truth they opposed the movement on the well-thought-out (if strangely self-defeatist) grounds that men and women were bound to vote differently and thus granting women the right would sow discord in families and, indeed, in the nation itself. But by 1912, following the trend in the rest of the country, the majority of Wellesley students supported women's right to vote.

These idealistic young women arrived on campus ready to change the world—in the latest fashions, of course. In their trunks were long, tight "hobble skirts," which, while they were the height of style, had a tendency to impede their wearers' strides thanks to the narrow hem. The girls wore them with low heels that made for easy—or at least easier—walking on the hilly campus paths, and tied up their hair in ribbon bows. One issue of the campus paper described the usual garb for a day of classes: "White buckskin golf shoes, a long narrow white linen skirt, shirt-waist with long sleeves and a negligee ruffled collar; the whole 'toned' by a dash of color in the form of a violent green sash two feet wide. This costume is usually set off by what might be called the 'society slouch,' which aims to give a bored listlessness to one's posture." In the privacy of their cluttered rooms, the girls wore

boudoir caps and played the latest dance tunes on their man-
dolins, guitars, or banjos. "Can you dance the Boston, / Can you
dip and gently rise?" they sang, scandalizing themselves ever so
slightly in the process. As an editorial in the paper saw it, "modern dancing" was a big problem for the Wellesley girl. "People
who wish to be broadly tolerant are countenancing dances which
their instincts tell them are disgusting, and which doctors have
pronounced full of danger from a physiological point of view...
We would not be prudish, and yet we would be decent."

Wellesley girls were a vibrant group of young women, curious about the world if somewhat more socially conservative compared to their counterparts at other women's colleges. In an
editorial to the freshman in the fall of 1910, the *Wellesley News*
encouraged the new class to "be alive, be awake and active in
every phase of college life into which you enter." But, like all
women away at school in those years, they operated under strict
rules of conduct. They were not allowed to go off campus without registering a time of departure, a destination, and time of return, which could be 7:15 P.M. at the latest, and leaving campus
in the evening without a chaperone was not allowed under any
circumstances. They were not to even consider entering "the
precincts of any men's college or building used as a dormitory for
the student of such college... [which] shall be understood to include the Harvard Yard." They could not be seen eating anything
on the street in town or "stand[ing] about the railroad station
without a hat," but they were venturing into the town of Wellesley more and more (an activity referred to by a local priest as "the
4 o'clock invasion") and even to Boston, where the ideal afternoon included a play and some shopping topped off by a marsh-
mallow fudge sundae. Their numbers on these outings could be
literally overwhelming—as a spoof poem in the *News* joked:

"One day to Boston I did go / To watch the crowd, the passing show, / I thought to walk on Tremont Street / And gaze on Boston's true elite. / But every swell at whom I'd stare / Had such an old, familiar air: / The truth at last came over me, — / The whole crowd was from Wel-les-ley!"

With its enormous parcel of land, Wellesley had ample grounds for recreation of other sorts within its own walls. There were plenty of playing fields as well as excellent aquatic facilities. Harriet herself played tennis, field hockey, and softball, and swam and rode horses when she could. In addition, a new class called "Physical Training" was required of all students in their first two years at the college, combined with a course in "Hygiene." "The department of Hygiene and Physical Education...seems to me a very important development of the College," asserted the college president. "Without health a woman's life is sadly handicapped. She is the natural guardian of the health of children. To maintain and improve her own health, whatever her walk in life, is one of the prime essentials of living; to instill right principles in those under her care is one of her highest duties." The era in which girls were expected to sit inside embroidering was at an end, and Wellesley was at the forefront of creating young women who were confident in both mind and body.

For her major, Harriet chose music and English composition, but it was the history of religion courses she began to take in her sophomore year that she always counted as her favorite. In them, she believed, she had learned that "if one strips each of the great religions down to its basic concept one will find that the philosophy is the same: a reverence for deity, kindness to one's fellow-man, and a belief in life after death. It is only when man himself adds a lot of superfluous ideas and customs that misunderstandings occur, even to a point of bloodshed. The answer is tolerance." These were the tenets of a noble life, and she held herself to them strictly.

The rigors of a Wellesley education were far greater than those of Barringer High School. Harriet was, by her own account, "an average student because of too many other interests." Among other things, she was deeply curious about the suffrage movement. She was an enthusiastic participant in the activities of the Wellesley Equal Suffrage League, which invited prestigious speakers on the issue and took note as voting rights were granted, state by state, over the course of Harriet's four years at Wellesley—Washington in 1910, followed by California in 1911; Arizona, Kansas, and Oregon in 1913; and in 1914, Montana and Nevada. At one point, the league went so far as to assert that "in any non-military country, woman suffrage is natural, logical and right." In early 1912, just after Chinese women were given the vote—a short-lived gesture toward equality that was taken away again almost immediately—the group implored in the News: "Let us... be glad for them, and then let us be a little bit ashamed of our own position in contrast, and buckle to change it! American women have public spirit and patriotism. Can we better show it than by assuming responsibility—and being worthy of it?"

After writing home exuberantly about her activities with the league at one point, Harriet received a chastening, if loving, letter from her father, reminding her that while suffrage was certainly important, she should not let it distract her from her studies. Her passion ran in the family, apparently. Edna wrote to her enthusiastically and often about the movement in Harriet's first years at school, saying gleefully at one point: "Are you a suffragette? *I am!*" Both girls were electrified when NAWSA announced plans to disrupt the inauguration of Woodrow Wilson—Progressive candidate Theodore Roosevelt had run and lost on the first pro–equal voting rights platform in history—with the March for Woman Suffrage. Scheduled to arrive in Washington on March 3, 1913, it was designed specifically to attract an enormous amount of attention from the press waiting to cover Wilson.

On February 12, 1913, twelve marchers left New York City to walk down to Washington for the parade, traveling through New Jersey on their way. "Next Wednesday morning between 9:30 + 10, the walking suffragettes are going to pass through Newark," Edna wrote to Harriet, with whom she was carrying on a lively exchange about the upcoming event. "Mrs. Harris has invited me to see them...I think I'll join the procession and walk to Washington eh! Meet my old friends Taft and Wilson halfway!"

When the New York marchers reached Washington, they joined more than five thousand other protestors behind the beautiful and charismatic Inez Milholland, who led the parade down Pennsylvania Avenue dressed in a white cape and riding a white horse. Tiara on her head, dark curls tumbling down her back, she brought her true believers to a stop on the steps of the Treasury Building, where they performed an allegorical pageant that depicted "those ideals toward which both men and women have been struggling through the ages and toward which, in cooperation and equality, they will continue to strive." Among the crowd were famed reporter Nelly Bly (whose piece on the march ran under the headline "SUFFRAGISTS ARE MEN'S SUPERIORS") and Helen Keller, who was scheduled to speak but was so exhausted by the effort required to cut through the masses to reach her post that she had to cancel. Thousands of men in town for the inauguration the next day had begun to heckle the marchers just a few blocks into the procession, shouting indecencies and, among other things, "Where are your skirts?" The disorderly conduct prompted a Senate hearing in the following days to determine what had gone wrong. There, one panelist pronounced: "There would be nothing like this happen if you would stay at home."

As for Wilson, he was warned in a letter carried by the New York marchers that advocates of suffrage would "watch your administration with an intense interest such as has never before been focused upon the administration of any of your predecessors." Alas, the missive was never delivered, and when approached by a delegation from the organization after he took office, Wilson, hedging, claimed that he had never even given much thought to the matter. It was hardly surprising, given his reaction to the presence of the March for Women Suffrage at the time of his inauguration. Arriving in town to accept the presidency on the day of the march, his staff was so unaware that one of them actually asked the police where all the people were. Though Wilson would eventually come to support suffrage, it would take another seven years before the vote was finally granted during his last year in office.

Cosseted up at Wellesley, Harriet could not participate in the march. But she continued to do her part with the Equal Suffrage League. She also enjoyed numerous other extracurricular activities. Paramount among her nonacademic pursuits was her role at the Wellesley Press Board, first as an enthusiastic member after its founding in 1912 and eventually as president. As it was at all of the elite eastern schools, image was of enormous importance to Wellesley, and the Press Board, like similar organizations at other schools, was designed to control the flow of news about the school to the outside world. It supplied local newspapers, primarily the *Boston Globe* and the major New York papers, with approved items about the goings-on at the cloistered women's college in the Massachusetts hills. If a student wished to send an item to her own hometown paper, she had to join the board temporarily and have the contents vetted. Prior to its formation, according to the *Wellesley News*, information got out through "the disconnected work of a number of students engaged by the newspapers for which they reported, and responsible only to these papers." In other words, the school had no say in how it was being depicted to the outside world. Among recent infractions at the time of the Press Board's creation was a story in a California newspaper characterizing a student who had recently been elected a fire captain for one of the college houses as "[a] Wellesley girl who ran the only hose-wagon in the country driven by a woman."

Clearly this kind of vile misrepresentation would not do. As a member of the Press Board, Harriet sent carefully worded news items about her beloved school to the *Boston Globe*, the *Newark Sunday Call*, and the *Newark Evening News*. An economics class had taught her about the plight of women factory workers and taken her on a tour through some of Boston's housing projects, but she was so sheltered from the world of financial concerns that she had never seen a check. When her first payment arrived from the *Boston Globe* in that form, she believed it was "for information only" and pasted it into the pages of her memory book as a souvenir. Though she later peeled it out, leaving an empty space in her book that always made her laugh in later years, she had clearly never experienced the necessity of earning a living.

In the spring of her junior year, Harriet, who had often found the task of warding off outside reporters and photographers in the name of school honor difficult, was watching an outdoor play being performed on the college green from a hidden vantage point in the school's woods. Apparently, she was not the only one who found it a choice spot for gathering material for an article.

She became aware, suddenly, that two newspaper photographers were also secreted in the foliage, preparing to take a picture of the girls onstage, who were dressed in tights. In addition to the other restrictions, Wellesley girls were not allowed to perform in men's clothing if men were to be present in the audience. Under no circumstances were they to be photographed wearing even pants, much less tights. "At that time Wellesley…even had the girls standing behind tables or stone walls when the town photographer came," Harriet remembered. She immediately took the interlopers to task, waving a threatening finger at them and crying out, "You can't do that!" As she herself told the end of the story: "A week later I saw myself in a newsreel with the title 'Wellesley Press Board member tries to stop the above picture.' The above picture was a scene of Wellesley girls cavorting on the green in pants. No one ever reprimanded me, but I learned a lesson which has been invaluable to me in being interviewed: 'Don't threaten the media!'"

Though the girls were not allowed to be photographed wearing masculine clothing, according to the mores of their time, they never shied away from filling in for their missing beaux on social occasions. As an editorial in the school paper chided, "Don't kiss each other in the public highway. It's awful to see a woman doing a man's work." Single-sex dances where the girls dressed up as men to "escort" their partners were de rigueur, as men — fathers excepted — were not allowed on campus. On Sundays they could not be entertained even in the village. The first great exception came in the winter of Harriet's junior year, when a senior dance with men was planned for the first time. "Tomorrow night is the Glee Club Concert and the Senior Dance, and of all the excitement!" one thrilled girl wrote home to her mother. "Of course the faculty are still rather careful about the whole thing, — make them stop at midnight, etc." In preparation for the big occasion, the faculty passed a rule that all dancers must maintain a three-inch distance from one another, so as to be "preventive of the 'turkey trot,' the 'bunny hug' and other recent substitutes for the staid old waltz and two-step...Some of the girls are considering the availability of crinoline gowns as a precautionary measure."

When the time came for Harriet's own senior dance, she invited Russell Vroom Adams, her old childhood playmate, to be her escort. He was so enthusiastic that he danced his date into a punch bowl at one point, leaving her little doubt as to his eventual intentions. But the dances were a rare exception; generally speaking, the sexes were not allowed to mingle unless in the presence of the proper chastening influence. "Young men who call on the girl students at Wellesley Sunday nights must attend divine worship in Memorial Chapel under a new rule just put into effect by the faculty," a Boston newspaper reported in 1914, adding grimly, "The young men must sit through the service."

For the most part, Harriet's years at Wellesley were uneventful and enriching. The spring semester of her final year, however, would give her the chance to prove herself to her parents and everyone else in a very different manner and under circumstances no one could ever have imagined.

In the earliest hours of March 17, 1914, around 4:30 in the morning, two of Harriet's fellow Wellesley seniors awoke to the smell of smoke emanating from the Zoology Laboratory across from their room. Seeing a red glow through the glass transom above the door, they jumped from their beds and ran to alert the night watchman and the college registrar. Another girl who had awakened in the meantime ran to a lower floor and rang the great Japanese dinner bell until the actual fire alarm bell could be reached. The other residents of College Hall, Wellesley's main building, filed out calmly. For all anyone knew, this was simply a drill and, as such, they reacted without panic. Some of them grabbed coats or robes, but many were barefoot and clad only in nightdresses as they made their way out into the foggy early morning.

By the time they reached the first floor of the massive brick-and-wood building, flames were already eating away at the upper floors. Within ten minutes of the first alarm, all the students were shivering in the chilly March morning as they watched their possessions go up in tongues of flame and smoke. Later the head of College Hall, Olive Davis, recalled the moment vividly:

> What few words can picture that scene forever etched on the mind of each who shared in this experience? Outside the darkness and the stillness of night; within, the light of flames and the clang of the fire alarm, the crackle of the fire's steady onslaught, the falling embers, the students' white, terror-stricken faces as they realized the danger, the quiet of voices broken only by muffled answers to the roll call, the quick, decisive order, the unhesitating obedience to recognized authority, the passing of the students out through the north center windows, the breathless, frightened run through smoky, deserted halls for the missing seven, the sharp order "Dangerous, All out," and College Hall was gone.

As the uncontrolled flames blew from west to east, all students and faculty were accounted for, and the crowd fell silent.

Then, all at once, several faculty members came to the realization that the ground floor of College Hall contained not only student records, class schedules, and the entire life's work of many professors, but also cherished antiques and furniture that had been part of the school since its founding. They dashed into the inferno to try to save what they could. In their wake, groups of students, including Harriet, who had rushed over from her dorm, began to form long lines—bucket brigades of a sort—from the smoldering first floor of College Hall to the library next door. As the columns of girls grew longer, faculty members inside the burning building began to hand their rescued treasures out to the eager pairs of hands, which passed them, girl by girl, to safety in the library. Before long, the students could see that there would not be enough time to save everything, and several of them joined the faculty inside the building to aid the process. Among them was Harriet, who later won a medal of honor for her bravery and was commended by a fellow student, Hazel Cooper, in a Newark newspaper account of the fire printed the next day:

> Miss Harriet Stratemeyer of 171 North Seventh Street...with several others, carried valuable records from the burning building. Miss Stratemeyer also helped organize the endless chains of students that passed things along...As the girls in the building or in the chain gangs became exhausted, others stepped in at a quiet word of command.

Within half an hour from the time the alarm had first gone out, the building was completely gone. The firefighters who had finally arrived had been unable to get enough pressure in their hoses to reach the flames high above, and within minutes of their arrival had turned their attention instead to protecting other structures. Henry Durant's prized hall, built upon the very first stones laid on the campus in 1871, had been reduced to a shell of brick wall filled with a pile of blackened, smoking timber.

Charred wood was found on rooftops as far as a mile away, and many speculated that only the cold, rainy weather, which had filled the calm air with mist, had kept the flames from spreading not only to other buildings on the Wellesley campus but to the town itself.

But Wellesley College would not be cowed. As the president wrote in her year-end report, "No one thought of Self; everyone thought for the College, and the result was greater than one could have believed." At 8:30 that morning, just three and a half hours after the building had come down, the students and faculty assembled for chapel at the regular time. Many were dressed in borrowed clothing, and the remains of College Hall were still smoldering nearby. The choir sang, "Oh God our help in ages past, our hope for years to come," and President Pendleton said a prayer of thanks for the preservation of lives, before announcing that school would recess for spring vacation two weeks early and would reopen on the planned day of return. As offers of lodging, money, and goods from the town poured in and the railroad began to make special stops at the Wellesley station to ferry students home, the girls quickly packed what they could and left campus. One cheery soul commented on their good fortune in that "the fire was before and not after Easter shopping!"

"Attired in costumes plainly not their own, and carrying little baggage save magazines and musical instruments, about one hundred Wellesley College students arrived at the Grand Central Station last night at half-past six o'clock, bound for their homes," ran an article in the New York Herald. Ever cautious of how they represented their school, many of the girls "refused to admit that there had ever been a fire." Coming at last upon a clutch of girls who had been separated from their chaperone, the dogged reporter was finally able to get some facts. He tried to interview Harriet as well, but she said that "she hadn't even seen the fire, living outside the college confines." Only after she got permission from the faculty adviser to the Press Board did Harriet feel free to discuss her experiences.

Others, however, did not hold back. A school janitor, quoted in one of the hundreds of stories about the fire that came out all over the country, was nothing short of awestruck at the girls' behavior in a moment of crisis. "This heroine has not been and cannot be excelled," he told his interviewer. "For they were calm, determined, and unafraid, and chatted in quiet tones as they worked in the cold damp morning, performing feats that would be tests for young men of their years." Harriet's own account of the fire included her assertion that "not one girl flinched or fainted at the work before them." Though she would not own up to it, she herself fit this description well. A letter from one of her first-year roommates that reached Harriet at home over the vacation attested to her bravery at the scene of the fire: "Some style to Billie [Harriet's nickname] the Heroine! I sent all those things (letter and all) to Mother so she can see what kind of a girl I roomed with. Meanwhile we are all bursting with pride."

Harriet's parents, relieved that she had made it home unharmed, were also touched by her ordeal. Edward gave a generous donation to the Fire Fund almost immediately. Soon thereafter, Harriet and her fellow Press Board members announced that they would be donating their annual earnings to the Fire Fund as well. As for Lenna, she wrote to her elder daughter in pure admiration: "Whoever you inherited the nerve from in the family to go thru such an ordeal I'm sure I don't know."

When the students arrived back on campus in early April, provisional classroom and office space was almost completed, in the form of a wood-frame building that was thrown up in fifteen days and nicknamed the "Hen-Coop." Other colleges and students donated money and laboratory supplies (it was thought that the fire had perhaps started in the Zoology Lab, and much of the college's scientific equipment was replaced through gifts from other schools). The freshman and sophomore classes at Barnard took up a collection and sent $400, and many publishers donated books to replace the more than five thousand that had been destroyed. Thanks to the quick and astonishing mind of the dean's secretary, Mary Frazer Smith, classes started up again without interruption. In the hours between the fire and the triumphant chapel service, she had sat down at the president's house and written out both the class and examination schedules for the remainder of the year from memory.

Miss Frazer Smith and the indomitable spirit of both faculty and students ensured that the year finished off successfully. Indeed, commencement week for the 304 graduating members of the class of 1914—which included a senior class play, a garden party, and various concerts—was a thoroughly joyous affair. Engraved invitations were mailed out to family and friends, and the festivities culminated in the commencement exercises on June 16, replete with music by Verdi and Handel and followed by a luncheon. The Stratemeyer family attended the full week of events and had a grand time. Edward, flushed with happiness over his daughter's success, also had some thoughts about her immediate future. Writing to a friend and business acquaintance, he said: "I am just back from Wellesley with the whole family. We had a most delightful time at Harriet's graduation, the exercises lasting a week. She came through with flying colors and was offered a position at the college this Fall,—and she has also received three other offers, to teach, etc. But I think she will take a much-needed rest for the present."

Edward had thought to take Harriet to Europe as a graduation present. But, as he wrote to a friend: "Everything in Newark is War and the excitement is intense. We are mighty glad Hattie and I didn't go to Europe, as once planned." Instead, Edward took his daughter to Maine for a vacation. Perhaps he was trying to distract her from the fact that he had forced her to turn down not just the job offer from Wellesley but all the others as well. Among them were a post at the *Boston Globe*, which had gotten to know Harriet through her work with the Press Board; a teaching job; and, most unlikely, a job as a pianist in the Poconos. Edward, however, would have none of it. He wanted his daughter home, where he could take care of her until she was safely married. She was allowed to take a course in practical nursing at the Newark YWCA and to volunteer at the Home for Incurables, but otherwise he expected her to remain under his care. It was a frustrating turn of events not at all to Harriet's liking, and she and her father wrangled for some time. "He felt that as long as a father could take care of his daughter, he should," she remembered later. Though he was employing several women writers by this time and clearly appreciated and admired their work (he was generous with praise in his letters to authors and never failed to compliment a scene or bit of dialogue he especially liked), they were a separate breed from his daughters. "His idea of a woman writing was to earn a living," Harriet said, "and this was unnecessary [for me]."

Though Harriet's headstrong personality had been tempered during her time at Wellesley, it was not banished for good. She argued with her father for so long that he eventually gave in and said that if she had to work, she would work for him. Not in the office in Manhattan, of course—he had recently moved his operations to 17 Madison Avenue, where he worked with his secretary, Harriet Otis Smith—for a true woman of the upper classes did not go into an office. Instead, a compromise was struck. Harriet would be allowed to edit manuscripts and galley proofs, but only in the privacy of her parents' home. Nevertheless, she managed to learn a great deal about her father's winning formula. Just reading the books, which she had not done much of before, taught her about ending chapters on a suspenseful note and making sure that the first page of each story was good enough to make a reader continue. Looking over a book manuscript one afternoon, she discovered an entire page of action that had been carefully written by a ghostwriter and then crossed out by Stratemeyer in the editing process. Instead, written at the top of the page was the single word "CRASH!" On another, the entire introduction had been replaced by one emphatic "Bang!"

But Harriet's career as a junior editor was to be short-lived. Just as her father had planned, it endured only until another man assumed responsibility for her well-being. Over the course of her first year home after college, her relationship with Russell Vroom Adams, who had been her ardent admirer for years, intensified. He had become an investment banker in the intervening period and felt he was prepared to take care of Harriet in the style to which she was accustomed. The match was approved, the couple got engaged, and the Stratemeyer household was thrown into happy chaos.

In October of 1915, Edward wrote to one of his most prodigious authors, assuming the role of the grumbling patriarch: "On the 20th, my older daughter gets married, so matters at our house are pretty lively just now." The wedding took place at the Stratemeyer home at 6:30 on a Wednesday evening, with the family's Presbyterian minister presiding. Harriet, who was given away by her father, wore an elaborate dress concocted of white satin and "real" lace, complete with a train and flared standing collar. Her veil was done up with a cluster of orange blossoms, and she wore as her ornament a wristwatch that Russell had given her. The bridesmaids wore pink and blue, and Lenna Stratemeyer wore deep purple velvet adorned with silver lace and a diamond or two. Though the guests numbered under one hundred, Edward spared no expense. The house was resplendent with yellow and white flowers and potted palms, and a string orchestra played well into the night. When the young couple left for their honeymoon in New Orleans by boat, Harriet was attired in a chic black traveling outfit, including a velvet hat trimmed with autumn flowers. It was a grand affair all around, lush and expensive.

One important element, however, cost nothing, for it was made of a family heirloom. Lest she should forget her bond to her family and her father, she would literally wear it on her finger every day. As she vowed to marry Russell and be true to him, Harriet accepted a wedding band that had been formed from a nugget of gold that her grandfather Henry Stratemeyer had dug up in 1849. Though she had changed her name to Adams, the ring, along with what was now her middle name, ensured that, devoted to Russell as she was and would always be, she remained a Stratemeyer.

4

HAWKEYE DAYS

"FROSH WOMEN WIN SWIMMING EVENT!"

"FROSH CO-EDS WIN IN INITIAL GAME!"

"HAWKEYE SWIMMERS GIVE EXHIBITIONS
AT THE BIG DIPPER!"

HEADLINE AFTER HEADLINE trumpeting athletic events at the University of Iowa—whose school nickname was the Hawkeyes—ran in the school newspaper, the *Daily Iowan*, in the fall of 1922. All of them attested to the triumph and dominance of Iowa's powerful sports teams. Seventeen-year-old Mildred Augustine, who had just arrived from Ladora—forty miles and a world away—was a member of many of them.

She played right guard on the basketball team, was on the freshman soccer team, and made a short-lived effort to run track as well. Most importantly, she was a proud member of the Seals Club, a competitive swimming team for women that specialized in "Style Revues," relays, and fancy diving. It had been formed just prior to her freshman year in order to promote swimming among university women and had been so successful that by 1922 the sport was "perhaps the most prominent and popular" for women at the university (a trend that reflected a new national interest in swimming for women as well). Membership in the Seals was by audition only, and the competition was fierce. The group often gave elaborate shows that displayed their cutting-edge swim attire (they showed most but not all of their legs, and bare arms were a matter of course).

But the Seals were more than just fashion plates. They had been formed as a counterpart to the men's swimming club, the Eels, and one of the special features of all Seals and Eels exhibitions was coed relays. On one occasion when the Eels were giving a show at the Iowa City municipal swimming pool, known as "the Big Dipper," this report followed in the *Daily Iowan*: "The feature event of the evening was the exhibitions given by Captain McCullough of the University 1923–24 team...In a mixed relay with a man swimming against a woman, Mildred Augustine touched the wall a few seconds before McCullough did." Even the captain of the men's team, older than her by several years, was no match for the slender first-year from Ladora.

At last Mildred had an outlet for all of her athletic talent and ability. She was unstoppable, and even at a school known for its strong athletics, she made an impression quickly. "AUGUSTINE WON NOVICE SWIMMING MEET LAST NIGHT," ran one headline in the *Daily Iowan* her sophomore year. The story underneath it announced that she had beat out thirty other girls for the honor.

Women's athletics, especially swimming, were a new and thrilling part of campus life, and the life of the nation as well. Swimsuits themselves were the fashion accessory of the moment, perfect for baring the boyish figure that was all the rage, while the caps that went with them complemented the new bobbed hairstyle very pleasingly. In 1926 nineteen-year-old Olympic champion Gertrude Ederle became one of the country's biggest celebrities when she not only became the first woman to swim the treacherous twenty-one miles of the English Channel, but did it faster than the five men who had done it before her. Americans had never seen such speed and daring from their girls.

The University of Iowa, started in 1855, moved to the former capitol building in Iowa City in 1857 (the state capital itself was moved to Des Moines that year) and was the perfect place for a girl with aspirations both professional and athletic. Founded at federal expense and situated on land ceded by a federal grant, it was big and rowdy and had, among other things, a long-standing reputation for progressiveness and equality. It had admitted men and women on an equal basis since the moment it began holding classes, the first public institution in the United States to do so. In addition, there were no restrictions on students of any race or ethnicity. By 1922, Mildred's freshman year, the university was well established. "The institution of the present more than justifies the hopes of its founders," said the president. In addition to the undergraduate liberal arts program, Iowa had a law school, a medical school, a dental school, an engineering school, a school of pharmacy, a school of education, and schools of public health, nursing, "commerce," and music. It was truly engaged in preparing its students for fulfilling, necessary places in the world. As for the energetic student body, its nearly six thousand members were experiencing a kind of idealism and freedom that to previous generations would have been unthinkable. The difficult war years were finally over, and everyone, it seemed, was ready to let loose.

For the young men and women of Mildred's generation, as for everyone, the Great War had been a bloody education in the unthinkable cruelty of humankind and the new powers available to the military world. The first massive bombing of civilians and the first use of chemical weapons like poison chlorine gas had left little doubt in anyone's mind that the world had entered a terrifying new era. Though the assassination of Archduke Franz Ferdinand in Sarajevo in the summer of 1914 actually set off the war in Europe, for most Americans it was the infamous sinking of the *Lusitania* by a German U-boat in the spring of 1915 that brought home the dangers of the western front. Americans were outraged, and though Wilson was reelected the following year on an antiwar platform ("He kept us out of the war"), he asked for permission to declare war on Germany in the spring of 1917, telling his fellow countrymen: "The world must be made safe for democracy." The first wave of American troops landed on French soil in 1917.

"Good-bye Broadway, Hello France, we're ten million strong," ran the lyrics of one popular song that year. "Good-bye sweethearts, wives and mothers, it won't take us long." Never before had America sent her troops to another land to fight for freedom, and the patriotic fervor it created ran high as the news from across the ocean grew more and more worrying. Service flags with blue stars for each family member serving and gold ones for those who had been killed hung in windows and over porches of homes across the country. Food was rationed ("Eat More Cottage Cheese, You'll Need Less Meat," suggested one propaganda poster put out by the Board of Food Administration), and prescribed heatless, wheatless, and sugarless days, along with drives to save scrap metal and buy war stamps and war bonds, became a feature of everyday life. "Uncle Sam needs that extra shovelful of coal!" the iconic red, white, and blue character cheerfully reminded.

In November of 1918 Germany surrendered at last and signed Wilson's armistice agreement. Though American soldiers fought only the tail end of the war, the boost of morale created by both the country's entry into the conflict and Wilson's role in bringing it to a close allowed America to emerge as a global power, ushering in a new sense of pride and well-being that colored the postwar years, even as the country retreated back into isolationism. "Above all in the 1920s," historian Sarah Jane Deutsch writes, "there was a pervasive sense of newness. To many it seemed that the world was made new after the massive destruction of World War I ended in 1918 — and that women were made new too."

Though it would not be until the Second World War that the image of the working woman on the home front was popularized, the spike in employment women experienced during the Great War had similarly transformative effects. They had gone over to Europe in droves as nurses and Red Cross aid workers in the early years of the fighting, well before the United States had committed any troops. It was, for many of them, the opportunity of a lifetime, as the situation abroad was so chaotic that "women who were daring and willing could easily assign themselves to duty." There were many such women to be found in America, all of them longing for something to do. After 1917 the ones who did not want to go abroad began to fill in for the missing men at their places of employment, often in iron factories and steel mills that were producing materials for the war effort. At one point during the fighting, women made up 20 percent or more of workers "manufacturing airplanes, electrical machinery, leather and rubber goods, food, and printed materials," and by the end of the war, more than one hundred thousand women worked for the railroad as everything from station clerks to dispatchers to rail-yard laborers. Their earnings were often two to three times greater than what they had made before the war, if they had made anything at all. When the fighting ended, they were understandably reluctant to give up these jobs, a turn of events that angered and worried the men they had replaced. In New York, where many women were employed in public transportation, the Amalgamated Association of Street and Electric Railway Employees wrote a little ditty to express their dismay: "We wonder where we are drifting, where is the freedom of the stripes and stars / If for the sake of greed and profit we put women conductors on the cars." Having come too far to be so easily dismissed, the women responded in kind: "The simple, tender, clinging vine / That once around the oak did twine / Is something of the past; / We stand now by your side / And surmount obstacles with pride, / We're equal free at last / And I would rather polish steel, / Than get you up a tasty meal."

The other great change that affected women in the post–World War I years was the advent of widely available birth control, thanks to a powerful movement spearheaded by Margaret Sanger. Any form of contraception — even literature about it, which fell under the obscenity laws even for married women — had remained illegal well into the early part of the century. Educated women had access to condoms and spermicide, which were often obtained from Europe, but for the masses, no such materials were available. The only options were unlikely abstinence, backstreet abortions, and, presumably, the less-than-effective rhythm method. Sanger's own mother, an Irish working-class woman, had gone through eighteen pregnancies and eleven live births, giving her daughter an unforgettable reason to fight for change. In 1916, after spending a few years in Europe after an arrest, Sanger returned to the United States and, with her sister, set up an experimental birth control clinic in Brooklyn, New York. She was promptly arrested yet again, which drew enormous attention to her cause. Women of all classes and education levels banded together to support her efforts, protesting and going to prison for handing out illegal pamphlets, and each time another group was arrested, the groundswell of support for legalized birth control grew. By the 1920s birth control leagues were ministering to women both nationally and internationally and fighting for the legalization of their services, a cause that had long since taken on a political aspect along with its medical one as women emerged from World War I with a clearer sense of their rights than ever before.

With a dramatically different idea about what might be possible in their futures, women enrolled in college in the highest numbers ever in the 1920s. This group of coeds, as they were known, was a jubilant bunch. Having gained the vote at last in 1920 — what was the point of fighting for democracy elsewhere when they did not have it at home, they had demanded to know — they turned their backs on the previous generation's activism and began to sunbathe, wear makeup, and dress in short skirts. They seemed, in fact, to take their new privilege for granted. As Mildred herself put it, "I always voted and I just accepted that it is a woman's right, but I never became involved in suffrage at all. I just took it as it came...I just assumed that we would get it, which we did." All of this presumptuousness was distressing to the leaders of the recently victorious suffrage movement. Watching America's young women take their freedom and run with it was too much for the older generation. As flappers descended upon the country with their spangles and cigarettes, they seemed to wipe out all of the struggles and high-minded activism that had brought them into being, leaving only the fizz of champagne and racy stories in their wakes. Heralding a swing of the pendulum, by 1924, as one historian notes, "popular magazines were running articles (written by men) with such titles as 'Is Woman Suffrage A Failure?' and 'Women's Ineffective Use of the Vote.'"

But the young women of the early twenties were not all just about razzle-dazzle. On the Iowa campus, the Women's Association was a powerful presence that threw parties for undergraduate women and made sure they were properly represented in extracurricular activities. The Women's Athletic Association was also strong, and there were numerous clubs for women only, including sororities and literary societies. Living conditions, too, were up-to-the-minute. Many women, including Mildred in her first year, were housed in the modern new Currier Hall, which had private bathrooms and telephones in every room and kitchenettes for students who got the midnight munchies after dining-room hours. It was a building of such opulence and calm that one alumna, upon entering it for the first time, felt that any girl living there would realize "that these college years mean her chance to do something, to be somebody; that these four springtimes at the big dormitory may be her planting and her sowing season for a lifetime of high efficiency and lasting happiness." And though the Currier Hall rules about table manners and attire were strict, they could not prevent the falling away of many old social codes. "Today's woman gets what she wants," ran one newspaper ad of the era. "The vote. Slim sheaths of silk to replace voluminous petticoats...The right to a career." Even a man as traditional as Edward Stratemeyer could see the change: "I see in your books you have a tendency to fearful and fainting girls and women," he chided one of his male girls' series writers. "Better cut it—in these days the girls and women have about as much nerve as the boys and men. The timid, weeping girl must be a thing of the past."

Dating—no chaperone necessary—was all the rage, and skirts went as far up as the knee. (Mildred confessed to wearing "short" skirts, but not "short short" ones.) Women cut their hair up to their ears and wore open collars, and corsets were a thing of the past. Perhaps all of this was what brought the president of Mount Holyoke College, Mary Woolley, to the Iowa campus to answer charges that young people, meaning young women, were more superficial than they had been twenty years earlier. They were considered "flighty and flippant" in some circles, but Woolley was careful to draw the distinction between those girls and the ones who wanted more out of life. "There are certain qualities which characterize the woman of today, qualities which her mother and grandmother did not have, and these are independence and initiative," she told an enthralled crowd. "These qualities can be over-emphasized but I do not believe that this is the case today. The average girl has not developed them to such an extent that she is unruly, but they have helped her to gain a confidence which the older generation of women did not possess and a poise which makes her feel perfectly at home in any society and enables her to rise to any emergency." This was the ethos of the new generation. Along with the enormous barriers that had spawned it, the collectivist impulse that had allowed women to conquer so much in the past was fading. Now, it seemed, it was each woman for herself. When the Equal Rights Amendment was introduced in Congress in 1923, instead of sparking a whole new women's movement, it simply died on the vine. The National Woman's Party, which had thirty-five thousand members in 1920, had been reduced to a mere one thousand by the end of the decade. These new pioneers believed that in order to succeed, they needed to move beyond the idea of themselves as a separate entity from men; what they wanted was simple equality. In a *Harper's Magazine* article called "Feminist — New Style," the female author commented on the current generation's regard for those who came before: "They fought her battle, but she does not want to wear their mantle."

This description certainly applied to Mildred, who, utterly of her time, remembered herself in college as "an impudent little pup" and an "individualist." It was the perfect moment for such a girl to enter college. The war years had changed the face of leadership at Iowa from masculine to feminine, just as it had changed the country's. In the absence of male students, women had taken many positions of power in student government and extracurricular activities that, like the women of the New York City public transit system, they were not about to give back for no good reason. The student newspaper had had its first female editor — in fact, the first female editor of any campus daily newspaper — in 1918. This in turn led to the founding of a chapter of the national journalism sorority, Theta Sigma Phi, which Mildred would join in her years at Iowa.

Though there was a certain amount of division in social clubs and regulations regarding entertaining the opposite sex after hours were in place as well, these rules were fairly liberal. Undergraduates were allowed to stay out as late as 1:30 A.M. after formal dances on campus — the Charleston was the step of choice — and though dancing was forbidden on weekdays, other social engagements, such as attending a play or a literary meeting, were not. The rules for women were stricter than those for men, but they were far less binding than in earlier years, and it was entirely possible to spend a pleasant evening ensconced in the backseat of a Model T and still make it back to the dorm in time for check-in.

But Iowa was a Big Ten school with a sterling athletic reputation, which meant that football, above all else, was the consuming passion among the student body, and games were the biggest social affairs of the season. When the win was big, there was no holding back the exuberance, as during Mildred's sophomore year, when the news of triumph came from the East Coast: "HAWKEYES BEAT YALE 6–0!" shouted the *Daily Iowan*. "CORN TRIUMPHS OVER CULTURE AT NEW HAVEN!"

In addition to sports, of course, there were any number of societies—literary, social, dramatic, and otherwise—and Mildred was an enthusiastic member of many of them. She continued with her xylophone performances both in the school orchestra and at the various banquets held by the students and faculty. "Miss Mildred Augustine of the University will render for your approval a musical program on her Xylophone," ran the ad for "Jerry's Jubilee" during her junior year. "Don't miss this treat. Miss Augustine is an apt artist on this instrument." She was a member of the Athena Literary Society, whose motto was "To be rather than to seem," and for which she once played the goddess herself in a pageant; a member and later president of the Matrices, a women's writers group; an editor on the yearbook—the only woman out of six that year; and a staff writer for the *Daily Iowan*. Perhaps her favorite organization among them in terms of the social life was the Cosmopolitan Club, created for "the promotion of a spirit of friendship among the students of the various nationalities enrolled at the University," of which there were a fair number. The members threw frequent "International Nights" to introduce American students to foreign cultures—Japanese night or Hindu night, for example—one of which led to the observation that "FOREIGNERS ARE MORE EARNEST IN THEIR WORK THAN AMERICANS." It was not long before Mildred was elected secretary of the club.

In general, Iowa students were encouraged to be morally well-rounded human beings. "Don't try to make a 'hit' the first week," warned the freshman section of the student handbook. "If you are above average, it will be discovered in other ways." Also, it reminded its readers, "Write home when you arrive and often during the year." Another of its provisos was "Don't get in the habit of 'cutting.'" While Mildred no doubt tried to take this to heart, she was not an especially good student and had no patience for anything other than English. Finishing high school in three years had not helped in the preparation department. "I always had one or two subjects that were really hard for me," she remembered. "It was a big jump from high school to college… especially languages. I was never one who could learn it decently by taking a course. I was very poor in math and I didn't take much science. I took whatever I could get that was English or English related."

Luckily for Mildred, her years at Iowa were the ones in which the school's famed journalism program began to take root. Registration for journalism classes, which were offered throughout the English department, had increased rapidly since their formal introduction in 1915. Among the offerings were "Reporting and Correspondence," "The Interpretation of News" (a class on editorial writing), a history of American journalism, a class on the mechanics of printing, and one on the business side of the field. Students enrolled in these classes worked at the *Daily Iowan* to put theory into practice, and the results of their training showed. The paper, started in 1901 as the first college daily west of the

Mississippi, became known by the early twenties as a breeding ground for smart young journalists. They were stringers for papers statewide, wrote for national magazines, and on rare occasions were called in to oversee the production of a daily paper as preparation for their futures. "WE NEVER SLEEP," ran a story about the hardworking newspaper crowd, only half jokingly.

Indeed, demand for journalism classes was so great that in the fall of 1920 a bachelor of arts program in journalism was formed for the first time. Many of the courses were taught by William Maulsby, the assistant editor of a newspaper in Springfield, Massachusetts. He had turned down a promotion at his paper to come to Iowa, and his students referred to him as "Major Maulsby" because, according to Mildred, he told "the most gory stories in class about the adventures of a reporter, and that really inspired me." One of the other revered professors in the department was a young graduate of the university's psychology program by the name of George Gallup. He had been the editor of the *Daily Iowan* during Mildred's freshman year and would go on to combine his training in psychology and journalism to create the Gallup Poll.

For Mildred, working on the *Daily Iowan* was a dream come true. By the time she was a sophomore, the paper had become a member of the Associated Press and had its own building on campus, which contained a printing plant. In addition to college news, it ran local Iowa City news and AP wire stories — it was one of only two college papers with the privilege of doing so — and it was generally understood to be one of the best college papers in the country. It sent both men and women graduates on to top journalism jobs all over the country. Nevertheless, she was as interested in campus news as she was in state news, especially if it had to do with women, swimming, or both. In an unsigned

editorial in the *Daily Iowan* entitled "Our Sardines," she had this
to say about unequal swimming facilities. "Iowa's new swimming
pool, the best of its kind in the world, will serve as a new spur
to the men who are to use it. Iowa women are also devoting
more time and enthusiasm to swimming...The women's pool,
twenty yards in length, which a number of years ago was ample
to accommodate all who wished to swim, is now cramped...
Swimming records at the women's gymnasium have been
slashed in the last three years...If Iowa women cannot have
more room in which to exercise their ambitious limbs, if they
cannot have high diving boards—then at least they should be
praised for the progress they have made in spite of handicap."
She had already developed a talent for telling the unvarnished
truth in elegant prose.

By 1924 the Iowa journalism program had expanded to include a graduate school. It offered advanced courses and inces-
sant instruction on the hows and whys of good journalism, many
of which were published in its magazine, the *Iowa Journalist*.
Among them was an ongoing list of "Faults in Expression":

> *Fair sex*—Write girls or women.
> *Female*—Do not apply the term to a human being.
> *Floral Offering*—A stock expression of indefinite meaning.
>   Tell what kind of flowers were sent or given.
> *Leaves a widow*—Obviously impossible. The most a man can
>   do is leave a wife.

Perhaps most important, there was a recurring column called
"Advice to the Young Reporter." One month it printed a list of
"essential qualifications of a good reporter," including one that
described Mildred perfectly: "Untiring industry and an unwea-
ried capacity for taking pains."

For in addition to her various athletics, clubs, classes, and work on the paper and yearbook, Mildred was also continuing to publish short stories in children's magazines around the country. Along with a series of tales about Midget, the athletic star of her first published story back in high school, were others that seemed to draw on the details of Mildred's life. One of them, "Wanted — An Idea," tells the saga of a girl named Margaret Howard working a summer job at a department store. When it becomes clear to her that the employees are disgruntled and lacking motivation to make sales, she comes up with, naturally, a brilliant idea.

"Mother, I know—a store newspaper!" Mrs. Howard looked surprised. "I don't see exactly what you mean," she said. "Why, listen," Margaret began in an excited tone of voice. "Not a news-paper of course—but a bulletin published weekly. In it one would publish the names of the people that had made the most sales for the week and whenever anyone furnished a new idea for the organization, an account would be in the paper." "People do like to see their names in print," Mrs. Howard admitted. "And competition is the life of trade," Margaret added.

With such great faith in the power of journalism, it was no wonder that Mildred made it her life. She graduated from the University of Iowa in the early summer of 1925, finishing in three years (later she admitted that she regretted it, just a bit, because, she explained, "I think you need the cultural effect of college just as much as you need the subject matter"). Unbound by the so-cial mores of the upper classes, she joined the ever-growing ranks of the middle-class working girl, promptly getting a job at the *Clinton (Iowa) Herald*. Movie stars had just recently begun to re-place politicians and other civic leaders as role models for young people, and on-screen many of them were doing just what Mildred was. The plots involving spunky women with guts and brains to spare "echoed the enormously popular novels that Horatio Alger had written fifty years earlier about poor young men who, through luck, pluck, and virtue, became rich. In the 1920s, it was working women who embodied this entrepreneurial drive...they were now in charge of their own lives." These women often did it by marrying their bosses and moving up, which Mildred had no intention of doing. Instead, she worked on the society pages of the *Herald* and joined Clinton's town orchestra, once again playing the xylophone.

In the fall of 1926, she reenrolled at Iowa, this time in the brand-new master's program in journalism. There, she soaked up more of the principles and rules of journalism that would serve her for the rest of her life. In a guest lecture, the editor of the *Sioux City Journal* charged the young hopefuls with a serious task: "I enjoin every journalist to make sacrifices to truth and in furtherance of truth. Write nothing that you do not know to be true. Check and double-check your facts. Do not crucify the truth for the sake of a good story. Invention should have no place in newspaper writing."

At the age of eighty-eight, Mildred could repeat these fundamentals as if she had graduated just the week before. She was still spelling out the name of her hometown tartly for reporters to make sure they got it right—"I came from the town of Ladora, Iowa, of course, and that's spelled L-A-D-O-R-A"—and telling them, "There's only two things I believe in—well a few more things than that—but I believe in absolute honesty and honesty in journalism...I don't think you should sacrifice a person for a story and I never have believed that and I've never done it, even if I've been ordered to do it."

After writing her assigned thesis, which she hated, on "Newspaper Illustration: A Study of the Metropolitan Daily, the Small City Daily, and the Country Weekly," Mildred became the first woman to graduate from the Iowa School of Journalism in the summer of 1927. She had fallen in love with a fellow student, Asa Wirt, whom she would marry in 1928. She was also at the beginning of another relationship that would have an impact on the rest of her life. It had started well before she joined the master's program, in the spring of 1926, when she answered an ad in the *Editor* magazine.

The Stratemeyer Syndicate, Edward Stratemeyer, proprietor, of Newark, N.J. and New York City, can use the services of several additional writers in the preparation of the Syndicate's books for boys, books for girls, and rapid-fire detective stories. These stories are all written for the Syndicate on its own titles and outlines and we buy all rights in this material for cash upon acceptance. Rates of payment depend entirely upon the amount of work actually done by a writer and the quality of same. All stories are issued under established trademarked pen names unless otherwise agreed upon...We are particularly anxious to get hold of the younger writers, with fresh ideas in the treatment of stories for boys and girls.

5

NELL CODY, HELEN HALE, DIANA DARE

IN THE SPRING OF 1914, just after Harriet had gone back to Wellesley to prepare for graduation, Edward Stratemeyer sent a note to his car insurance agent. He had recently bought himself a small new automobile, and he wanted to straighten out a pressing matter. "I wish it understood that the car is to be driven not alone by myself but also by my two daughters, Harriet and Edna C. Stratemeyer." The relationship between cars and girls was one that Stratemeyer was intimately familiar with by then. He had insisted on teaching both of his girls to drive in their teens and, seeing their enthusiasm (Edna turned out to be quite good behind the wheel), had started a successful series in 1910 called the Motor Girls.

A spin-off (unsurprisingly) from a popular boys' series called the Motor Boys, the Motor Girls books detailed the touring adventures of Cora Kimball and her chums the Robinson twins, Bess (plump, as Nancy Drew's chum Bess would be, too) and

Belle. In the opening chapter of the first title, Cora receives a car of her own as a gift from her mother, a wealthy widow. Further confirmation of Cora's independent spirit is only a few pages away. Offered a driving lesson by one of her brother's friends, she immediately retorts, "This is my machine, and I intend to run it." Cars are a part of the matriarchal lineage in the Kimball family, a heritage that reflected the trends in reality.

Just two years before the Motor Girls were introduced, Henry Ford's mass-produced Model T debuted, along with Ford's cheeky marketing campaign: "You can paint it any color, so long as it's black." Priced at $850, its immediate popularity with both men and women sealed America's fate as a nation of car lovers; suddenly a car was a fact of life rather than a luxury item. Cora Kimball gave little girls a taste of what lay ahead when they grew up, a kind of freedom unthinkable to their mothers' generation. Left alone with her gift at the start of the series, Cora bathes her newfangled "machine" in an affectionate gaze, exuding pure, rapturous excitement (and no small degree of technical knowledge): "The girl stepped over to a window and looked out. There, on the driveway, stood a new automobile. Four-cylindered, sliding-gear transmission, three speeds forward and reverse, long-wheel base, new ignition system, and all sorts of other things mentioned in the catalogue. Besides, it was a beautiful maroon color, and the leather cushions matched."

It would be another few decades before a truly car-obsessed girl made it to the pages of a young adult book: In 1937 Noel Streatfeild's *Ballet Shoes* featured the charming Petrova Fossil, a girl who goes so far as to wear mechanic's coveralls for the entire second half of the book despite a career in dance; and in 1955 Beverly Cleary's intrepid Ramona Quimby took her favorite doll, Chevrolet, to show-and-tell. But surely no girl could fail to adore lucky, modern Cora and the promise of her new vehicle. There were a few comments on the oddness of girls driving cars in the book, no doubt intended to bring a chuckle to readers who could no more imagine not being able to drive than they could not being made to go to school, but Stratemeyer made sure to put them in the mouth (and uneducated dialect) of a hayseed who relied on horses: "Wa'al, I'll be gum-swizzled!" exclaimed the farmer. "What's this, anyhow? Auto-mobiles? As I live! Wa'al, I swan t' goodness! An' gals a-drivin' of 'em! Ho! ho!"

The Motor Girls series—which took its heroines through plots involving stolen fortunes, family heirlooms, and other stock features of mystery books—went on to run for seven years and ten volumes. Cora and her pals were ever young and single, and in that sense they differed enormously from the heroines of girls' books in the previous century, most of whom were locked in some kind of domestic drama involving death or hardship. There were the long-suffering March girls of Louisa May Alcott's *Little Women* and the little band of siblings in the *Five Little Peppers and How They Grew*, Margaret Sidney's famous tale of a pious family fallen on hard times after the death of the father, but ever cheerful and Christian in the face of poverty. A classic example of the genre, *Five Little Peppers* was first published in 1881 and reprinted repeatedly, including in 1907, when one of Edward Stratemeyer's editor friends sent him a new holiday edition that he passed on to his daughters (both of whom, it should be said, enjoyed reading it). But in spite of the ongoing popularity of such old standbys, new entries into the world of girls' series books were gaining ground in the early part of the twentieth century as publishers realized they had a virtually untapped market before them. Forty-six new girls' series were started between 1900 and 1910, and another ninety-four were started in the following decade. Girls who read were no longer considered poor relations to their brothers and pals: They had been discovered as a demographic, and the Motor Girls series was specifically designed to take advantage of that fact.

They were not, however, Stratemeyer's maiden effort in the field. Though he got started somewhat late—a slip that, he confessed in 1906, "comes of my ignorance concerning girls' books and those who pen them, for I have devoted nearly fifteen years of my life to boys' books and boys' periodicals"—he was quick to catch up. That year he began writing to various women authors, hoping to engage someone to write his first line of girls' books. "Among other things, we want one line of stories for girls," he wrote to one candidate that same year. "If you know anything about my Rover Boys Series...you'll know exactly what I mean...We do not ask for what is commonly called 'fine writing,' (usually another name for what is tedious and cumbersome) but want something full of 'ginger' and action."

The result of these efforts appeared in 1908 in the form of fourteen-year-old Dorothy Dale, who was, according to the subtitle of the first book in the series, "a girl of today." "Dorothy Dale is the daughter of an old Civil War veteran who is running a weekly newspaper in a small Eastern town," announced the first volume. "Her sunny disposition, her fun-loving ways and her trials and triumphs make clean, interesting and fascinating reading." She is also missing a parent—her mother, who died giving birth to her youngest brother—and runs her home with the help of a loving housekeeper who is like a member of the family. Her devoted father refers to her as "Little Captain," and her adventures take her from coast to coast, to boarding school, to the mountains and the ocean. At least they do until the second-to-last book in the series, which proved to be the kiss of death for the young heroine: *Dorothy Dale's Engagement* was the first indication that little girls of the new century did not care to see their role models grow up and marry. Admitting to a friend that she's smitten, Dorothy says, "I have too much good sense to lose the chance of showing the man I love that he can win me, because of any foolish or old-fashioned ideas of conventionalities." The conventionalities happen to be an enormous fortune Dorothy is due to inherit at any moment, which she happily agrees to forgo if she can just have her Gerry. Luckily, he makes a good business deal of his own, and at the book's end she pledges to wait for him to earn a fortune. In that instant, Dorothy's devoted readers lost interest and sales dropped off, a lesson the Syndicate never forgot. Much later Harriet wrote herself some general guidelines on writing stories for young people. Among the key points was this one: "Must appeal to children. This excludes love element, adult hardships. Marrying off Nancy Drew disastrous."

Dorothy's misguided betrothal did not come until 1917, however, by which time Stratemeyer had plenty of other girls' series in the works. As always, he was ahead of all his competitors in this new field, largely due to his wise marketing techniques. One of the advertising catalogs he worked up for his books included a special section called "Books Especially for Girls" that reassured parents and booksellers that he understood their problems in finding reading material they could trust would be up to their standards. "To get good books written for girls has always been a difficult problem, the reason probably being that many girls prefer to read boys' books or to jump to the regular novels of the day—the latter a particularly bad habit, since their minds are not sufficiently developed to sort out the good from the bad among what are commonly called 'the best sellers.'" Stratemeyer continued to have strict policies when it came to content. As he wrote to the author of the Motor Girls books when she turned in a manuscript that departed from his wishes: "I have never permitted a murder to occur in any of our boys' books and naturally would not permit that sort of a thing in a book meant for girls from ten to fifteen years of age. Nothing is said of such a thing in the outline given for the story."

STRATEMEYER HAD A new reason, on top of all the usual ones, to be wary of too many unsavory scenes in his books. Childhood as a whole, no longer just children's books, was suddenly coming in for more examination than it had ever borne before. "It is the Century of the Child," boomed the *New Republic* magazine in the fall of 1926. "Childhood has ceased to be a terra incognita taken for granted. Like the North Pole, it has become worth much adult attention." Theodore Roosevelt had established the White House Conference on Children and Youth in 1909, designed to deal with "all children, in their total aspects, including those social and environmental factors which are influencing modern childhood." Thanks to the Child Labor Act of 1916, which limited the working age to fourteen, and the advent of labor-saving devices like vacuums, electric irons, and refrigerators—by 1927 nearly two-thirds of American homes had electricity, and running water was a given—kids were working far less both in and out of the home than they had in previous years. Where they had once held factory jobs and turned over their pay to help support their households, they now went to school and had time for idle pursuits.

The golden age of radio dawned just in time to help them fill their suddenly relaxed days. By 1924 two and a half million

American households owned a set, and children's programming proliferated on the airwaves. Shows like *Buster Brown's Radio Club, Uncle Don,* and Sunday night bedtime story hours were immensely popular as children followed their parents' cue and gathered around the family radio. These entertainments—along with the unrivaled success of nickelodeons patronized almost exclusively by children after school and on the weekends, without their parents—were the first signs that young America had been recognized as a segment of society worth not only paying attention to, but serving. But even as they were given ever more independence from the burdens of adulthood and marketers began to zero in on them, children were also being viewed as innocents who needed to be protected from the ills of the grown-up world. By the end of the 1920s, parenting had gone from a duty to an all-consuming profession of sorts. One middle-class woman who spoke to researchers in 1929 practically bragged to them: "I accommodate my entire life to my little girl."

A large part of this newly intense interest in raising children found its expression in education, and as schooling came to the forefront of childhood—with fewer children working, they had more time to go to school—so did opinions about how and what children should be taught, including what they read. New magazines devoted to analysis and criticism of children's reading and books sprang up, like the *Horn Book* and the *Bookman.* Publishing companies were setting up children's departments, an annual Children's Book Week designed to bring attention to the best and brightest new books and authors had been established, and the prestigious Newbery and Caldecott awards for children's books were launched. The previous eight years, according to the author of the *New Republic* piece, had seen "a trebling of the numbers of children's books published annually." In 1925 alone, by one estimate, more than twenty-five million children's books were printed.

None of this attention, however, was designed to encourage the sales of the Stratemeyer Syndicate. For along with the rise of children's literature had come a renewed effort to demonize series books. Various critics had been harassing Stratemeyer as far back as the turn of the century, but even their sustained effort could not much affect the financial fortunes of books like Stratemeyer's. Still, they made their voices heard. The year Stratemeyer started his company, a well-known child psychologist published an article pointedly titled "What Children Do Read and What They Ought to Read." A decade or so later, a book called *The Guide to Literature for Children* opined that "much of the contempt for social conventions for which the rising generation is blamed is due to the reading of this poisonous sort of fiction." But perhaps the biggest potential blow came in 1914, when Franklin K. Mathiews, chief scout librarian of the Boy Scouts of America—then 127,000 members strong with enormous influence over the habits of American families—published a screed entitled "Blowing Out the Boys' Brains." In the language of the battlefield, the widely circulated piece deemed series books nothing short of sinister, permanently life-altering forces. "The harm done [in reading them] is simply incalculable," Mathiews moralized. "I wish I could label each one of these books: 'Explosives! Guaranteed to Blow Your Boy's Brains Out.'"

In addition to being righteous and pedantic, Mathiews and his ilk were absolutely right about one thing: Series books were enormous moneymakers. Even when the Newark Public Library had removed all of Stratemeyer's books, along with Horatio Alger's and Oliver Optic's, from its shelves in protest earlier in the century, it had done little to hurt him. "Personally, it does not matter much to me whether or not my books are now put back on the shelves of the juvenile department," he wrote to the chairman of the library's book committee at the time. "Taking them out of the Library has more than tripled the sales in Newark." Matters remained much the same throughout the 1920s. At a New Jersey Federation Women's Club Convention in 1921, Magdalene Stratemeyer heard a speech lambasting her husband delivered by the head of the Brooklyn Library children's department. She reported back to Edward, who found himself in a quandary. The talk had been given by none other than his old nemesis, the same woman who had contrived to excise his work from the Newark Library in 1901, and Stratemeyer now considered suing her for libel. There was a problem, however, which he confessed to Lenna in a letter: "Maybe I'll scare her into something. But in order to get damages I have first to prove them—and *how* can I prove such talk hurts the books while the sale keeps up?" Indeed, the following year, the Stratemeyer Syndicate earned $9.1 million, $1 million of which was from sales of a single series, the Outdoor Girls.

"He has probably influenced youth more than any writer in America today, and in 30 years he has amassed a sales distribution of between 15 and 20 millions of copies," sighed one admiring journalist. Nevertheless, Stratemeyer worked as hard as ever to sell more books. Competition with the five-cent nickelodeons that were attracting children in swarms sparked his latest revolutionary scheme: He priced his books at a mere fifty cents. The days of books costing a dollar or more had passed, in his opinion, like a plague. Parents could afford fifty-centers, and children with a reasonable allowance or an after-school job could, too. Boys had paper routes and flower carts; they blacked shoes and carried telegrams. Girls, who did not have jobs outside the home for the most part, also had their methods, as one of them confessed: "It is so easy for a girl, when sent to the corner grocery for 15 cents worth of coal oil, to get a dime's worth and save a nickel." No matter where they were getting their cash, children gladly spent it on series books.

Stratemeyer didn't hesitate to spend his, either. Unwilling to settle for what the publishing houses called "publicity," he routinely put up his own money to buy mailing lists of children's names and addresses from various youth organizations and then helped his publishers create booklets packed with teasers, color pictures, and intriguing tidbits of plot and adventure, which were soon winging their way through the mail to every corner of the country. On the back page of these catalogs was a form that could be used to write down "the names and Addresses of other boys and girls to whom you want us to send catalogs." It was a clever way to appeal to modern children, who, with all their newfound leisure time and social status, were often, as one assessment put it, "too busy shooting marbles to look at book announcements." It was also pure marketing genius. One kid empowered with a pen and a catalog was enough to make an entire neighborhood crazy for fifty-centers, and the numbers bore it out. By 1934 Cupples & Leon, one of the big three juvenile series book publishers, estimated that their mailing list was half a million names long. Whole gangs of children were comparing notes about what they were saving up for and what they were prepared to swap, and they frequently wrote letters to publishers with comments and suggestions and demands. The catalogs had done the trick, functioning, in the words of one disapproving writer, like "an insidious narcotic with the habit-forming properties of opium."

The result was that while series books were viewed darkly by many parents and educators, they soon acquired the highest stamp of childhood approval: Over back fences and during school

recesses, they served as private black-market currency. Two Tom
Swifts might be worth a baseball bat or a bag of marbles. Tales of
boys in fast cars and rocket ships offered an escape from reality
in thrilling, page-turning prose, and their reach was seemingly
limitless. "No matter where you are, there is a [series] book," one
pleased young writer from Kentucky mentioned in his fan letter
to a publisher. "If I had enough money saved up, I would get the
rest," wrote another, from Milford, Illinois, referring to the Rover
Boys series. Not only the characters, but their fake, pseudonymous authors had become friends to the youth of America. "During adolescence Roy Rockwood had always been one of my
favorite people," confessed one of Stratemeyer's eventual ghostwriters, about the famous "author" of the Bomba the Jungle Boy
series. "I pictured him seated at his desk, pen in hand, white shirt
open at the throat, a bulldog pipe in his teeth." Children wrote
in to the Syndicate and their favorite authors by the dozens. They
asked for autographs and for information about the authors for
book reports; they inquired as to whether or not the characters
were real people, hoping to resolve arguments about the books
that cropped up in their circles of friends by going straight to the
source; they requested replacement dust jackets for their well-
worn books, which the Syndicate provided without a fuss; they
sent in suggestions for plots ("Write a mystery about a ferret") and
asked to star in the books themselves as a way to break in to a future as a movie star.

By 1926 Stratemeyer was more prosperous than ever. His offices on fashionable Madison Square Park in Manhattan were
buzzing, and his secretary, Harriet Otis Smith, had become an
integral part of the Syndicate, reading manuscripts and making
suggestions. Certainly Stratemeyer needed the help, for by this
time he had twenty-four series running, and the Syndicate had

sold somewhere between three and four million books the previous year. Stratemeyer, knowing he had yet more to offer his publishers, was also busy making plans for the future.

But first a few changes had to be made. Writing to one of his biggest publishers, Cupples & Leon, he berated them for what he considered to be an inferior jacket on a recent title in one of his series and then went on: "You will perhaps be interested to know that during the past two months my Syndicate has been conducting a campaign for new writers and out of the great number who applied I have found several magazine authors who are crackerjacks. So I am expecting better manuscripts than ever in the future." The response to his ad in the *Editor* magazine had been immediate and overwhelming; letters came from New York and Nebraska; from a hopeful town called Fertile, Minnesota; from Washington, D.C.; Waynesboro, Virginia; Framingham, Massachusetts; and Cuyahoga Falls, Ohio. A missive also arrived from 730 Ninth Avenue, in Clinton, Iowa. "Dear Sirs," it began:

> I understand that the Stratemeyer Syndicate can use the services of writers in the preparation of books for boys and girls and also in the short story field. Will you kindly furnish me with information concerning this work and your terms?
>
> I have sold twenty-eight stories in the past two years to St. Nicholas Magazine, Lutheran Young Folks, Young People, Youth's Comrade, and similar magazines and papers. In addition, I have sold a number of articles, feature stories and fiction, and have turned out about six hundred printed inches of newspaper material each week for the last year.
>
> In September I am planning to change my location to New York City.
>
> Yours very truly,
> Mildred Augustine

Before entering Iowa's journalism program, Mildred had apparently been laboring on a scheme to move to the big city. Perhaps her newspaper job in Iowa, with her duties on the society pages, had not been all she had hoped for; certainly she longed for a more cosmopolitan existence than could be had in small-town America. No doubt she thought it would make sense to have some contacts in New York before throwing herself on its mercies like so many young women before her had, and, as she was eager to break into books, Stratemeyer's ad had seemed just the thing. He responded immediately, asking her to send stories if she wanted. She did.

"I have looked over these stories with a great deal of interest," he wrote to her in May, "and it is just possible that in the future I may be able to use your services, provided we can come to terms." It was enough to encourage her. That July, on her way home from a tour through Europe (which she paid for with money she had earned at the *Clinton Herald*), Mildred stopped off in New York and met with Stratemeyer. His impression of her in person must have solidified his belief in her as a fresh new voice for his books, for she came away with a promise of eventual work. When she went back to the University of Iowa for her master's degree — clearly her backup plan when no immediate job was offered — she made sure to send Stratemeyer her new address in Iowa City so that he would be able to find her easily. Just a few days later, he wrote to ask her if she would undertake the next title in his Ruth Fielding series, which was about to lose its originating writer.

Of all the girls' series Stratemeyer started in the early part of the century, Ruth Fielding (1913) was his greatest success, centered on one bold young movie star/director heroine who knew what she wanted and how to get it, even in the male-dominated, fast-paced world of Hollywood. By the time Edward sent Mildred a two-and-a-half-page outline for *Ruth Fielding and Her Great Scenario; or, Striving for the Motion Picture Prize*—scenario meaning screenplay—Ruth had been established as a go-getter and had made the shift from solving tame crimes at her boarding school to cracking Hollywood cases, even as she kept up a back-breaking workload in the movie industry. The basic plot of Mildred's first effort for the Stratemeyer Syndicate, as described by Edward, was "a bitter rival learned that Ruth was writing a prize scenario and laid a plot to rob the girl of the rewards of her labor. A fascinating tale of mystifying adventures." But in spite of being all of that, set at a summer resort and replete with explosions, theft, and suspense of all kinds, the story was also about the more mundane, if no less important, aspects of Ruth's existence namely, her love life.

For Ruth Fielding, like her predecessors Dorothy Dale and Cora Kimball, is nothing if not a thoroughly modern girl—and not always in the most reassuring way. Just as Cora had put up with being harassed about driving a car fifteen years earlier, Ruth has to cope with Americans' slowly regressing ideas about women and work, which manifest in her relationship with long-time beau, Tom Cameron. "Through all her exultation and excitement, Ruth felt a tiny ache of conscience when she thought of Tom. He was being such a sport about it—as indeed he had been all along." Eventually, she gives in to Tom's fondest desire, albeit with some ambivalence. Not twenty pages of *Ruth Fielding and Her Great Scenario* go by before we learn that "the engagement ring on her finger... told Ruth's friends that the girl did not always intend to remain a single business woman. But Ruth wanted a career as well as love."

This inexorable, newly resurgent pull of domesticity was drawn straight from the daily headlines. As one historian notes, thanks to the flash and frivolity of the Jazz Age, "Many Americans had begun to fear that the family was being destroyed. If women were free to vote and live in apartments on their own, and if wives were working outside the home in increasing numbers, then who would keep the home fires burning?" Perhaps some of the fear was also economic; the last decade had introduced many women to the rewards of the workplace, but having made an enormous effort to educate women, society now had no careers to offer them. Though more women were working, fewer were entering the male-dominated fields like science and academia, and employers began to prefer hiring women who did not have college degrees. Mostly they held clerical jobs at which their bosses invariably called them "girl" regardless of their ages, or else they did work from their homes. They also did not earn nearly as much as their male counterparts.

Not getting married had become a pitiable social faux pas, and once a woman succumbed, chances were her husband wanted her at home taking care of the children, who were supposed to be bright and fresh and pressed at all times lest they should cast doubt on their parents. "What do the neighbors think of her children?" read one 1928 detergent ad's copy in the *Ladies' Home Journal*. The number of women who never married, which had once been as high as 20 percent, dropped to 5 percent by the end of the decade, and even education seemed to have very little effect. According to one study, "Most college women surveyed claimed they aspired above all else to the role of wife." Vassar College went so far as to invent a school of "Euthenics" that ran courses like "Husband and Wife," "Motherhood," and "The Family as Economic Unit." The issue was no less pressing for lower-class women, who, while they needed to work, could not escape the prevailing sentiment that they were hurting their children by doing so. "Can the devoted wife and mother conduct a successful business outside the home?" questioned another ad in the *Ladies' Home Journal.*

As always, Stratemeyer's books took reality and made it tidier. *Ruth Fielding and Her Great Scenario* is filled with moments in which the pliable Tom Cameron not only pledges wholeheartedly to take a backseat to Ruth's brains and brilliant professional life, but also would never dream of making her change her ways to keep him. Unlike her real-life counterparts, she would not have to give up a thing to achieve both peace of mind and a career. "Ruth, I'll never say a word about your career," he says at one point. "Not even if you decide to open a moving picture studio on the moon! I only want you to know that when you're ready for a home, I'll be right at your doorstep—waiting." When one rather backward—but actually completely au courant—suitor in another of her stories protests that "woman's place is in the home," Ruth's closest chum Helen flies into a rage and puts him in his place once and for all: "Bosh! Let me tell you, the modern woman can do something besides wash dishes and darn socks." The enraged indignation practically flew off the page.

Perhaps this was because the young woman who was ghostwriting the book was facing the same issues in her own life. She was on the verge of matrimony, but like Ruth Fielding, she did not intend to enter into it without embarking on a career of her own. Though many women were once again working, as Harriet Adams had, for only the short period of time between school and marriage, Mildred was determined to learn the business of book writing before she settled down, and to have something of her own even after she married. Her intentions ran absolutely counter to what America expected of its young women at the end of the 1920s. The tide had shifted, and she was going against it. "What had looked like vigorous independence and strong-mindedness in the flapper now seemed careless, selfish, and superficial," writes one historian of the period. "Now family was about self-fulfillment, consumption, and nurturing the newly discovered psyche of the child...A whole generation was tempted by an older, comforting vision of mom as a plump, slightly frazzled woman who could be relied on to sacrifice herself...and make it all better."

Mildred, however, was not one of the tempted, and so she wrote the first six chapters of *Ruth Fielding and Her Great Scenario* at her parents' house in Ladora, where she was staying before heading back to school, and sent them in to Stratemeyer for his opinion before she went any further with the text. As was his custom, he sent back a detailed edit and a letter explaining some general Stratemeyer Syndicate writing guidelines.

Mildred had had a difficult time with Ruth and the world in which she operated. Writing about romance was never her strong suit, and the character, she later admitted, had "fought her on every page," not least because she knew almost nothing about the motion picture industry, a new and wild world cropping up on the West Coast. But she was a relentless worker and a quick study, and she knew how to take criticism, no doubt from her journalism classes at Iowa. She wrote back to Stratemeyer immediately, and in the process displayed both graciousness and an incredible efficiency as a writer.

> Dear Mr. Stratemeyer:
>
> I regret that the chapters of the Ruth Fielding serial were not satisfactory. I have attempted to rebuild the story, and appreciate your criticism. In the first chapter I have changed a number of speeches and have entirely rewritten the second and third chapters. I had the first eighteen chapters finished when I re-

ceived your criticism, but if you find the enclosed ten chapters suitable, I can polish it up, and place the entire manuscript in your hands within a few days.

By the end of October, after a few more back-and-forths, *Ruth Fielding and Her Great Scenario* was done. From Stratemeyer's short outline, Mildred had spun out 208 vigorous pages that portrayed Ruth as a forward-thinking, multitalented girl who always kept her head in an emergency and was by far the most well-informed, capable person, male or female, in any situation. Despite his stern comments, Stratemeyer knew he had not chosen wrong in Mildred Augustine. He was accustomed to training talented new writers in the style and methods of the Syndicate, and he expressed his utter faith in Mildred, lest she should be discouraged, telling her, "I think you can do this work when you catch the idea of just what is wanted."

It was not an accident that Ruth Fielding was turning into a detective of sorts, for a nationwide craze for mystery novels was on. Agatha Christie—who had been responsible in large part for the trend when her first Hercule Poirot book, *The Mysterious Affair at Styles*, was published in 1920—could barely write her new books fast enough for her devoted fans. Dashiell Hammett had begun to publish his crime stories in pulp magazines, and S. S. Van Dine's Philo Vance mysteries and the early books of Erle Stanley Gardner, who would go on to create the inimitable Perry Mason, were also selling like crazy. Stratemeyer believed the passion for mystery was bound to trickle down to children, and he had an eye toward exploiting it when it did. Around the time Mildred was turning in her first Ruth Fielding, he contacted a young

Canadian writer named Leslie McFarlane—who was churning out the adventures of underwater explorer and deep-sea diver Dave Fearless for him at the rate of a book every three weeks—to see if he was interested in taking on a new series of mysteries.

Stratemeyer had already devised a pen name for his new idea—Franklin W. Dixon. The series would feature "two brothers of high school age who would solve such mysteries as came their way. To lend credibility to their talents, they would be the sons of a professional private investigator, so big in his field that he had become a sleuth of international fame. His name—Fenton Hardy. His sons, Frank and Joe, would therefore be known as...The Hardy Boys!"

With that, the series that would go on to be one of the Stratemeyer Syndicate's best loved and most enduring was off to a running start. The outline for the first story, *The Tower Treasure*, went off to McFarlane in the mail. It was soon followed by the outline for Hardy Boys number two, *The House on the Cliff*. By March of 1927 Stratemeyer was confident enough in his new series and its writer to suggest a fourth title even though the first three had not yet been published (they were intended to come out simultaneously as a "breeder" set that would give children a chance not only to get to know the series well but to hanker for more).

When the breeder set was published in mid-May 1927, little boys went wild for Frank and Joe Hardy. Lindbergh had flown across the Atlantic and now the Hardy Boys had arrived in the bedrooms of America's youth by motorcycle. (As McFarlane later joked, they were somehow talking at the time. "Don't ask how they managed this with two motorcycles going full blast. They just did.") Boys clamored for more stories about these bright, modern heroes; by mid-1929 more than 115,000 Hardy Boys books had been sold. In the meantime, Stratemeyer had begun to dream up another detective, though he had neither convinced a publisher to take on a new line nor settled on a name for his heroine. He did know one thing, however, and that was who would write it for him. "For this series I have in mind one of our younger writers, a woman who has just graduated from college and who has written one book already for my Syndicate and a number of stories for St. Nicholas and other high-grade magazines," he wrote to one potential editor. "She writes particularly well of college girls and their doings, both in college and out, and I feel that she could make a real success of this new line."

By February of 1929, when Stratemeyer was more anxious than ever to get his new series going, he was still just as sure that Mildred was the one to do it for him. She was ready and waiting to go to work. All that remained was to find a name for the main character and a publisher to take her on. She might be called Nell Cody, Stratemeyer thought. Or Stella Strong. Or Nan Nelson, Diana Dare, or Helen Hale. Or, possibly, Nan Drew. Whoever she was, she was everything America had been waiting for.

6

NANCY DREW LAND

IN MAY OF 1927, as the Hardy Boys stormed the juvenile book world, Mildred received a letter of hearty congratulations on her master's degree from her editor. In spite of his attitude toward his daughters' education—certainly neither of them would have been permitted to go back to school for an advanced degree with an eye to employment—Stratemeyer thought her accomplishment "a fine thing," telling her, "I hope it will do you much good." But Mildred did not take her new credentials out to find a job immediately. Instead, she spent the following summer at home in Ladora, selling stories to *St. Nicholas* magazine and, as she told Stratemeyer, "attempt[ing] to improve my style of writing." A year later the probable cause for her holding off on full-time employment in an office was revealed. In May of 1928 she wrote to Stratemeyer from Ohio, telling him her news and making sure he did not mistake her for a newly minted housewife of the kind that were popping up all around the country: "A few months ago I married Mr. Wirt, who is a member of the Associated Press staff here at Cleveland. I have of course continued my writing, and am doing special articles for Cleveland trade journals in addition to my juvenile fiction." Her letter was signed "Mildred Augustine Wirt/Mrs. A. A. Wirt."

Asa Wirt, a Nebraska native, had a great sense of humor and, like his new wife, loved to travel and to work hard. A fellow student, he had taken a year of technical classes at the Iowa School of Journalism while working for the Associated Press in Iowa City and then transferred to Cleveland. After a small March wedding in Chicago, attended by only a few family members and friends and followed by dinner at the ritzy Palmer House hotel, the couple moved to Ohio to start their life together. But it was clear from the start that Mildred was also going to continue her life apart from Asa. Even in the short note informing Stratemeyer of her nuptials, change of name, and change of address, she did not fail to mention her eagerness to write another book for him. Soon she would get her chance at last.

"As perhaps you know, I was talking to Mr. Grosset about the steady popularity of our 'Ruth Fielding Series,'" Edward wrote to his editor at Grosset & Dunlap in the summer of 1929. "For the past four years I have had a young western woman (newspaper woman) doing this line and making the series more popular than ever. This author is now anxious to start a brand new line and I am wondering if it wouldn't hit you. At present our line is weak on girls books with a single heroine. We have 'Outdoor Girls' and 'Blythe Girls' but not a single line in which a single character dominates the page, like 'Tom Swift,' 'Ted Scott,' and 'Don Sturdy.' This author could do this line under my directions and do it well."

A few months later, Stratemeyer mailed off his one-and-a-half-page description of the new series to Grosset & Dunlap, including a pen name and the plots and possible titles of what he envisioned to be the first five books. Under the heading "Suggestions for a new series of girls' books. From Edward Stratemeyer. Confidential. Please return," he laid out his general ideas for the cast of characters, the star of which was a teenaged sleuth, and the basic tenor of what he planned to call the "Stella Strong Stories." Then he listed plots for the first five stories in thrilling, telegraph-style prose, each one attesting to the enormous ingenuity and generous spirit of Stratemeyer's new invention:

STELLA STRONG AT MYSTERY TOWERS
How Stella visited the old Tower House and met the rich and eccentric maiden ladies, Patricia and Hildegarde Forshyne, who were much disturbed by many unusual happenings about the place. She learns that some relatives are trying to get possession of the Forshyne fortune. Stella was once made a prisoner, but turned the tables and made a most startling exposure.

THE MYSTERY AT SHADOW RANCH
A thrilling tale of mysterious doings at various places in the valley. Many thought that robberies of rich homes were contemplated. It remained for Stella Strong to clear up the perplexities.

THE DISAPPEARANCE OF NELLIE RAY
In this tale either a rich girl or an eccentric rich lady disappears under most puzzling circumstances. The authorities were at their wits' end to locate her. Stella Strong unearths one clue after another and followed a perilous trail to triumph.

THE MISSING BOX OF DIAMONDS

Stella arrives at a summer hotel to find great excitement because of the disappearance of a box containing some famous diamond jewelry. Stella gets mixed up in the affair, but finally manages to clear herself and find the valuables.

THE SECRET OF THE OLD CLOCK

A large estate remains unsettled because of a missing will. Some domineering rich folks claim the entire estate. But Stella Strong thinks it should go to two deserving poor girls. A letter is found stating that the location of the will is described in a paper secreted in the old family clock. This clock has disappeared and efforts to find it had been in vain until Stella hears that is had been taken to a summer camp miles away. She arrives at this camp to find that the place has been looted and the clock is gone. How the old timepiece was finally recovered and how this led to the finding of the will makes interesting reading.

Looted treasure; poverty; kind, eccentric rich people and mean, ordinary ones; the opportunity for endless Robin Hood scenarios with a little bit of danger thrown in—as with the Hardy Boys outlines, all the elements that would make the series an instant hit were right there in his two pages. Grosset & Dunlap jumped at the idea (though they weren't exactly crazy about Stella, so they pulled "Nan Drew" from his other suggestions and lengthened it to Nancy). They wrote to Stratemeyer immediately, saying they would take on this new girl detective, but that they had new names for the series and for most of his plots as well. "If the titles are acceptable," Stratemeyer's longtime editor at Grosset & Dunlap wrote to him, "the stories can be written in some consecutive order around them and we shall be very glad to have them worked out along these lines…We very much like your title THE SECRET OF THE OLD CLOCK, and the other titles suggested are: THE HIDDEN STAIRCASE, THE HOUSE OF MYSTERY, THE MISSING JEWELS, THE MYSTERIOUS GUEST, THE SEVEN BLACK PEARLS."

Stratemeyer was ecstatic, and he wrote to Mildred to tell her of his coup: "I have just succeeded in signing up one of our publishers for a new series of books for girls, the same length and make-up as the 'Ruth Fielding' books. These will be bright, vigorous stories for older girls having to do with the solving of several mysteries." He wanted her to write the first three books right away, turning out each manuscript in about four weeks' time. She accepted the offer, and by October 1 the Nancy Drew Mystery Stories by Carolyn Keene (a change from Louise Keene, Stratemeyer's original suggestion for a pseudonym), were contracted. The first three titles in the series would be *The Secret of the Old Clock*, *The Hidden Staircase*, and *The Bungalow Mystery*, each of them hewing to one of the plots Stratemeyer had hatched in his initial proposal. They were to sell for fifty cents each, returning a royalty of two cents per copy for the Syndicate. Mildred would be paid $125 for each manuscript and, as usual, would sign away her rights to the stories and characters as soon as she handed in the manuscripts.

Sending his first three-and-a-half-page outline for *The Secret of the Old Clock* to Mildred, Stratemeyer impressed upon his young writer the difference between the kind of girls' books she had been writing for him and the new line, which was to be less about niceties and more about being brave and adventurous. The plot of *Old Clock* remained just as he had first envisioned it, with a full complement of selfish rich people (the Tophams) and virtuous poor ones (the Horner girls), and a possibly fictitious missing will that would set everything straight if only it could be found. "I trust that you will give this outline and also the note above it a very careful reading. In reading over the plot, you will, I am sure, see the advantage of bringing out the disagreeable points of the Topham family and especially of the daughters and also the advantage of stressing old Abigail's poverty and then her sickness and also the poverty of the Horner girls. All these things will increase the interest in what Nancy is trying to do…" Signing off, he expressed absolute faith in Mildred and in his new creation. "With best regards and trusting that you will be able to give us a first story that will make all girls want to read more about Nancy Drew, I remain, yours truly."

Sixteen days later the stock market crashed, throwing the country into uncertainty and despair. By the spring of 1930, the average income of the American family had sunk to $1,428 — between 1929 and 1933, it would drop a full 40 percent. In 1930 alone, more than a thousand banks would fail as America plunged ever deeper into recession. Ten million women, now celebrating the tenth anniversary of their right to the vote, had gone out to work over the past two decades, many of them out of financial necessity, but seven out of ten American women overall still believed firmly that the place for them was in their own kitchens. From 1930 to 1940, the number of women who worked outside the home would increase only a smidgen, from 24.4 percent to 25.4 percent, as all the progress that had been made in the early part of the 1920s seemed to wither away under the duress of the country's newfound morality and the strictures of the Depression. Thanks to the scarcity of jobs, a new debate cropped up: Should married women whose husbands were employed even be allowed to seek jobs? Those who did were now vilified in the media, and one popular women's magazine featured a piece in which a former career woman proclaimed, with no apparent angst, "I know now without any hesitation...that [my husband's] job must come first." Women had more reasons than ever to stay at home washing the clothes, the baby, and everything in between. To those lower on the economic ladder, of course, such debates were a luxury they couldn't afford. In many slightly better-off families, women who had never before considered it were forced to find work of any kind in order to help pay the bills.

There was also a third, untouchable category of Americans— the very rich, who made up a minuscule portion of the country. Though many of them lost an enormous amount of money in the crash, the more conservative ones, like Stratemeyer and his fam- ily—including Harriet and Russell—did not give up much of any- thing. Instead, they had trouble hiring and keeping good help, an insignificant problem compared to what most of the country faced.

It was into this world that Miss Nancy Drew, well-to-do plucky girl of the twenties, arrived on April 28, 1930, dressed to the nines in smart tweed suits, cloche hats, and fancy dresses— including "a party frock of blue crepe which matched her eyes." From the very first moments of her life on the page, it was obvi- ous that she knew how to keep her head above water in any kind of situation. Even the Great Depression would prove to be no match for her. Pretty enough to be exceptional, but not so pretty that she would alienate readers, she was also in possession of not only an admirable intellect, but a shiny blue roadster, the latter a birthday gift from her devoted father. Her mother had died when she was three, and so she was the sole wise mistress of her charming upper-class household, which she ran superbly with the help of a grandmotherly servant named Hannah Gruen. The blond, blue-eyed teenager, affectionately called "Curly Locks" by her father, was an all-around knockout, "the kind of girl who is capable of accomplishing a great many things in a comparatively short length of time. She enjoyed sports of all kinds and she found time for clubs and parties. At school, Nancy had been very popular and she boasted many friends. People declared that she had a way of taking life very seriously without impressing one as being the least bit serious herself." As Mildred Wirt later confessed, she was everything her author — or any girl, in fact — wanted to be, and then some.

As in so many of Stratemeyer's books, there was nothing in the Nancy Drew Mystery Stories that might break the spell of this new fictitious world. The sixteen-year-old sleuth did not attend school (she had graduated some time in the recent past and did not plan to go to college) and had no worries about money, career, or marriage. She did not even have a boyfriend yet (though Ned Nickerson would show up before too long). Her wardrobe expanded to fit whatever sleuthing or social occasion befell her, and she was free to do exactly as she pleased, even if it meant getting tied up or kidnapped in pursuit of a thief. Her father's faith in her was unshakable. River Heights, Nancy's attractive midwestern town, was hermetically sealed off from the unemployment and hard times that were crashing like tidal waves over the country. Even as Eleanor Roosevelt began serving seven-cent meals in the White House to show her solidarity with her husband's citizens, Nancy Drew was shopping at a posh department store in downtown River Heights for "a frock suitable for the afternoon party she had been invited to." She reminded everyone that the good old days, the days of frills and festivities, of tea parties and a maid to do the cooking, were not so far gone and thus, perhaps, not too far off, either.

As for moral character, Nancy's was established from her very
first sentences, written for her by Stratemeyer himself. "It would
be a shame if all that money went to the Tophams! They will fly
higher than ever!" she cries out to her father, who is reading his
evening paper by lamplight, the epitome of cozy authority. By the
end of her first adventure, the inheritance in question has been
removed from the greedy, already-wealthy Tophams and restored
to the deserving Horner girls. To achieve this result, Nancy endures, among other mishaps, near death while driving through a
"rain[storm] blinding in its violence"; "a paralysis of fear" when
trapped in a deserted summerhouse with a "rough-looking man";
and being tied up and thrown in a closet by this man and his
dastardly henchmen. "Left to Starve" (the less-than-subtle title of
chapter 16 of the book), she panics, then reminds herself, with
awe-inspiring pragmatism, that it is unproductive. "She began to
think of her father, of Helen Corning, and other dear friends.
Would she ever see them again? As despondency claimed Nancy
she was dangerously near tears. Resolutely, she tried to shake off
the mood. 'This will never do,' she told herself sternly. 'Surely,
there is a way to get out of here. I must keep my head and try to
think of something.'" Moments later, fueled anew by her own optimism, she uses the hanger rod, which she's managed to tear
down in spite of her high heels and narrow skirt, as a lever to
break the door hinges.

Underneath her matching sweater sets, Nancy, as her decisive
last name implies, was a force unto herself from the first, all action, and it prevented her from being an unredeemable goody-
goody. She was also not beyond a petty moment or a petty crime
if either should be called for. Encountering the Topham girls
while on her downtown outing at the beginning of the story, she
passes judgment with a confidence born of the spiritual high

ground: "'Snobs!' Nancy told herself. 'The next time I won't even bother to speak to them!'" Later on, in mad pursuit of the solution to her mystery, she steals the all-important clock of the title and endures a harrowing ride in her blue roadster with a police officer next to her and the contraband on the floor in the backseat. Spurred on by adversity, Nancy Drew can make even cattiness and thievery seem brave and right.

The trick to this is that she does it all in the name of rising to a challenge, a quality most people wish they had but can only hope to approximate. Nancy is never better than when she's in trouble. Trapped in a spooky barn with a band of quarreling robbers approaching, she reacts with the calm of a true professional: "While Nancy Drew hesitated, uncertain which way to turn, her mind worked more clearly than ever before." Under pressure, she relies entirely on herself, a trait developed perhaps in reaction to her lack of a mother to guide her. The absence of that role model is not only sympathetic but serves her well in some senses. There is no one to nag her about chores or clothes or to worry about her gallivanting around; her brilliant, charismatic father dotes on her. Most importantly, Nancy never runs the risk, as so many girls did in her day (including the dreaded Isabel Topham of *Old Clock*), of having a mother whose "ambition [was] that some day she marry into a wealthy family." She would never betray her readers as Dorothy Dale and the Outdoor Girls had by getting hitched. She would never, like Ruth Fielding, worry over the feelings of a fiancé or agree to wear his ring.

The combination of Stratemeyer's outline and editing with Mildred's efforts had produced a fantasy girl with a few touches of the real—possibly touches of the Mildred, who had added some of Nancy's bolder moves and snappier dialogue to Stratemeyer's outline. Together, they had created a star, and Stratemeyer knew it. Though it would later become a part of Mildred's lore that he had disapproved of her first rendition of Nancy, thinking her too "flip," no evidence of this reaction exists. In fact, Edward had no problem with Mildred's interpretation of his outline. He was especially pleased with the second half of Mildred's manuscript for *Old Clock*, and, after giving her some pointers and telling her he would go ahead and fix up the first half himself, he sent off the outline for Nancy Drew Mystery Story number two.

The plot of this book, *The Hidden Staircase*, involved a creepy haunted mansion inhabited by two rich, elderly sisters who need Nancy's help. Mildred, fresh off a fishing trip in Canada with Asa, dug right in, and when Stratemeyer read over her manuscript, he found, to his delight, that she had gotten the tone just right. "Dear Mrs. Wirt," he wrote to her just before Christmas of 1929. "I have received the manuscript of The Hidden Staircase and read it with much satisfaction. It seems to me it ought to interest any girl who likes mystery stories. I shall make only a few changes and those of small importance... I think the new outline [for *The Bungalow Mystery*, the third book in the series] will appeal to you, as it is full of action and with many good holding points. Of course, keep the girlish part girlish and don't get the dramatic part too melodramatic. The second story was very well handled in this respect."

In addition to providing the requisite thrills, the final book in Stratemeyer's breeder set also had to fulfill a very specific function: making every girl who finished it desperate to buy Nancy's next adventure. At the end of *The Bungalow Mystery*, after Nancy has escaped sinking boats, lightning, a near miss with a falling tree, and being knocked out by "the butt of a revolver" and tied up in a dank basement ("You're a smart detective, but your smartness won't do you any good this time!" the villain sneers at her, of course encouraging Nancy to prove him wrong within a few pages), a tantalizing promise is dangled before readers. "It was written in the annals of the future that before many months had elapsed she would be engrossed in a problem as puzzling as the bungalow mystery — a problem which would tax her mental powers and ingenuity to the limit." In other words, dear reader, stay tuned.

As it turned out, no manufactured temptation to read *The Mystery at Lilac Inn* and *The Secret at Shadow Ranch*, books four and five, would be necessary. The first three volumes did the job nicely all on their own. Nancy's clever, privileged ways struck a chord instantly with little girls. The blue-and-orange volumes, with their brightly colored dust jackets featuring America's first full-time girl detective mid-adventure and in gorgeous attire, sold out of stores by the thousands. Less than a year later, other publishers were looking enviously at Nancy Drew as a model for bestsellers — the books were, in the words of one competitor, "selling like hot cakes."

Indeed, if the Nancy Drew Mystery Stories became essential to girls almost immediately, they became critical to Grosset & Dunlap just as quickly. In a market weakened by the Depression, the publisher soon counted on the girl sleuth to bring in money just as faithfully as the needy characters in her books did. They knew that if a Nancy Drew was in their catalog, they might be assured at least of survival, if not huge profit. "We expect to publish a few juveniles in September and would like to have a Nancy Drew to feature on this list," Laura Harris, the series editor at Grosset, wrote to the Syndicate in May of 1931. "Can you let us have the manuscript as soon as possible, and no later than July 10? There will only be three or four titles brought out then and the Nancy Drew is one of the most important." By Christmas of

1933 they were outselling most other series books, even the Syndicate's other big winner of the moment, Bomba the Jungle Boy.

NO DOUBT STRATEMEYER would have been as thrilled as his publishers with his instant success, had he only lived to witness Nancy's ascent. He was home sick in bed for most of the winter of 1930 with pneumonia, and even through the final editing of the first three Nancy Drew books, he had relied heavily on Harriet Otis Smith. Letters flew back and forth between the Stratemeyer home, where Edna was caring for her father, and the office in Manhattan. "Dear Miss Stratemeyer, and poor Miss Stratemeyer, nurse, housekeeper, and business woman," Otis Smith wrote in January, upset over the slow pace of a ghostwriter's work. "I am in my first real jam over here, and will turn to you to know how much I can ask of your father, for I do not wish to throw worry on him that may impede his recovery." It was she, not Stratemeyer, who had read Mildred's manuscript for *The Bungalow Mystery*, the third Nancy Drew book, and made the final decisions about it with her employer's blessing. Stratemeyer was confined to bed and to dictating letters to his daughter, who bore her burden, if not lightly, then at least with a certain amount of humor. Lenna was by this time an invalid, and Harriet had four young children, as well as a host of club and Sunday school responsibilities that took up her time, so it was Edna who sat with her father daily, bringing him food and serving as his secretary. "This is all Dad has to say, Miss Smith, and now he will eat his orange and be a good patient," she added on to one of her father's letters that January. "Think he is tired of this kind of life and much prefers the office. Think I need a course in shorthand in order to keep up with his messages, besides a nurses' uniform when doing the other jobs."

By March Edward was back in the office happily dealing with his series again. But his health did not hold. Sending the outline for *The Mystery at Lilac Inn* to Mildred in late April was to be one of his final acts as head of the Stratemeyer Syndicate. By the following week, he was too ill to even look at illustrations for a book that was about to be published. Harriet Otis Smith wrote to one of his editors, "It is a question—as always in pneumonia—as to how long an already weakened heart can stand the strain."

The answer turned out to be not very long at all. On May 10, 1930, just twelve days after the launching of Nancy Drew, Edward Stratemeyer succumbed to pneumonia at his home in Newark at the age of sixty-seven. The response was immediate and passionate. "Your Husband and Father was every inch a man, and deeply admired and respected by all his friends and business acquaintances," wrote one publisher to the Stratemeyer family. The newspapers weighed in, too. "Now Mr. Stratemeyer...has laid down his pen," mourned the *New York Times* in their second piece within a week about his death. "Who is to write tales of adventure for the boys of the airplane and television age?" Letters of condolence poured into the Syndicate offices in Manhattan, from authors, publishers, magazines, and the charities toward which Stratemeyer had been uncommonly generous. Everyone who came into contact with him seemed to have been changed for the better by the experience. "He was the 'grand old man' of the Juvenile book world," Alexander Grosset wrote to Magdalene Stratemeyer, "and his passing will leave a place that will be difficult to fill."

In particular, many of the young writers he had nurtured with his patient comments and kind soul wrote in to pay their respects. Leslie McFarlane, author of the Hardy Boys, wrote to Harriet Otis Smith, "Although I had never met him personally I felt that I knew him as a real friend by reason of my five years' association with him in the writing of the books he assigned to me. His kindness to Mrs. McFarlane and myself at the time of our marriage and on the occasion of the birth of our daughter betokened a personal interest that we appreciated more than he possibly imagined. I think he must have been a very kindly and warm-hearted man...My work for Mr. Stratemeyer helped me so much in days of my literary apprenticeship that you may be sure this letter is no hollow and conventional expression."

Mildred, too, wrote Harriet and Edna a heartfelt note to say how sorry she was to lose him. In a letter to Otis Smith, though, after brief condolences, she was all business. Bringing up the looming issue on everyone's minds, she wrote, "Dear Miss Smith: It was with the deepest regret that I learned of Mr. Stratemeyer's sudden death...As you requested, I will forward the Nancy Drew volume as soon as completed, which should be sometime this month. As soon as you know what is to be done about future work, I will appreciate being notified."

What *was* to be done about future work? With Nancy Drew and the Hardy Boys and all the offspring of the Stratemeyer empire? With no sons to inherit the family business, Edward had made provisions in his will for it to go to his wife, with the idea that it could be sold (it was valued at some half a million dollars) and the proceeds used to support her (to each of his daughters he had left the sum of $20,000). But he had not counted on the Depression, and suddenly the odds that anyone would have the cash or inclination to buy the company were questionable. Then there was the matter of secrecy. Other than Harriet Otis Smith, there was no one, not even Edward's own family, who really understood the workings of his Syndicate or its history. He had planned it that way, though he also understood the trouble it might create. As Edna wrote to Harriet many years later, "His one complaint was that at his death everything would die with him." Anyone taking it on would have an enormous job just understanding it, much less trying to keep it going into the future under such difficult economic circumstances and without its founder's genius for plot and character creation. Everything was suddenly in question, including the fate of his final contribution, the teenaged detective with blue eyes and gumption to spare.

7

SYNDICATE FOR SALE

AUTHOR, JUVENILE. Executors will consider bona fide purchaser for nationally known and prosperous syndicate of boys' and girls' books, including rights in many well known series. Reply, E.C.S., care of *Publishers Weekly*.

THE FIRST DAYS after Edward's death were, for his family, an odd combination of grief and urgency. Given the economic conditions of both the Stratemeyers and the country, the future direction of the Syndicate had to be charted as quickly as possible. Neither Lenna nor Edna had any earning power, and though Harriet was well-off thanks to Russell's work as a stockbroker and her inheritance, she could not afford to support her mother and sister in their current lifestyle. Nor, with four children of her own, could she be expected to do so. The first order of business was to transfer the task of executor from Lenna, who was in no position to make decisions, to her daughters. Newly in charge, Edna and Harriet soon found themselves awash in information about their father's work and world that was entirely unfamiliar and often overwhelming. As Edna exclaimed less than a week after his death, "I never dreamed of so much red tape before." The legal matters involved in a business that employed writers-for-hire and had all of its revenues tied up in rights and royalties as opposed to actual book publishing were maddeningly intricate. In addition, Edward had begun to sell radio and movie rights to some of his stories, adding another complication.

With Harriet Otis Smith as their only guide — she had agreed to stay on in her current role for the foreseeable future, saying that "Mr. Stratemeyer was far too kind to permit of any other course" — Edward's loyal daughters began to wade through the papers in the Madison Square Park office in order to determine how best to consolidate and sell the business. No other course of action seemed possible. Neither sister had any business experience, nor had they participated in the work of the Syndicate in any serious way for years. Certainly they knew nothing of the day-to-day details involved in bringing a series from inspired idea to finished book. Nevertheless, they were committed to making the most informed decision possible about the future of their father's brainchild. While Edna tackled some of the accounting at home, such as paying salaries and money owed to ghostwriters, Harriet took it upon herself to become the public face of the Syndicate. For Edward's publishers were not only saddened but unnerved by his death. They counted on the Stratemeyer series as a big part of their business and were panicked at the thought of either a great delay in their production or a cessation altogether. As Otis Smith knew well, "If these publishers suddenly lose the right to bring out not only new volumes in their big paying series, but the right to issue any new book at all by their very popular 'authors,' it will be a serious loss to them of both money and prestige." Someone had to take on the responsibility of assuring them that the house of Stratemeyer would not go dim, even if that someone was not entirely sure of it herself.

With a clear division of labor established, Harriet wrote a note to her father's trusted assistant just eight days after Edward's death, demonstrating her desire to get a handle on the situation as well as her obvious ability to do so. That Wellesley education and strong spirit, it seemed, were going to come in handy after all. "My dear Miss Smith," she wrote. "At this time, of course, we are still bewildered, and must acquaint ourselves with more of the details before coming to any decision. To this end, we shall interview the various publishers with whom my father had business associations, and try to get their point of view. Grosset and Dunlap have asked for such an interview on Tuesday, and as my sister is unable to go, I shall go to their office myself. Will you get ready for me on Monday or Tuesday morning if possible, a short summary of the dealings my father had with these people — number of years, number of series, number of books, series running now which are considered good, and any other data which you think would help to make my conference with them an intelligent and helpful one. I will come into the office some time the latter part of Tuesday morning. Very sincerely, Harriet S. Adams."

Though they had remained very personally close all through her married life — she had even named her second son after him — Harriet was so far removed from her father's business life that she did not know the difference between Bomba the Jungle Boy and Joe Hardy. Yet she was determined to learn as much as she could and proceeded to do it with an energy that, while not uncharacteristic, might have surprised those who did not know her well. Happily settled with her brood in the plush New Jersey town of Maplewood, Harriet was, by this time, every inch the well-to-do young matron. As a newspaper article on the Syndicate would later muse, "Were it not for the extra spark, we would be tempted to nominate Mrs. Adams for the role of typical Maplewood householder and clubwoman." She was active in the New York Wellesley Club and wrote for the newsletter of the Maplewood Women's Club. She also taught Sunday school and was the mother of two boys — thirteen-year-old Russell Jr., known as Sunny, and five-year-old Edward, the baby of the family; as well as two girls — Camilla, who turned eleven in the summer of 1930, and Patricia (Patsy), who was eight. Harriet had help both with her children and her household, and was able to devote some of the time she usually spent on her other activities to Syndicate business, if not full-time, then at least enough of the time to make some headway toward getting things in order to sell.

In addition to dealing with nervous publishers, she had to consider the few offers to buy the company that were trickling in. In this, as in everything during those first few months, Otis Smith's wisdom was critical. Though she was, as she put it, "the only person who has a knowledge of this business as a whole," she harbored no illusions about who was really in charge, and as such was the ideal helpmate. "If you are interested in the buying of the Syndicate, you might apply to his daughters and executrixes, Mrs. Russell V. Adams and Miss Edna C. Stratemeyer, 171 North Seventh Street, Newark, New Jersey," she wrote to one interested party, warning him, "It is a rather large business and will require considerable capital to run it, but either Mrs. Adams or Miss Stratemeyer can give you details." Polite business correspondence notwithstanding, she confessed her real opinion about this prospective new owner to Edna and Harriet lest they should rush into something ill-advised: "I think he is just a foolish boy and does not know what he is talking about and doubt if he could raise two thousand dollars."

It did not take long to confirm that the prospects for selling the Syndicate were dismal at best. The Depression had severely limited the number of people with the means to purchase the company, and those who were left, like the foolhardy young man, hardly seemed appropriate. As the sisters began to wonder what course of action to take next, Otis Smith warned them against further indecision. "If the books do not get under way before long the publishers can hardly have them, at least not more than one or two of them, for early spring publication...The greatest danger is that if things drift too long the authors will be immersed in other things and cannot go on with the Syndicate books, for, after all, their needs will continue in spite of the law's delay, and that, just at this time of readjustment, would be perhaps an irreparable loss." She also enlightened them on the matter of just how difficult it was to find writers suited to the unique work of the Syndicate. "Authors cannot be picked out of the gutter at will—or out of a garret, the traditional place for authors to live. Nor have the new authors ever done perfectly satisfactory work until after a preliminary training under your father's methods on some three or four or five books. The first volumes have always had to be written in part, talked over, usually rewritten and then in the end heavily edited." To lose any one of their writers at such a critical juncture would deal a blow to the company and its publishers that could prove fatal.

By early June Harriet had begun to take a more active part in the business, if only to make sure it did not fail. She handled all the correspondence with the Syndicate's publishers (who tended to respond with letters addressed "Dear Sir") and tried to amass a more complete understanding of the company even as she and Edna continued to hope for its sale. Otis Smith was editing the final manuscripts that had been received before and just after Edward's death, and a decision was made to solicit no new work until things could be gotten back on track.

Among the stories on Otis Smith's desk was the fourth Nancy Drew title, *The Mystery at Lilac Inn*, which Mildred had sent in, as instructed, in early June. Though she had made the error of hinting rather obviously at the solution to the mystery too early on in the plot, her work otherwise met with Otis Smith's approval. Ever the responsible employee concerned with the quality of the product, Otis Smith wrote to Mildred to tell her so. "The manuscript of 'The Mystery at Lilac Inn' was received here in this office yesterday afternoon," she acknowledged. "I am afraid the story will need a little jacking up, but so little that it can be done easily in this office…The changes will consist largely in cutting off the last sentence in various paragraphs in which 'Nancy' states her unalterable belief in the innocence of those whom the police, and with very good reason, suspect. The executrixes of the estate of course have charge of all financial matters, and I will notify them at once of the receipt from you of this manuscript." In the middle of the chaos, it was Otis Smith who kept a firm hand on the practicalities. While Harriet and Edna struggled, she ensured that the Syndicate had continuity, writing letters very much in the tone Edward had always used.

As Otis Smith continued to press on with the books and manuscripts the Syndicate already had in progress, Harriet tried desperately to keep up with complexities at the office and Edna stayed at home and waited for reports from the front. "My sister stopped by last night and told me of the office doings," Edna wrote to Otis Smith in June. For her part, Otis Smith was pleased with the progress she saw, writing to Edna a few weeks later, "I really think that Mrs. Adams has assimilated most wonderfully all the information that has been poured over her as though it were an avalanche."

But there was one critical function that Harriet, no matter how ambitious she was, could not perform. The writing of the outlines her father sent to authors as the basis for each volume in a series was utterly beyond her, as she was not familiar with the individual series and the casts of characters in each one, nor was she even acquainted with the various ghostwriters. Most importantly, she had no knowledge of where her father had planned to send his much-loved characters next. It fell to Otis Smith to divine her former boss's plans for four of his most popular series, Nancy Drew, Honey Bunch, the Ted Scott Flying Stories, and the Bobbsey Twins—all of which had volumes due for publication in 1931. By the time of Edward's death, she had been the sole other member of the Stratemeyer Syndicate for fifteen years, but even for her the task was going to be formidable.

In light of that, Otis Smith knew that the most important thing was to get the series' practiced, reliable authors on board. Writing to Mildred in early July, while the future of the Syndicate was still hanging in the balance, she indicated yet again how vital Nancy Drew, and by association her author, had become to both the Syndicate and its publishers:

> *Before Mr. Stratemeyer's death Grosset & Dunlap OK'd a title for a fifth volume in the "Nancy Drew Mystery Stories" for publication in 1931. Mr. Stratemeyer had indicated briefly to the publishers, as he always did, the direction the story was to take.*

He had not, however, elaborated that nucleus for the author. The publishers are asking for their manuscripts for their 1931 output, and this morning I wrote out the outline in full for this new "Nancy Drew" tale. Mr. Stratemeyer's heirs, and I as well, hope you will undertake this new volume. Also the publishers are eager to have the author continue with this line. I should like to hear from you if you think you can undertake the work. The executors, Mrs. Russell V. Adams and Miss Edna C. Stratemeyer, will have to settle the financial part, though I shall offer now on their part the same compensation you have been getting. Hoping to hear from you soon a favorable reply, and if I do and as soon as I do I will send to you the outline for the new tale.

The book in question was *The Secret at Shadow Ranch,* which Mildred happily agreed to write. She and Asa were also feeling the squeeze of the Depression, though they had wisely removed all their money from the bank before the stock market crash and were storing it, rather whimsically, in the tubes of Mildred's xylophone. Otis Smith sent off her outline, revealing in a letter to Edna later that week that all she had had to go on while writing it was the extremely slim description Stratemeyer had sent to Grosset & Dunlap some months before: "A thrilling tale of mysterious doings at various places in the valley and around the ranch. It remained for Nancy Drew to solve some perplexing situations." It was enough to reassure Edna, anyway, who wrote back that she was sure "the books on the way having my Dad's touch will be quite alright and the writers will help all they can to do their part." Upon receiving the outline, which detailed adventures at a "a real Western ranch" in Arizona, including riding horses through yet another blinding storm ("loved by me as space fillers," Mildred later confessed) and being stalked by a lynx in the forest, Mildred settled down to work.

Back in the quiet, sunny offices on Madison Square Park, Harriet had settled down to work, too. Her interest had been sparked, and though Otis Smith still handled much of the day-to-day work, Harriet was finding the opportunity to have a career, however temporary, not entirely unpleasant. Edna, meanwhile, remained at home, steadfast in her belief about what to do. She was losing interest in the Syndicate and was wrapped up in daily life with her mother, who, despite having a nurse attending her, required constant care. "My sister keeps me informed somewhat of the New York business," she wrote to Otis Smith somewhat wearily. "She is trying hard to learn a great deal and I give her credit but personally I feel that the sooner we get people interested in buying the syndicate the sooner some real progress will be made." In another note several weeks later, she reiterated her worry, even lowering her standards a bit: "Personally I am very anxious to hear from any one interested in buying the business whether their price fits our approval or not, just to get a working basis at least."

In a last-ditch effort, Harriet and Edna decided to run an advertisement in *Publishers Weekly* to see if they could drum up any interest. Written in the vaguest of terms, it ran for several weeks in July of 1930. It did not mention the name Stratemeyer or any of the names of series or "authors." The only indication it gave of the success of the Syndicate, in fact, was a single word: prosperous. That alone may have been enough to scare off anyone reading the ad. In 1930 it was as good as saying the company was unaffordable to anyone but the very rich.

Whatever the reason, the ad failed to produce a buyer, and by late July the sisters were faced with the only alternative. They would run the Stratemeyer Syndicate themselves. Edna wrote to

Otis Smith on the nineteenth of that month, somewhat re-
signedly, "In spite of ourselves it looks as if we must carry on."
Though she enclosed a few ideas for the next volume in the
Hardy Boys series—admitting, "I have not read any of the books
and I only have the advertisement of them in another book"—it
was clear from her tone that she was barely more than a reluctant
participant. For Harriet, on the other hand, it was the chance of
a lifetime. She had always loved a challenge, and this one was
hard to pass up. Not only would she be able to work, as she had
so wanted to do after college, but she would be the boss. Perhaps
most importantly to a woman who valued family and tradition
passionately, she would be able to make sure her father's series
and his name carried on.

With the enormous decision made at last, she threw herself
into the one aspect of the business she had not been over with a
fine tooth comb in the previous months. "Your sister went home
armed yesterday with books and outlines and casts of characters
for a new volume in the 'Buck and Larry' series to try her hand
at this work," Otis Smith wrote to Edna after spending a day in
the office with Harriet. "It is far from easy." Now that the decision about the Syndicate's future had been made, the trustworthy
assistant did not plan to stay on, and it was imperative that Harriet and Edna learn the creative side if the company was to continue successfully. For her part, Edna began to read the Hardy
Boys books, and by a week or so after her first letter on the subject to Otis Smith, she found herself with "a better idea of the stories already." A few days after that, the sisters had procured
Stratemeyer Syndicate stationery with their names on it.

There were, however, a number of contingencies that had to
be dealt with before it was possible to really get down to work. First

and foremost was the fact that Harriet was a mother. In spite of employing a nanny, she could not leave her children every day for an office in the big city, close as it was; that was strictly for men. Edna did not have the constitution for such a commute, nor could she leave Lenna, who was growing weaker and more difficult by the day. Something had to be done, and the answer was surprisingly simple. "Perhaps my sister has been into the office, and has told you of the idea of bringing the office to Newark, making it convenient for us both and less expensive," Edna wrote to Otis Smith. In due course, the bright offices in Manhattan were sublet and the sisters rented space in East Orange, New Jersey, a fifteen-minute car ride away from their homes. For Harriet, especially, the decision to go to an office every day, no matter how nearby it was, and to run a company was an enormous break from not only the way she had been raised, but the upper-class world in which she lived. Cushioned as she was, the Depression had not made it either necessary or acceptable for her to work, but the death of her father had given her the only possible excuse to do just that. Luckily, she had chosen wisely in Russell, who knew his wife's strengths and encouraged her to put them to use in spite of social mores. "I was 38 when [my father] died, and my youngest child was still a baby," she recalled decades later. "But my husband and I talked it over and he agreed with me...Oh, it was a radical thing to do all right, and some of my friends didn't think I should work. But my children have turned out all right, so I guess I was right." Unlike so many women during the Depression, she did not think her husband's job should come first, and neither did he.

The remainder of the summer was spent streamlining the company for the sake of saving money. The sisters took a hard look at their inventory and begin cutting failing series. They also devised a new one about a girl detective named Doris Force—

modeled on the Ruth Fielding books but "more youthful, as several volumes must be written before there is any hint of matrimony"—which was assigned to Mildred that fall along with another Ruth Fielding. They began work on new outlines for existing series, including one for the next Nancy Drew book, *The Secret of Red Gate Farm*, which Edna concocted. *The Mystery at Lilac Inn* and *The Secret at Shadow Ranch* were both ready to go to press, giving Harriet a chance to try her hand at some publicity for the first time. The blurb for *Lilac Inn* that she sent Grosset & Dunlap that fall showed she had already started to master her father's talent for the ambiguously exciting sentence-long pitch. "While working on the mystery that had its inception at Lilac Inn, Nancy Drew finds she must think quickly and act instantly both to solve the mystery and to extricate herself from some dangerous situations." It was the best she could do on such short notice: Unlike her father, who conceived of each book himself before advertising it, she had probably only read *Lilac Inn* once, and hurriedly at that.

In early October Harriet and Edna said good-bye to Harriet Otis Smith and moved to the offices in East Orange. The letters they wrote during the fall and winter of 1930 show that they had spent considerable time studying their father's methods and had picked up a great many of them. They gave authors tips on their writing ("We would advise that you keep up a tone of excitement from the beginning, although the outline, of necessity, had to be rather explanatory in the first part"); they reassured publishers that series would be carried on "satisfactorily"; they chewed out writers who did not meet their new standards; they even began to respond to fan mail, a task their father had considered critical to his business. In the process, they were putting their mark on his company and his books, transforming both, bit by bit, into their own endeavors. In writing back to fans, for example, they began to weave personas for the pseudonymous authors. Where Edward had simply said that so-and-so was not a real person, or that he or she was "a good American," Edna and Harriet offered something more personal. "My dear Robert," began one of their efforts to a young fan of Victor Appleton, author of numerous series. "Mr. Appleton is not able to answer your nice letter just now, and has asked us to tell you that he is very pleased that you enjoy the Don Sturdy books so much. And it is splendid that your geography mark has improved so quickly."

Except for ongoing and generous offers of help from Howard Garis, one of Stratemeyer's original writers and the by-now famous author of the *Uncle Wiggily* books — published under his own name — Harriet and Edna were alone with their father's creations. Though the company was solid and the two were well-off in their own rights, they were aware that the Syndicate's financial position was precarious. Book sales were far from brisk, so in addition to canceling failing series, the sisters began writing to long-time authors of their less important series asking if they would temporarily accept a fee reduction from $125 to $100. Still, once all the new office arrangements had been made and Garis had signed on as a kind of godfather, the prevailing sentiment was not of worry, but excitement. The Syndicate was sound enough that Harriet and Edna could not really fail to make a go of it, regardless of the general economic malaise that surrounded them. It would take many months of errors to bankrupt their father's financial stores, which gave them a safety net.

Soon after the move to East Orange, a letter went out from Harriet to Miss Otis Smith, describing the exhilarating chaos that had marked the time since her departure from the company. "As you will see from the above address, the 'reorganized' Strate-

meyer Syndicate is in full swing in Jersey. We had a great time
moving, finding many hidden treasures beneath piles in the back
room. The duplicate books are still piled upon the floor here and
we are still trying to decide how to dispose of them. If we so
choose we might make them an aid to our Christmas budget, but
with times the way they are I presume they should go directly to
charity. Although not as quiet as the room on the 18th floor, this
office is a very pleasant one and very handy for both my sister and
me. Things are going along nicely, and I am most happy to report that my sister has become very interested in the doings here,
has written several corking outlines for new books, and really en-
joys coming to the office." She finished off, "I suppose the doings
of Bomba, Ted Scott and Ruth Fielding seem like a dream to you
now. As you travel about perhaps places and peoples will remind
you of your work with my father, but I trust that you will recall
us all and let us hear from you often."

For Harriet and Edna, the doings of Bomba, Ted Scott, the
Hardy Boys, Nancy Drew, and all the others were anything but a
dream — they were the new reality. As Edna would later write to
an old high school friend, "I am sure you will be surprised to hear
from me and especially on this stationery. For I am a business girl
since the death of my father…I little dreamed when I was at
Townsends that I should some day be in this kind of work. We
handle many boys' and girls' books, carrying on the literary syndicate along the lines my talented father laid down. It is intensely
interesting, and I can give my imagination free reign, [sic] and
you know that is always a pleasure for anyone." Pleasure was only
a small part of it, however — at least in Harriet's mind. "Getting
courage out of the air," as she later recalled, and much to their
great surprise and seeming contentment, she and her sister had
become businesswomen.

8

AN UNFORTUNATE BREAK; OR, THE CLEVELAND WRITER COMES INTO HER OWN

THE START OF 1931 rushed in new and full of promise—not only for Harriet and Edna, who had begun to settle into their offices in earnest, but also for Mildred, who was embarking on the most productive period of her creative life. Over the next two years, twelve books written both under her own name and under several pseudonyms would be published. Nancy Drew was thriving, too, on that western ranch in Arizona, in the company of Harriet Otis Smith's final innovation before her departure from the Syndicate—otherwise known as Bess and George, the matched pair of girl chums would soon become as much a part of Nancy Drew's legend as her blue roadster.

One a dark-haired tomboy, the other giggly and blond, cousins George Fayne and Bess Marvin appeared for the first time in *The Secret at Shadow Ranch*, published in early 1931. Mildred later acknowledged that of all the stories she had worked on, it was one of her favorites because of its setting, which she had a grand time researching at the Cleveland Public Library. She wrote many of the chapters in the tiny kitchen of the rental apartment where she and Asa were living in Cleveland, on a typewriter set up on an overturned orange crate. While Asa worked the night shift at the Associated Press, Mildred wrote and attempted to perform the duties of a housewife that were currently so in vogue, the latter out of a sense of obligation rather than any interest in or proficiency at the culinary arts. While writing *Shadow Ranch*, she later recounted, she had become so engrossed in the plot as she hammered away on her typewriter that a can of condensed milk she had boiling on the stove for a caramelized dessert was left too long and exploded onto the ceiling. There, she recalled, "it splattered a huge blob of dark brown goo on the white wallpaper above my head. As a result of this mishap, we moved to a better apartment."

It was no wonder she was distracted, considering the adventures that befall the teen sleuth in *The Secret at Shadow Ranch*. The story opens with "an enticing invitation" to a ranch owned by Bess and George's Aunt Nell, a woman "of a practical turn of mind, but always in for a good time." It also establishes a very specific pecking order among the three teenagers, a structure that would remain unbroken for decades. "Look at this straight hair and my pug nose," George wails at Nancy soon after the cousins drop by to tell their friend about the invitation:

"And everyone says I'm irresponsible and terribly boyish."

"Well, you sort of pride yourself on being boyish, don't you? Your personality fits in with your name, you will admit."

"I do like my name," George admitted, "but I get tired of explaining to folks that it isn't short for Georgia. Bess doesn't have half the trouble I do."

As she spoke, George glanced up at her cousin as though trying to discover the secret of her dignity and composure. Elizabeth was noted for always doing the correct thing at the correct time. Though she lacked the dash and vivacity of her cousin, she was better looking and dressed with more care and taste. Yet, had a stranger entered the room, he undoubtedly would have looked first at Nancy Drew, for though she could not be termed beautiful, her face was more interesting than that of either of her companions.

So begin the adventures of the three female musketeers — pretty, timid Bess; rough, athletic George; and indescribably, almost inscrutably fascinating Nancy. The introduction of two recurring characters provided girls with an even greater opportunity to identify with the Nancy Drew Mystery Stories; if you were not as perfect as Nancy, surely you were at least interesting enough to be like — and thus to be — one of the closest chums of the queen bee.

From this moment, the plot moved along at an almost feverish pace. After securing permission for the trip from Carson Drew ("Four girls ought to be able to take care of themselves," George insists, including her aunt in the band of capable women), a flurry of shopping, and a train ride on which Nancy meets a mysterious stranger named Ross Rogers, who just happens to live in the town nearest to Shadow Ranch, the girls arrive at their breathtakingly scenic destination. Along the way, George explains the origins of her odd name to readers by way of explaining it to a crotchety ranch hand, also named George, who growls, "That ain't no name for a gal!" While boyish nicknames were common — Harriet was still called Billie, her college nickname, by her college pals and by Russell — an actual boy's name was another matter. George defends herself with a piece of lore that must have been extremely satisfying to little girls who loved her tough edge and were tired of watching their brothers get selected to carry on family traditions: "Every one had given up hope for a boy in our family by the time I came, so I was named George, just plain George, for my grandfather."

Then, while Bess laments the practically geriatric cowboys at hand ("Not one of them is under forty years of age!"), further emphasizing her flighty, boy-crazy qualities, Nancy immediately asks to see the ranch's resident broncos. Free from insecurities about her femininity and her single status, she has all the time in the world for adventure.

She's also the only one of the three with the maturity to tackle life's little surprises, no matter what form they take. When the girls go out on a long horseback ride a few chapters later, their guide calls Nancy aside to tell her about yet another impending storm. "I don't want to alarm the others," he says to her in hushed tones, transporting her instantly from the world of jittery, inexperienced teens to the Olympus of capable adults. From then on out, it's clearer than ever who's in charge, so it comes as no surprise when Nancy, somehow an expert horsewoman in spite of the miles she logs in her trusty roadster, rescues pitiful, terrified Bess from a raging stream a few pages later. Riding into the swirling water on her pony, she first calms the beast, and then her friend, who exclaims, "I never was so frightened in all my life... You saved me, Nancy." Just another day in the life of America's teen sleuth.

There was, however, one new wrinkle in Nancy's character. As edited by Harriet and Edna instead of their father, she acquired a new patina of modesty. "All I did was to grab hold of the bridle," she responds to Bess's grateful sighs. Where she would once have simply remained silent on the matter, she now feels compelled, at this and many other moments in *The Secret at Shadow Ranch*, to remind others that, while she may be brilliant and capable, she'll also be the last to admit it. The Wellesley motto — "not to be ministered unto but to minister to" — was already kicking in. Still, she remained the quintessential detective. After a few more treacherous trail rides and the discovery of a cabin in the woods inhabited by a mean old woman and a little girl dressed in rags, she's utterly in her element: "Was it not possible, she asked herself, that she had accidentally stumbled on a mystery?"

Yes, it was. And in order to solve the puzzle and discover the true identity of the little girl and her relation to her miserly keeper, as well as sort out a subplot involving another girl's missing father, there is work to be done. When a picnic in the mountains is planned a few pages later, Nancy receives yet another vote of confidence from the grown-up world in the form of a bit of advice from her friends' aunt: "If you girls go alone, I'm going to insist that you take a revolver," Aunt Nell tells them, after which George adds, "Nancy can tote the gun because she's the only one that could hit the broad side of a barn." Though she'll later prove to be a crack shot when she fells a wild lynx in hot pursuit of the trio, the evolving Nancy of course assures her chum that "it would have to be a big barn." In later years the Syndicate was much maligned for such politically incorrect scenes, which were eventually edited out, but as Mildred herself pointed out in the 1990s, "at the time, long before animal rights or violence became an issue, [they] seemed quite natural."

Such stunts were merely a sideshow for the larger story, not even its highlight. After one more chase through the woods, a dance in town to which the girls wear "their best party frocks," and a run-in with a villain named Zany Shaw, Nancy straightens everything out. The friends head back to River Heights content-edly, having solved a double mystery and reunited a long-lost fa-ther and daughter. "I'm beginning to think it may be wise to protect my practice by taking you in as a partner," Nancy's father jokes with her when she gets home. "All right," she tells him. "Put out your sign. 'Carson Drew and Daughter.'"

Nancy was not the only character being whipped up in Mil-dred's Cleveland kitchen, either. Around the time that the sleuth made her thrilling trip to Arizona, Mildred achieved enough fame to merit a profile in the *Cleveland Plain Dealer*, in a series called "Chats with Cleveland Writers." Accompanied by a photo of the youthful-looking twenty-six-year-old author with her dark bob and bangs, the piece mentioned—in parentheses—that she was married, but it also noted that "she signs her name Mildred Augustine to most of her short stories and magazine articles." Mildred was, in other words, a thoroughly modern young woman, and just the sort that parents should wish as a role model for their girls. Over the course of the article, it became clear that perhaps one of the reasons for the popularity of everything she wrote, even from a Stratemeyer outline, was her willingness to take her audience seriously. "One must be careful not to insult the intel-ligence of the youthful reader by making the words too simple," she told her interviewer, perhaps thinking back on her own frus-trating childhood reading efforts. "And I try never to have impos-sible situations, as I would not have my readers lose confidence in me." The profile ended with some talk—or chat—about the changes in children's literature and one final flourish: "Mrs. Wirt tactfully combines what children want with what they need.

There is artistry here. Perhaps this is why, even in 1931, publishers are taking her books as fast as she can write them."

The Stratemeyer Syndicate also made an appearance in the *Cleveland Plain Dealer* article. Clearly aware of the debt she owed Stratemeyer, Mildred acknowledged that the Syndicate had started her off as a writer of books, and also that Edward had been an exceptional talent. But she was not aware, apparently, of the necessity of keeping the details of her work for the Syndicate out of the press, so Mildred allowed the *Plain Dealer* to name all three Syndicate series she was working on, including Nancy Drew, as well as their publishers and the fact that she wrote them under pseudonyms. The pseudonyms themselves went unmentioned, and perhaps Mildred believed this was enough to keep her promise of anonymity.

Whatever her motivation, she had clearly not received the lecture Stratemeyer had given many of his other authors by mail. "The work for our syndicate is done sub rosa by the majority of our authors and...it is well understood that they are only authors in part," he had reminded one loose-lipped ghostwriter. "All of our stories are written on our complete outlines and...we frequently make many alterations in the manuscripts received...As I told you on your last visit, I have no objection to an author saying he is 'doing work for the Stratemeyer Syndicate,' but to be fair he ought to add that he is working on our complete plots and outlines."

Though Harriet and Edna had yet to fully appreciate it, this kind of tortured relationship was at the heart of all the Syndicate's work. While each series was invented and edited by the company, it also relied heavily on its ghostwriter, who had been specially picked and trained by Edward Stratemeyer for success.

The sisters were about to find this out the hard way. "We have had an extremely busy year," Harriet wrote to Harriet Otis Smith in June of 1931, "and I sometimes wonder how we accomplished all we did." She, especially, was exhausted and worn down. "Today it looked like Christmas around here with so many bundles," she wrote to Edna at one point that spring, giving some indication that madness was barely being kept at bay. "Books and more books. Another manuscript and yet another manuscript, to say nothing of page proofs and sheets and sheets of Estate work." Though Edna had the burden of caring for their mother, Harriet's children ate up all the extra time she had. When she finally escaped the office later in the summer for a trip to her family's farm in rural New Jersey, Edna reprimanded her in a letter for her relentless work ethic. "Was not surprised to learn your blood pressure was low. I've thought that it wasn't humanly possible to lose so much sleep and carry such a strenuous program at your time of life without developing something besides loss of weight."

Still, they were having some fun as well. When one or the other of the sisters was away, letters flew back and forth with high-spirited details about various series and the office goings-on. "Other high-lights from the Lone Syndicate Sister and her lonesome Secretary will follow," Harriet wrote to Edna, who had taken Lenna and her nurse off to the Jersey Shore for some relaxation. Edna wrote back with a telling, if amusing anecdote about her perspective on their newfound careers: "We all dropped a penny in the slot of a palmistry machine. We all got quite different fortunes—Mine said in part 'About middle of life great good fortune falls to you through a death; see that you use it wisely'... Did we laugh!"

Back in the office that same summer, Edna wrote to Harriet, "Dear Pardner: Well, you can see we're on the job. Miss Pearson [Agnes Pearson, the secretary who had replaced Harriet Otis

Smith] and I think we have turned out a corking good outline and we are sure now it contains enough plot, sub-plot, and what have you, to make a readable story. We will be glad to hear your comments on the enclosed outline." Edna's somewhat defensive description of her latest effort came in response to a complaint from Mildred, who had suggested in the letter she sent in with *The Secret of Red Gate Farm* manuscript that the sisters had yet to fully master the skill of writing an outline. "Dear Miss Strate-meyer: I am submitting 'The Secret of Red Gate Farm,' today by express and hope that it will fulfill your requirements," Mildred wrote. "I venture to call your attention to the length of the plot which, you will note, is a full page shorter than usual. In writing the story it was difficult to find chapter endings with sufficient suspense, and the book ran some chapters short. To lengthen them out I added a few incidents but even so it was necessary to dwell upon the 'cave' scenes a bit too long. I believe that I would be able to handle the denouement with better technique if the plots were somewhat longer."

Harriet, who opened the letter while Edna was on vacation, both took Mildred's criticism to heart and seemed to be grateful for the extra work Mildred had put into the book to make up for the lack of plot. "Dear Edna: Before I shut up shop here and take two dozen eggs down to Aunt Etta I shall report progress up to date," Harriet dashed off to her sister. "Nancy Drew has arrived here from Red Gate Farm and, according to Mrs. Wirt, solved the mystery satisfactorily. However, her 'guardian' says in a letter that she was very shy of plot and had to add a great deal on her own account. I read the first chapter and it sails along breezily and en-tertainingly, and I have great hopes that the whole book will be of the same tenor." Perhaps because she had written the outline in question—her first, admittedly—Edna reacted rather differently. "Well, we got to be gray heads to know everybody's whims," she huffed by return mail. "Certainly men writers write with much less written outline, I should say." Still, her letter later in the summer showed she had registered Mildred's comments.

Whatever Harriet thought of Mildred's complaint, she behaved impeccably toward her. She knew she needed her, not only for Ruth Fielding and Nancy Drew, but for the new Doris Force series, which was intended to capitalize on the girl detective genre. "We are sorry that you found the outline short, and, although we have not as yet read the story, we hope that the material which you inserted will hook up well with the story without seeming like intruding insertions," she wrote to Mildred. "I read a couple of chapters, and up to that point the story is excellent...Thank you for getting the story back to us so soon. The publishers seem to like Nancy Drew and her adventures and have already been asking for this volume. It is possible that they will request a second one for this year and, if so, we shall communicate with you."

That request soon came, and Mildred began working on *The Clue in the Diary*. She was busier than ever on her Underwood typewriter but sent the manuscript in that August as promised. In mid-September the sisters asked her to take on two more Doris Force books and another Nancy Drew, but there was a catch. The publisher of Doris Force was wavering a bit about the future of the series, they explained, and "because of this, and because of the great drop in sales as shown by our July statements from publishers, we are going to ask you to take a reduction on these manuscripts of twenty-five dollars each — in other words, we will pay one hundred dollars for each story. We hope that business is very soon going to take an upward turn, and that we shall be able to return to the former standard of payment." Harriet concluded,

"We hope that you will be willing to carry on with us through this period, as we enjoy working with you, and do not want to make any shifts on these series." Harriet and Edna had held out as long as they could on pay cuts for the authors of their best-sellers—Leslie McFarlane and Mildred—but by now they were too worried about falling Syndicate revenues to keep even those writers at full salary.

Mildred wasted no time responding. Though she was cordial, it took her only until the second sentence of her reply to address the main issue and to make a pointed remark about the Syndicate's pay rate. "I...am sorry to learn that business has not been as good as before with the syndicate. I have always tried to cooperate in every way possible, but I feel that I cannot take less than one hundred and twenty-five dollars for each manuscript—an average of about one-fourth cent a word." She proceeded to lay out her reasoning, which not only displayed her complete understanding of her own progress as a writer, but highlighted a problem that Edna and Harriet had no way around: Unlike their father, they commanded very little loyalty from their writers, nor had they made an effort to. "At the time I started to work for the syndicate, about five years ago, I believe, I accepted this rate, for at that time I had not had a great deal of experience in book writing. I have never requested a raise although my work has improved, as you will note by comparing it with my earlier volumes. Then, too, after the first year, Mr. Stratemeyer always gave me a bonus, which helped out. As the rate now stands I am receiving less than I did when I first became associated with the syndicate."

Indeed, Edward had always given a generous annual Christmas "present" to the writers who were doing the Syndicate's best work. Harriet and Edna had decided that they couldn't afford to make that gesture, but its disappearance was a blow that many of their ghostwriters must have taken as a sign that the Syndicate as they knew it was gone. Though some surely attributed the loss to the Depression, several other writers who refused the lesser rate mentioned the lack of bonuses as well. It turned out that many of them had been writing Stratemeyer books for a price they knew was low in relation to the market in general largely because, as one of them explained, with the annual bonus "my books averaged about $175.00 each as compared to the $125.00 I have been receiving for the past year, constituting an actual reduction of fifty dollars on each book under the present regime." Another longtime author wrote in to say, "I am sorry that I cannot accept the reduction of $25 that you propose on payments for subsequent books...Only my attachment to the memory of a dear friend and my earnest desire to be of real service to the new organization have kept me at the work at the sacrifice of my own personal interests. I do not feel that I can go any further in that direction."

For Mildred, too, not accepting the lowered fee was a matter of pride — as she wrote in another letter to Harriet, who had asked one more time if she might reconsider. "I realize what difficult times we are passing through and would have been willing to accept some reduction were the amount paid not already as low as I feel I could accept with justice to myself." But it was also a matter of practicalities. Though the country was in an economic crunch, Mildred, it seemed, was not. She had so much work that she was juggling "clients," and though she was sorry to stop her work for the Syndicate, she was also able to. "Since writing you I have signed for a new girls' series and have other work in prospect. In my negotiations with the publisher I reserved time for my syndicate work but unless I hear from you soon I must fill up this vacancy," she informed Harriet rather impatiently. And then, as if to soften the blow, or perhaps simply to keep relations good, "I trust that the future will produce happier circumstances which will permit a resumption of our relations. With best personal regards and kind wishes for the continued success of the Stratemeyer Syndicate, I remain, Yours truly."

Mildred was not alone in feeling insulated from the effects of the Depression. Though they were worried about the company, neither Harriet nor Edna had given up the lavish lifestyle in which they had been raised. Each of them had her own income from Edward's estate, Russell was still earning a good living as a stockbroker, and Edna was living at home with Lenna, who had an income of her own as well as royalties and securities from Edward's estate. In fact, there was so much money to be spent that no one was even accounting for it, as Edna complained in a memo she wrote for her sister entitled "Resume of the Management of Monies and Welfare of Mother."

Certainly no one in the Stratemeyer family had even been ostentatious, but Edward's death seemed to have brought it out in Lenna. "It doesn't seem necessary to pump everything up and live so grandly because Dad died," Edna sighed. Lenna and Edna were paying a full complement of servants, including a chauffeur, a nurse, a couple to keep the house, and a variety of other staff. Lenna had gotten into the habit of giving them money to keep them happy, something she apparently felt she needed to do and that resulted in them, as Edna put it, "not wanting to follow my instructions in matters, then going behind my back and getting mother to say they don't have to do it." Edna was also beginning to resent her role as caretaker of her difficult invalid mother. "It certainly works me up and to get no co-operation and no thanks for a hard job is I think the last straw," she informed Harriet at the end of the memo. "Think it over." Though she was aware of how hard Harriet was working at the Syndicate in addition to making time for her young family, Edna could not hide her petulance.

She also had a somewhat different take on the Syndicate's financial problems than Harriet — or at least on the people who refused to help alleviate them. Just as she had once been willing to sell the Syndicate as quickly as possible, she now saw little reason to hang on to pesky writers like Mildred, whom she considered arrogant. When Harriet forwarded her Mildred's letter refusing the lower fee, she wrote back immediately and in great annoyance. "Dear Hat: Received letter from you enclosing Mrs. Wirt's tale of woe. Of course she is getting a swell head and doesn't choose to take less. Well, I think if your letter to her doesn't make her change her mind we better consider Mr. Karig."

So, after five years and thirteen books, Mildred was suddenly no longer writing for the Stratemeyer Syndicate. A letter went out to Walter Karig, who was writing the Perry Pierce mystery series for the Syndicate, asking him to take on Doris Force. When he agreed, they sent him an outline and a few significant pointers about the difference between writing for boys and girls, according to the Stratemeyer Syndicate: "You will notice that the story contains adventure and characterization but that the idea of the secret oil well is kept from being too prominent. While girls like action in their stories, they are not as interested in the details of things like these as boys are, and therefore such ideas are merely used as background."

As for Mildred, Harriet and Edna decided to try to keep her "on reserve" for Nancy Drew in the event that Walter Karig proved incompetent, a plan that involved treating her with a graciousness they did not necessarily think she deserved. "My dear Mrs. Wirt," Harriet wrote. "Of course, we were disappointed that you felt you were unable to acede [sic] to our request in regard to the writing of certain books, but we are really delighted to hear that you are making out so well with your own stories. As we do not want to hold up any of your own work, we thought it best to write you that we have been able to place the writing of the Doris Force books with someone else. As the Nancy Drew story would not have to be decided upon immediately, we are reserving our decision in this matter. If we should decide that we would like you to do it we will communicate with you at a little later date … We wish you every success with your new girls' series."

It was not to be, however. When Walter Karig handed in his first Doris Force book, in spite of the fact there were "some places where they conversation is perhaps a bit too mannish," Harriet and Edna decided to give him more work, no doubt at least in part because he was willing to accept a lower payment per manuscript than Mildred. "All in all, the story was so well handled that we are asking you if you will for the same price undertake work on a girls' mystery story," Harriet wrote to him in October. "You may already know the NANCY DREW books." This latter was a rich display of false modesty if ever there was one, for by the end of 1931, there were very few people, especially people involved in the juvenile book world, who had not heard of Nancy Drew.

THE OPENING PAGES of Nancy Drew Mystery Story number seven, *The Clue in the Diary*, published in 1932, noted that, in addition to all of the teen sleuth's other stellar qualities, "in any crowd, she unconsciously assumed leadership." Even when her peer group was made up of all the other juvenile series that occupied the ravaged world of book publishing in the early 1930s, she did not disappoint. "Sales are not up to very much," the series editor at Grosset & Dunlap wrote to Harriet in April of that year. "But NANCY is still thumbing her nose at the depression and shows a good increase in the first quarter."

If anyone could rise above the bad economic climate, it was Nancy Drew. Surely the fact that the Depression did not exist in the well-appointed world of her stories was part of their appeal, but Nancy herself had just as much to do with the books' success. Her adventures provided an escape from the humdrum dailiness of childhood just as surely as her world provided an escape from the Depression. Slouched fashionably against a table as she questioned a dastardly suspect in Russell Tandy's frontispiece drawing for *The Clue in the Diary*, she was unmistakably a girl of great daring and strength. Neither the proper white-collared suit and high heels nor the blond curls that spilled from beneath her beret to frame her lovely, inquisitive face could diminish her force — especially not when the third character in the drawing, the suspect's wife, was frozen for all time with a shrill expression and a gaping mouth. The picture caption attested to the sleuth's powers: "'Don't give in to Nancy Drew!' his wife screamed."

The poor swindler, did, of course, give in — on the very next page — just as everyone else had. When an article about the fifty-cent juvenile industry came out in *Publishers Weekly* that summer, it noted that as a general rule "one of the first hard facts which successful publishers of fifty-cent juvenile series learn is that their best-seller boys' series always run into far higher figures than their best-seller girls' series." This was due to the same basic cause that Stratemeyer had diagnosed some years earlier: "Girls are unashamed readers of boys' books, while boys are notoriously loath to be seen with anything as effeminate as a book whose hero

is a heroine." But while boys may not have been picking up her
stories — she was still a girl, after all, George Fayne's influence
notwithstanding — Nancy Drew was thumbing her nose at publishing trends as well as the Depression. The article went on,
"Today the Nancy Drews stand as the top-notch sellers of the
many best-seller juvenile series published by this firm."

In record time the teen sleuth had captured the hearts and
imaginations of girls as well as the market. She did not even require many expenditures on the part of her publisher, because
"boys and girls like them [top-notch sellers] so well that they
themselves do the advertising by talking enthusiastically about
them with each other," the *Publishers Weekly* article continued.
Had they paid the author — in fact, they did not even know about
her before her article came out in June — Harriet and Edna could
not have asked for better publicity.

It seemed fortuitous, then, when that same writer, Edna Yost,
contacted Harriet to say she was working on a second article on
her subject and was hoping for an interview. "They have commissioned me now to do another featuring the personalities of the
authors of the various series," she explained. "Yesterday I talked
with Mr. Arthur Leon [of Cupples & Leon, one of the Syndicate's
main publishers] and he referred me to you for material on Lester
Chadwick, Roy Rockland [Rockwood], Alice B. Swann, and Frank
V. Webster." All of these were Syndicate pen names, a secret so
well kept that even the intrepid Ms. Yost was not entirely sure
whether or not they were real people. "The Weekly wants only
fact material — and is not interested in discussing any of the series authors under nom de plume," she told Harriet. "Will it be
possible, then, for me to include material on any of the above
list — and if so, will you let me have it and how?" In the event that
the answer was no, Harriet could still serve a purpose, which was

to illuminate the readers of *Publishers Weekly* about a great legend who had made it his business to stay out of the limelight. "I also want to write about Mr. Stratemeyer who — Mr. Leon says — was your father."

Harriet replied immediately, clearly flattered by the attention. She informed Yost that the list of authors she had inquired about were, indeed, all pseudonymous and thus useless to her for "portraying the lives of writers of certain series." She did not even mention the names of the real ghostwriters, much less offer them up for interviews, lest the secret of the Stratemeyer Syndicate should be revealed. "Because of the credulity of the young reader this fact is never made public," she wrote with chirpy authority. "Why dispel their illusions!"

If anyone was poised to know something about the credulity of young readers, it was Harriet. For one thing, she was privy to the loads of letters from children that arrived at the Syndicate each month and worried about how best to perpetuate the legendary lives of the adored pseudonymous series writers. "Fan mail is indeed heavy," she had recently written to Arthur Leon. "We shall be hard put to it to properly answer these letters so that the juvenile minds in that section will not become suspicious that their beloved authors write under pen names." She was also living with such minds under her own roof. Practically since the start of her work at the Syndicate, Harriet had become accustomed to consulting her children on some of the details of the books she was working on. "Another phrase where our correction was erased was, 'Atta boy,'" she once reprimanded Laura Harris, her editor at Grosset & Dunlap, regarding one of the Buck and Larry Baseball stories books, her father's final pet project. "I took the trouble to ask my son about this phrase when I was correcting the manuscripts, and he informed me that it is already obsolete."

On the matter of the title for Nancy Drew number six, she had again consulted with her offspring, this time Camilla. In writing to Harris, she gave her daughter's opinion every bit as much weight as the conversation that had taken place between her, Edna, and Agnes Pearson:

> We have talked this matter over in this office and really do not favor the name 'The Red Gate Farm Cavern.' We think the last word a bit grown-up, and it sounds very much like tavern...Incidentally, my ten year old daughter, who is also a devotee of the Nancy Drew series, has read this manuscript and prefers the first title mentioned below:
>
> The Plot at Red Gate Farm
> The Adventure at Red Gate Farm
> The Cave at Red Gate Farm, or, The Red Gate Farm Cave.

Fully confident in her children as arbiters of taste, Harriet was also not beyond using them as a kind of litmus test when she was in an argument with a publisher over the content of a book. "In regard to the first Doris Force book, we feel that perhaps we are putting too much stress on the opinion of one [editor]," she wrote with some annoyance to the publisher. "Two other series approved by her have been written by the same author, and we do not feel that this author would have put anything into the Doris Force books which girls 12 to 14 should not read. Acting upon your suggestion we have carefully gone over various approved series, and are really at a loss to understand how your critic can find this story so different from the others. I, myself, have a daughter nearly 10, and I should not hesitate one moment to let her read this book, and I have a reputation for being perhaps over-careful in the selection of reading for my children."

Harriet was, indeed, a conscientious, generous mother. Her

letters to Edna and Lenna through the 1930s are filled with details from her children's lives that make it abundantly clear that in spite of her heavy workload, she found the time to attend the recitals, parties, and various festivities that were part of their happy upper-class childhoods and took great pleasure in doing so. "We are wondering whether your Fourth of July was mostly spoiled by rain as ours was," she wrote to her sister in 1932. "The school races were held in the morning and Camilla went through her part drenched to the skin, and along with several others made a mud slide for home run." Rarely, however, did a letter get mailed with only family news. Even on the sidelines of her children's sporting events, Harriet was always thinking of new series book scenarios. "I had an idea for a Betty Gordon plot," she continued in the same note, "but in order to write it up I have had to go through some of the former volumes, so I have been very busy reading today."

Her devotion to both home and family eventually delivered Harriet into a crisis very familiar to her modern counterparts — she lost her child care. "Tomorrow I have a Scotch-Irish woman of 36 years coming to try the position for a week," she told Edna. "She comes highly recommended, and seemed to like the place and want to come. While I expect to be in the office part of tomorrow, I hardly feel it wise for me to go off to New York and leave her there, even though I am keeping Swanee on for a week, so that if the new lady and I do not agree at the end of that time I will still have somebody able to carry on."

Harriet was in unfamiliar territory and probably had no one in her immediate social circle with whom she could discuss it. Instead, she confessed to a fellow working woman, her editor Laura Harris at G&D. "I am sorry I could not accept the luncheon invitation for some day this week," she wrote, "but several matters have come up in the office to keep me here. Furthermore, I am changing servants at my home, a mighty difficult and frightening procedure for anyone who has to go away from the house each day, and often all day." There were no support groups for working mothers and no friends with full-time jobs she could turn to. Harriet was essentially a CEO, but she was still responsible for every element of running her home. There was no question that she wanted to run the Syndicate as well, but the worry she felt about leaving her family was just as real as her desire to work, and the pressure she must have felt from her peers, who had already made their opinions about her choices clear, as well as the overwhelmingly male world in which she worked — the all-female Syndicate staff was still receiving letters that addressed them, routinely, as "Gentlemen" — must have been enormous. "When I took over the Syndicate from my father, was it harder for me to get along with the outside world than it was for him? The answer definitely is yes," she admitted many decades later. "For years and years I felt as if publishers were treating me as if I were the little girl in the country." True to form, however, she was determined to fight this prejudice and resolve her situation no matter what it took. Her letter to Laura Harris ended on a note of optimism that, if it did not quite cover her nervousness, nonetheless showed her characteristic determination to make things come out right. "However, I am pinning my faith on a Scotch-Irish lady who, I trust, will be as efficient as Nancy Drew's housekeeper, Hannah Gruen!"

She employed the same upbeat attitude at the Syndicate and sought it out in others, too. "I enjoyed my few hours with you and Mr. Reed the other day," she wrote to Laura Harris on another occasion. "It is a real pleasure as well as a mental uplift to meet and talk with people who can smile and be optimistic despite a depression, and, as Mrs. Easy Ace says on the Radio, 'Be willing to take the bitter with the better.'"

But despite Harriet's efforts to stay positive and hide her concern, reality kept encroaching on the little office in East Orange. Sales of many Syndicate series slowed down, and publishers canceled orders—Doris Force, as suspected, did not last past 1932, and the Outdoor Girls, the Blythe Girls, and Perry Pierce, among others, were gone by 1933. Many of the Syndicate's writers were looking desperately for work: "This year, like every other writer I know, I have experienced a disastrous setback," wrote Leslie McFarlane in the summer of 1932. "My markets have been wrecked. Having lost my old newspaper contacts it is impossible to get a job. It is a straight bread-and-butter struggle." As financial matters worsened, Harriet let down her cheerful guard. "We have heard so much lately about all of us having turned the corner that somehow or other the phrase has become ridiculous," she wrote to one of her authors in the spring of 1933. "Don't you think so?" He, like many others, was looking for work and had just accepted her offer of $85 a book. "Although we try to be optimistic," she finished, "it does seem either that we have turned the wrong corner or that so many of us turned it at once that there is a traffic jam."

Even Mildred, once too proud to accept a lesser fee, had come back to the fold. Less than a year after she had departed, she received a letter from Edna asking her if she would undertake the next Ruth Fielding, which was to be called, appropriately, *Ruth Fielding and Her Greatest Triumph; or, Saving Her Company from Disaster*. Having learned, thanks to Walter Karig, a little bit about how much work it was to train a new writer, Edna must have changed her mind about Mildred's worth because she offered Mildred the highest possible fee the Syndicate could afford. "Our price for the volume is $100.00. We will furnish you with a complete outline as formerly. We are sorry that the original remuneration which you received cannot be offered, but as sales on all books, these included, are too uncertain to warrant an increase we will have to again ask you to cooperate with us."

Mildred was feeling the pinch of the Depression at last. Two of her girls' series had been canceled in 1931 and 1932, but, still, she was not going to admit to Harriet and Edna that she had less work—or, at least, she was not going to admit it outright. "In regard to writing the new volume of the Ruth Fielding series, I have been taking this under consideration," she wrote back. "Providing arrangements can be made with you so that this does not interfere with my regular work, I am willing to do the book at your price."

Ruth was headed for marriage, however, and it proved fatal for sales. Apparently little girls, unlike their mothers, still did not think catching a man was the be-all and end-all. Mildred wrote the final two books in the series, *Ruth Fielding and Her Greatest Triumph* and *Ruth Fielding and Her Crowning Victory,* before it was canceled by the publisher, leaving Edna and Harriet to cast around for some new characters to fill the void. They knew "from talking with other publishers and reading articles such as those which appear in the *Publishers Weekly* that mystery stories for girls far outsell any other variety." Accordingly, they conceived of two more girl detective series, the Kay Tracey books and the Dana Girls. The first featured Kay, flanked by a pair of chums who resembled George and Bess, and the second a pair of school-aged sisters named Jean and Louise who solve mysteries between classes at their boarding school. Both series made their first appearances in 1934. By design, the Syndicate and Grosset & Dunlap were flooding the market with Nancy Drew–inspired girls—the Dana Girls were even being written by the famous Carolyn

Keene. As Leslie McFarlane, the series' first author, characterized the invention of the Dana Girls many years later, "Nancy Drew and the Hardy Boys were doing so well that the Syndicate decided to launch a new series which would combine the best features of both. The Hardy Boys had shown that two heroes were better than one, because they always had someone to talk to and they could take turns in being rescuer and rescuee. So why not *two* Nancy Drews?" By the time Mildred had sent Ruth Fielding off into the sunset with Tom Cameron, the Danas and Kay Tracey were well on their way to production.

Harriet and Edna, meanwhile, had other problems on their hands. Edna Yost's follow-up article in *Publishers Weekly* had come out, and they were none too pleased with her work. She had revealed a number of their secrets and, even worse, had attacked not only the values of their company, but the reputation of their dead father. In spite of her experience with the Wellesley Press Board, it was in Harriet's nature to look for the best in everyone, and that included the media. She fancied herself something of an untouchable at the top of a famous company and felt that she had treated Yost graciously, so she was entirely unprepared for the broadside.

The sisters responded to Yost in the only way they could, with a letter to the editor of *Publishers Weekly*. They were angry that "certain facts [were] published without our permission" and hurt by the slur against their father:

> . . . *there is a sentence which is most unjust, if not actually libelous. I quote from page 1596:*
> *"The late Edward Stratemeyer hired a staff to produce the actual writing of dozens of series books—a process which is devoid surely of either literary sincerity or literary merit."*

> *As we are carrying on the work of Mr. Stratemeyer's Syndicate, and bend every effort to produce books of literary merit and true worth, we feel that the above quotation as well as other parts of the article need an explanation, both from Miss Yost and your concern.*
>
> *As subscribers to The Publishers Weekly, we heartily disapprove of the kind of criticism found in the article entitled: "Who Writes the Fifty-Cent Juveniles?", and as executrixes of Mr. Stratemeyer's Estate and owners of the Stratemeyer Syndicate we ask that you retract the latter half of the above-quoted statement.*

They had had no experience of such things before, and the high-handed tone of their letter did not provoke the reaction they no doubt expected, which would have included a retraction. Instead, the editor of the magazine wrote back to put them in their places. "My dear Mrs. Adams: It is very doubtful whether literary estimates by a reputable critic could by any stretch of the term be considered libelous. Edna Yost is an experienced writer, and she developed the two articles we printed about children's books out of a desire to study an interesting phenomenon, i.e., the enormous sale of books for boys and girls in fifty cent series. The Publishers Weekly point of view is a booktrade interest, but we give authors of signed articles the usual freedom of expression."

The result was that the Syndicate decided to make it as hard as possible for journalists to write about their business practices, their founder, and their ghostwriters. Harriet refused from then on to give out any information about her father, intending to write a biography of him herself some day (she never did). Their solution to the ghostwriter problem, on the other hand, was as simple as it was bizarre; they would pretend the series writers were, in fact, real people. They put their plan into effect just a few weeks after Yost's article came out. *Who's Who*, an encyclo-

pedia of noteworthy Americans, had been asking for information
on the various series writers, and the book's editor was to be the
first victim, as it were, of their ruse. "Enclosed also is a letter
which we should like to have you copy on your own stationery
and send out," they wrote to Laura Harris at Grosset, as well as to
all their other publishers. "We have had several requests from
WHO'S WHO for life sketches of Carolyn Keene and Laura Lee
Hope. We think it best that these letters be answered in the way
suggested, and trust that this will meet with your approval. We
think it is inadvisable to inform the publishers of WHO'S WHO that
these names are pseudonyms, thus making it unnecessary to reveal any of the business secrets which are held in contract between Grosset & Dunlap and The Stratemeyer Syndicate." The
enclosed letter itself, though brief, did nothing short of bestow-
ing personhood on fake pen names. "We have forwarded letters
from you addressed to Miss Carolyn Keene and Miss Laura Lee
Hope, and you may rest assured that if the authors wish to have
biographical sketches in WHO'S WHO IN AMERICA, they will write
directly to you, giving such dates. Yours very truly, Grosset &
Dunlap."

It was the first step in what would eventually become an all-
out campaign to create personas for the Syndicate's most valued
pseudonyms, brought on at least in part by the long-standing tradition of anonymity, but also, as the years went on, by the desire
to keep the Syndicate entirely under the control of the family. If
they were the only ones who knew who wrote the manuscripts,
then they were the only ones who could produce them for publishers, which gave them invaluable leverage. Eventually, every
"author" would acquire stationery with his or her name at the top
of it, a bit of biographical background, and a signature, generally
forged by Harriet whenever it was called for.

Carolyn Keene, of course, was the Syndicate's most illustrious author. "We have received our royalty statement, and thank you for it," Edna wrote to Grosset & Dunlap in the summer of 1933. "We wish that all our books might sell like the Nancy Drews, but considering the times we are satisfied." Walter Karig had by this time written three Nancy Drews — *Nancy's Mysterious Letter*, *The Sign of the Twisted Candles*, and *The Password to Larkspur Lane* — but they were to be his only volumes. Though Karig's titles were selling as well as Mildred's had, Edna and Harriet found that his manuscripts required extensive rewriting when they came into the office. They were also annoyed at him because of repeated failures to keep his work for the Syndicate secret. As far back as 1931, Harriet had reprimanded him for talking about it, to which he had replied — with characteristic jubilance — "Your mildly implied rebuke for violating a rule of anonymity with which I was not familiar is hereby taken to heart and indelibly engraved upon that organ, which is a mass of similar memoranda."

Whatever the cause for his departure from the series, by early 1934 the sisters had decided to try to convince Mildred to come back to Nancy Drew. The next title, *The Clue of the Broken Locket*, had been chosen, and the book was to be featured in the summer Sears Catalog, which gave it the potential to sell even more copies than usual. For Nancy's biggest outing yet — her chance to really break into the mainstream of America — Harriet and Edna hoped to have her originator back on the case. Despite Laura Harris's repeated queries about the progress of the manuscript, though, the sisters were slow to assign it. Perhaps reasoning that Mildred could turn it around as quickly as she always had in the past because she was familiar with the basic parameters of Nancy and her stories, Edna held off writing to her until March of 1934. When she did, she filled the note with compliments, possibly to soften the blow of an even lower fee. "We wonder whether you have any time in which you might write the next volume in the Nancy Drew series...We were very much pleased with the latest Ruth Fielding. We thought the story especially interesting and well done, a fitting climax to that long series. In view of the fact that this particular set of books has been completed, we trust that you will be willing to arrange your own writings, so that the new mystery story can be done conveniently, and that we will not lose contact with you. We will pay $85 for this story. Trusting to hear from you favorably at once."

They were not disappointed. Not only did Mildred agree to take on *The Clue of the Broken Locket;* she promised to bring all her expertise and even affection to the task. "I have always been rather partial to 'Nancy,'" she replied, "and it will seem quite like old times to be writing about her again."

9

MOTHERHOOD
AND NANCY DREW

"'I'M NED NICKERSON,' he declared with a warm smile. 'Anything I can do?'" With these seven immortal words, a relationship for the ages was set into motion. Ned Nickerson, blond, handsome, and always willing to assist, was on the case — as a sidekick, anyway. In his first appearance, he rescues Nancy, George, and Bess from a fender bender they've gotten into on the way home from investigating a suspicious fire. "You girls haven't seen the last of me," he calls after the departing trio at the end of the scene. "I know the road to River Heights and you mustn't be surprised if I follow it one of these days." Indeed, Ned was soon to become a regular fixture in Nancy's hometown and elsewhere, ever ready to ingratiate himself with his teen love, ever second fiddle to a good mystery. A college man, he takes Nancy to well-chaperoned dances and eventually finds friends for Bess and George as well so they can triple-date, all without receiving so much as a peck on the cheek in return. Strong and dependable, he nevertheless remains the epitome of the downtrodden boyfriend. Finding Nancy in a dangerous situation that could easily have gone awry toward the end of *The Clue in the Diary*, he chides her, only to be out-chided. "'Perhaps it was a daring plan,' Nancy admitted with a pleased little laugh, for she could tell that her friend was actually disturbed, 'but it worked, and that's the most important thing.'" As written by Mildred, Nancy was as clever as ever and still just a little bit of a know-it-all.

Ned, on the other hand, was doggedly useful, but only up to a point. He was designed to be that way, a plan made abundantly clear in the letter Edna sent to Mildred along with the outline for 1934's *The Clue of the Broken Locket*. Having been off the series for only three books since *The Clue in the Diary*—the 1932 book in which Ned made his grand entrance—it was unlikely that Mildred would have forgotten Ned's defining quality. But just in case, Edna wanted to remind her that while Ned may have been perfect husband material, a husband he would never be. In fact, she had another word altogether for him. "He does not appear...in the new Nancy Drew," she informed Mildred, "unless you should choose to use him as a filler."

The men in Harriet's and Edna's real lives—their professional lives, at least—were, alas, not nearly so easily controlled. Around the time that Mildred was working on *The Clue of the Broken Locket*—she chose in the end not to include poor Ned at all, even as an appealing distraction—a writer for *Fortune* magazine named Ayers Brinser became the latest person to turn unwelcome attention on the Syndicate, after sending Harriet a note saying that he was working on a piece about "boys' books in which the major efforts will be devoted to analyzing the phenominal [*sic*] sale of these publications. It is, of course, particularly important that the Stratemeyer Syndicate be consulted."

Fortune, the brainchild of Henry Luce, was only a few years old at this point, and the story Brinser was working on was a perfect example of the hybrid journalism the magazine was printing. It was, first off, a tale of business that went behind the scenes and included all the nuts and bolts of the series book publishing game. But it was also a story about the colorful series themselves, which Brinser described at several spots in the piece with obvious glee: "It has few literary pretensions; it is a flat-footed account of the superhuman exploits of adolescent *Ubermenschen*...Holding each volume together are the threads of some hair-raising adventure. Poverty empties the pockets of dastards only...Virtue and success are synonymous...In order to hold the reader breathless, the fifty-cent plot whirls lickety-split from the first to the last chapter like an express train." Last but certainly not least, his piece attempted to delve into the real issue, the identities of the writers responsible for the endless perpetuation of these two-dimensional yet somehow utterly compelling characters. This made it precisely the kind of story that put Harriet and Edna on the defensive. They agreed to help Brinser to a certain degree—aid that consisted, in the end, largely of them refusing to answer any of his more intrusive questions—and then asked to see a copy of the article before it went to press, thinking they could change it at that point.

Brinser complied with this last request, though it turned out to be no more than an empty gesture. His article came out in the April 1934 issue of *Fortune* under the portentous title "For It Was Indeed He." ("He" was Edward Stratemeyer, of whom Brinser wrote: "As oil had its Rockefeller, literature had its Stratemeyer.") It included not only a photo of Edward Stratemeyer but a photo of the Stratemeyer home and a general exposé of how fifty-cent series books came into being. He had not included any of Harriet and Edna's suggestions, but instead supplied readers with a prominent description of their work habits, which, while it paid them a compliment or two, had a gently mocking tone about it:

> …the Stratemeyer daughters have inherited from their father not only that genius particular to fifty-cent juveniles, but his business acumen. After his death they moved the office from New York City to the top of East Orange's Hale Building. There they sit today at their ponderous roll-top desks dispatching the affairs of fifty-cent juveniles with a sincerity and belief in their work equal to that of the most serious adult novelist. Obscured in a fern-filled corner is a secretary. The only other occupants of the office are immortal. Tom Swift, The Motor Boys, The Rover Boys, Dave Dashaway and dozens of others who exist in the 800 fifty-centers that line the wall.

Brinser could not resist taking a jab at their dramatic flair for secrecy, either, continuing on, "One…might readily mistake the Stratemeyer Syndicate for a private detective's office. As a source of open-handed information about fifty-cent juveniles, it might just as well be that. Miss Edna, who always stays at home managing affairs, waggles her bobbed gray head emphatically and says that their business is their business. Mrs. Adams, who takes care of personal contacts with New York publishers, smiles graciously and says the same…So greatly do they feel the need of maintaining the illusion of these fictitious literati [the pseudonymous authors] that, in spite of the great veneration in which they hold their father, they have refused to authorize any of the many attempts to write his life history."

Harriet and Edna were both offended and bewildered by Brinser's product. For all his insouciance, however, Ayers Brinser did do the Stratemeyer Syndicate several favors. In addition to placing its books squarely at the top of the juvenile heap, he confirmed the status of the Syndicate's star detective in no uncertain terms.

> Nancy is the greatest phenomenon among all the fifty-centers. She is a best seller. How she crashed a Valhalla that had been rigidly restricted to the male of her species is a mystery even to her publishers—for "Tomboy" rings like praise in the adolescent female ear, but "Sissy" is the anathema of anathemas to a boy...Nancy Drew tops even Bomba, the most popular of modern male heroes. The speed with which the public consumes this fabulous series is shown by the sales figures of one of the larger retailers, R.H. Macy & Co. In the six weeks of the last Christmas season Macy's sold 6,000 of the ten titles of Nancy Drew compared with 6,750 for the runner-up, Bomba, which has fifteen titles to choose from.

The super-sleuth was flying higher than ever, and even the continued publication of articles that disparaged her and her kind made no difference. "The cat is out of the bag at last," one critic announced smugly (apparently not realizing that it had been out since Edward's books were banned from the Newark Public Library in 1901). "Series books are the menace to good reading." Still, as even its librarian author had to admit, it was essentially hopeless to try to stop them. "There are always aunts and uncles and cousins, who give books for Christmas and birthdays," she practically sneered, "to say nothing of the underground library by which children obtain almost anything they want to read and into whose workings we should do well not to inquire too closely." Alarmism aside, there was no going back. By the end of the decade, inquiries about using Nancy on everything from children's clothing to radio would flow into the Syndicate, and she would become a movie star as well. In a few short years, Nancy had gone from being a girl detective to being a commodity. Complaining about the jacket art for *Broken Locket* in a 1934 letter to Grosset & Dunlap, Harriet displayed a shrewd understanding of the brand she was helping to create: "The picture should have had a more mysterious atmosphere, which might have been portrayed by a less bland look on the face of Nancy...Is the picture finished? If so, let us hope that the names Nancy Drew and Carolyn Keene, together with the title, will make sales for this volume rather than the picture itself." Then, with some of that business acumen Brinser had noted, she told her editor, "I really do intend to come soon to have a long chat with you about next year's Syndicate output for your concern, and also to discuss shop in general, that we may make some plans to help the unsuspecting public to use some of its money on fifty cent juveniles."

Nancy had become the Syndicate's most important asset, and Harriet and Edna — but especially Harriet — guarded every aspect of her development, from her clothes to her circle of friends. Fine-tuning her appearance and manners was as important to them as plotting the mysterious cases she solved. When Mildred sent in her manuscript for *Broken Locket*, for example, Edna was generally pleased, but the few minor tweaks she did mention in her return letter were all for the sake of making the book more girlish and formal. "Among the changes we were forced to make, was to soften the boyish glibness and swagger of George Fayne," she wrote, as well as to "round out a personal description of the characters; smooth out abrupt sentence endings, and delete a number of colloquialisms."

Under Harriet and Edna's guidance—which had perhaps grown more forceful during the period when Walter Karig's manuscripts for the Nancys had created a good deal of extra work for them—the books were evolving in a way that Mildred seemed, however subtly, to disagree with. "I am sorry you did not like the way I handled George Fayne," she responded, "but in the early volumes of the series she was the 'slangy' type, and thinking that her character had been changed in the latter volumes, I tried to represent her as she was in the beginning." Though she was writing from outlines, Mildred had, at least on the subject of the Nancy Drew Mystery Stories, a longer institutional memory than the Syndicate's current owners. She clearly felt proprietary about the series on some level, as well as believing that she had the right to at least be heard, if not agreed with, on the subject of George's character.

Times had changed, however. Harriet and Edna had taken to writing much longer outlines for their ghostwriters than their father had, a practice they claimed was a response to writers' complaints about doing the same work for less pay, but one that also gave them greater control over plots and characterizations. When Mildred requested that her fee for the next book, a Kay Tracey, be raised to $100, Harriet wrote, "We have tried to equalize depression prices by sending outlines which are much more detailed than those which you formerly received. We have felt that in this way you would not be required to spend as much time as if you had to plan all the fillers yourself." It soon became clear that what Mildred wanted was more freedom, not more pre-scribed action, in her stories. Contrary to being helpful, the longer outlines were precisely the problem. "I do think that the last Kay Tracey story had a slightly hurried and abrupt tone, al-though I spent fully as much time and thought on the manuscript as usual," she agreed in a reply to some criticism from Harriet. "Recent plots seem to be running somewhat long in detail, and…I had difficulty in getting all of the scenes into the story even by cutting many of them short…I think I could give you a much better story if you would grant permission for me to elim-inate minor or filler scenes if I find the material running long for a chapter. This will give me an opportunity to enlarge and em-phasize the more important points of the story, and I believe make for a smoother, more powerful tale."

No doubt part of the reason for her chafing was her growing experience writing her own books from start to finish. In the same letter in which Harriet gave her reasoning about the longer outlines, she also congratulated Mildred, working woman to working woman, on the recent acceptance of several other books by publishers. "There is so much competition in the juvenile field today," she wrote, "that one may feel justifiably pleased to have stories accepted."

At last, Harriet had gotten a firm grasp on the business world. While she remained utterly devoted to her family, she was also taking no small amount of pleasure in her status as a woman in full command of her intelligence and power in the world. Her enjoyment also pervaded aspects of her life that had nothing to do with the Syndicate. In a letter to Edna describing a riotous family outing to Manhattan, complete with trips to the NBC Stu-dio and Chinatown, she also included the details of a meeting about the Sunday school curriculum she was writing for her church. "My conference with the minister, the paid head of our young people's activities, the head of the Sunday School, and one of the Senior department teachers last Friday evening was very satisfactory," she told her sister proudly. "There were several times during the evening when I could hardly keep from laughing aloud as I realized that I, lone female, was 'sitting in' with these church dignitaries and discussing points in psychology, child education, theology and a long list of other subjects."

In addition to being a happy mother and a businesswoman, Harriet was also still very much the dutiful daughter. She wrote frequently to her invalid mother—and had Agnes Pearson type up the letters—to tell her of the doings at the Adams house. Filled with details about the children and the garden and all the rest, these missives rarely mentioned her hard work at the Syndicate office. She was also devoted to her other, lost parent. "Yesterday Russell and I went first to the cemetery at Elizabeth," she wrote to Edna in May of 1934. "We thought that a coinciding date of Mother's Day and another May anniversary [was] an appropriate time for flowers." Four years after her father's death, she was still unable to articulate her feelings about it, referring to it obliquely even to her sister.

She was soon to have another gloomy date to mark in May. Just a year later, in 1935, Lenna died. "Mrs. Adams and I gratefully acknowledge your kind letter of sympathy," Edna wrote to Harriet Otis Smith, who had dropped the sisters a note on hearing of the news about her former employer's widow. "We try to be reconciled to our mother's passing, as she had been an invalid for seven years, and within the last six weeks she suffered severely from her serious heart condition, so we should not wish her back. Did you realize that it is exactly five years since my father passed away? They were both born in the month of October and they both passed away in the month of May. These have been five busy and swift years with all our responsibilities."

Harriet took a few days off from Syndicate work, but then got right back to the next Kay Tracey book. The new series was selling well, and the Syndicate remained solvent, so there was plenty to do. Work was also a panacea for the new Kay Tracey's author, who had recently finished the next Nancy Drew under equally difficult circumstances. "Dear Miss Stratemeyer," Mildred wrote. "I was very sorry to learn of your sad bereavement. I realize what a grievous loss you have suffered and I wish to extend my heartfelt sympathy to you and Mrs. Adams. I am glad that you like 'The Message in the Hollow Oak,' for it was written under somewhat trying conditions. My father has been in very poor health of late, and it was largely on this account that I made my recent trip to Iowa." She had asked specifically that the outline for the book be mailed to her in Ladora, no doubt so that she could escape into her work when the going got especially rough with her father, who, after several years of illness, would eventually die in 1937. Still, her writing was so good that Harriet and Edna decided to put her on to the Dana Girls books as well. For the next five years, she would be responsible for writing every book in the Syndicate's three biggest girls' mystery series, a staggering workload she combined with a number of other books written under her own name.

While she might not have admitted it to everyone, Harriet's ambition was neither less fervent nor any less tied to personal satisfaction than Mildred's. When writing to Wellesley to thank them for refusing to give Ayers Brinser her yearbook photo as an illustration for his *Fortune* article after she had refused him one herself, she had passed off her demanding job with a quick throwaway phrase: "Fortune is publishing an article in the near future...in which some work I am doing will be mentioned," she wrote on a piece of "Mrs. Russell Vroom Adams" stationery.

But the real story was altogether different. In a letter to a dear college friend that same year, Harriet spent the first half confiding about how hard it was to find reliable help to keep her household running while she ran the Syndicate. Even with all her money, she was not immune to the problems of balancing motherhood and career. "As soon as the children were all home and my sister leaving for a month's vacation, my housekeeper-maid told me that she was leaving...So at present, along with many other things, I am looking for a satisfactory woman, and am in a quandry [*sic*]...sometimes I can hardly figure out how I am going to swim out of all the things I am trying to do."

It was all, however, for the sake of her profession, which now that she had it, she would not dream of giving up. "You and I, Rig, were such infants in college we missed a lot," she finished her letter. "And though it is pleasant to feel that one's life is beginning at forty, nevertheless, it is regrettable to realize that one missed so much from fourteen to forty. All we can say is that we are glad we are not going to miss it entirely."

Rai! Rai!
Elephants, Charms, Indians,
Drugs, Snakes, Treasure,
Nancy Drew! Nancy Drew!
Rai! Rai! Rai!
Will Mildred Wirt please come forward
to receive her Cum Laude.

So BEGAN a giddy letter from Harriet to Edna in mid-1936. "Rai" was the name of a sinister circus elephant trainer in the latest Nancy Drew book, *The Mystery of the Ivory Charm*, from which the references to drugs, treasure, and all the other exotic items listed in Harriet's epistolary cheer also came. Nancy—who begins *Ivory Charm* "neatly dressed in a blue traveling suit, her golden hair bound snugly beneath a modish little hat"—is soon caught in a death grip by an escaped jungle snake and plunged headlong into adventure. The superstitious Rai, who believes Nancy is saved not by the animal trainer who calms the snake but by her own powers, gives her a tiny ivory elephant as a token of his admiration. Being, apparently, an amateur art historian, Nancy does not make "the mistake of believing that it was a cheap, crudely made trinket." Her sleuthing instincts are confirmed when Rai tells her, "It has a story which fades far back into the past—a strange tale of a little known, mystic province of India. This charm was once a prized possession of a great ruler—a Maharajah who is said to have been endowed with supernatural powers." The charm, naturally, has a much more significant secret than this vaguely delineated myth. Nancy eventually uncovers it, but not before she takes in a runaway circus boy who turns out to be a lost rajah, gets to shout "Arrest that man!" and gives mouth-to-mouth resuscitation to the boy king at a critical moment "with a sureness of method that surprised even the detectives." The story ends with Ned trying to persuade her not to go to India at the invitation of the young royal. "'I'm sure I'd love India,' the girl said musingly. 'But it's so far away,' Ned protested. 'Perhaps,' Nancy agreed, smiling. 'But I would go to the very ends of the earth to find another mystery.'"

Mildred pulled it all off without a hitch, including the collapse of a secret tunnel that almost buries Nancy and her father alive, several trances, a kidnapping, a helpful if somewhat meat-headed intervention by Ned ("Why didn't someone tell me I was carrying jewels?" he mutters after spilling the precious cargo on the ground), and a kind of mini-tour of the customs and traditions of India placed in the mouth of a helpful professor Nancy consults about instructing her new charge. Harriet was thrilled.

"[The check] went out by mail today," she continued jubilantly in her letter to Edna, who was at the Jersey Shore. "We think the lady in Cleveland did herself proud, and as we are always more adverse in our criticism than you, we have no doubt but that you will find the story excellent. We shall mail it to you tomorrow for your perusal. I did not have the pencil in my hand until I had reached Page 60. I think the story will need so few corrections that I might as well do it as I go along." With Nancy Drew number thirteen, published in 1936, Harriet, Edna, and Mildred had reached the apex of their working relationship.

It was all the more impressive considering Mildred's schedule. Though it would take America's entry into World War II to really put an end to the Depression, book publishing was finally recovering somewhat and orders were rolling in almost faster than she could keep up with them. In that same year, a Dana Girls book and two Kay Traceys she had written for the Syndicate were published, along with two books in her new Mildred A. Wirt Mystery stories (put out by Cupples & Leon), a stand-alone girls' novel called *Carolina Castle,* and the first three books in her Penny Nichols series, also mysteries, written under the name Joan Clark. In 1937 another eleven books in those and other series—including two more Nancy Drews—were published. It seemed the more pressure she was under, the faster and better she could write.

For not only were Harriet and Edna pleased with *The Mystery of the Ivory Charm*, they were complimentary about Mildred's recent work on the Kay Tracey books as well, in spite of getting after her to keep her characters speaking the way they thought girls should express themselves. "We have found this story well handled as a mystery. It is baffling, and the revelation is interestingly delineated," Edna wrote to her. "[But] we will have to round out and develop the conversation between our heroine and her chums, tempering their speech at times. For instance, you often say 'she informed,' which is decidedly abrupt and not youthful."

It was only logical that a person who had been in as much of a hurry to grow up and speak like an adult as Mildred might occasionally lose her grasp on someone else's idea of girlish talk, and her journalism training probably didn't help, either. But Harriet and Edna became more and more disapproving of Mildred's characterization of girls and the kind of language she had them use in almost every manuscript. "Our only criticism is that we believe Kay and her chums at times speak too sarcastically and audaciously for growing girls. The story has a boyish ring throughout which we will temper to conform with more girlish ideals," Edna wrote to her at one point. The following year it was a similar line: "The writing is well done and the only changes we are making are along the lines of softening the characters of both Kay and the tramp. The heroine seems a bit too officious at times."

Mildred's portrayal of Nancy Drew, too, came under fire. "Enclosed is the outline for the new Nancy Drew story, *The Clue of the Tapping Heels*," Harriet wrote to her. "As you write, will you please bear in mind two things — in your zeal for synonyms in the latest manuscript you included a generous number of words beyond the comprehension of the average girl reader of our stories. We think you have improved a great deal in your writing during the past few years, but once in a while the phraseology is really too good—in other words, a bit adult for our yarns." In particular, she thought, Mildred was unaware of what it meant to behave like a proper girl. "We have already mentioned to you the idea of making the heroines too officious. This does not occur very often, but once in a while Nancy or Kay will get beyond the bounds of respectfulness for their elders. After all, they are a bit young to order around police officials and doctors!"

While Mildred was surprised by all of these comments, she was not unwilling to alter her style. "It never occurred to me that the use of 'she informed' was brusque or unusual," she replied, "and there are perhaps other expressions of mine which could be altered to meet your wishes, if I know just what they are." No doubt she felt she had plenty of other places besides Syndicate books to make her girls talk as she wished. Indeed, Sally Lansing, the heroine of *The Hollow Wall Mystery*, the second title in the Mildred A. Wirt Mystery stories, both "grumbled" and "declared in a low tone" within the first few pages of the book. Her chum Victoria, not to be outdone, said things "firmly" and also "commented grimly." These girls talked the way Mildred talked, with an edge that served them well in a world where men and boys were still mostly in control.

Still, the Syndicate remained a major supplier of work to Mildred, and assignments and outlines flew fast and furious through the mail to Cleveland in the first half of 1937. In January of that year, Edna wrote to her to ask if she would be interested in doing another Kay Tracey volume. Mildred replied with a shot of her usual brisk professionalism: "I am just completing a book but will have it finished within ten days and will be very glad to write the new Kay Tracey for you, forwarding it in approximately the usual time."

Her next paragraph, however, contained a revelation that made her ability to write so much and so well even more astonishing. "You and Mrs. Adams may be interested to know that early in November I gave birth to a blue-eyed, red headed baby girl," she wrote. "My work this past year was somewhat difficult, but at present I am in excellent health, thoroughly enjoying both my writing and the new baby." In contrast to many of the other writers for the Syndicate, fathers included, who asked for extra time when there was a new addition to the family, Mildred had not only not breathed a word of her situation, but had worked harder than ever while expecting. Motherhood had no doubt loomed as an unwelcome specter for a woman who, unlike Harriet, was not invested in family life or parenthood in the slightest. The relentless writing, in addition to providing some extra cash in anticipation of the new family member, was probably her best effort to make sure her career did not slip away from her when the baby arrived, a necessity for someone who measured her self-worth by the number of pages she could turn out each month.

Harriet and Edna were amazed. They sent her the plot for *The Secret at the Windmill* later that month, saying, "We hope you will find this story interesting to write and that it will not take too much time away from your new baby. It is a mystery to us, a la Kay Tracey, how you were able to manage so well with your writings and your household last year. We do congratulate you upon the birth of a daughter and should like to hear her nom de plume. That wisp of red hair sounds most intriguing."

Though her daughter was only two months old, Mildred kept right on going, cheerily informing the Syndicate sisters, "The new baby's nom de plume is Margaret Joan, and most fortunately, she seems to be a very good baby!" She was called Peggy for short, and Mildred kept her employers apprised of the child's development from time to time, even as she kept up a breakneck pace with her writing. In addition to the three girls' mystery series she was writing, Mildred took over the Honey Bunch series, which was for the age group the Syndicate referred to as "children," the assumption being that from ages six to nine, boys and girls would read essentially the same kinds of stories (the Bobbsey Twins also fell into this category).

She was, by this time, well aware of her value to the Syndicate, and she used her leverage to angle for the raise she had been seeking. "I am pleased to note that book sales have been picking up recently," she wrote to Edna, at the same time accepting a few more assignments. "I do hope that it will soon be possible for the Syndicate to reestablish the old rates which were in effect before the depression, as I feel that I should begin to increase my income if I am ever to do so." She had found her preferred method of parenting as well, and it included less involvement than Harriet's. "Our vacation this year extended over six thousand miles, quite too strenuous a trip for little Peggy Wirt, who only went a part of the way and spent her time with a doting grandmother," she wrote to Harriet at the end of 1937. "She seemed to thrive on it for she came home talking a blue streak!" When Asa was transferred by the Associated Press the following year, the young family moved to Toledo, and Mildred continued to keep the ladies of the Syndicate updated on her life. "We are well settled in our new home now, and have just sold our residence in Cleveland," she wrote to Edna. "However, as yet I cannot say that I like Toledo, as it seems a rather dirty, noisy city." But despite her distaste for her new surroundings, which she found "at best... smoky," thanks to the factories for the glass, automobile, and other industries that made up a huge part of the city's livelihood,

Toledo would prove a boon for Mildred. Its huge public library downtown provided her with information for many of her series books, and its newspapers—the *Toledo Blade* and its morning edition, the *Toledo Times,* where she got a job during World War II—would be her journalistic home for the rest of her life.

Even as Mildred began to experience the joys and trials of motherhood, Harriet was leaving them behind. "Your son goes to Colgate this fall, does he not? It is exciting, having children about to leave for college," she wrote to the current writer for the Bobbsey Twins, also a woman. "My oldest is headed for Princeton. Now that our big children will be away we shall have to adopt the Bobbseys as small charges to take up our attention!" Harriet took great pride in the accomplishments of her children as they began to make their own lives. "I must tell you what happy occasions Class Day and Commencement at Blair were," she wrote to Edna when her eldest son graduated from prep school. "Perhaps you read in the Newark News that Sunny made Cum Laude."

She was equally admiring of her daughters, who were turning out to be the kind of independent young women she herself had wanted to be. Instead of being confined at home during vacations, they were going out into the world and being encouraged to nurture their interests both as hobbies and professionally. "News from our house includes the fact that Patsy has decided to accept the job offered her by Miss Deucher. Did I tell you or write you that the head of Pathfinder's had asked her to become play director for the summer?" she continued on in her letter to Edna. Then, writing about a family friend, she extolled the virtues of work as a vital organizing force. "Jean is getting pretty discouraged about her play acting part, and I am about to suggest that she plan some form of work, either from the house or a few hours a day away from it. I really think the poor girl needs it. She is wonderfully fine and brave, but one cannot live pretense forever without a change of scene."

No matter how busy Harriet was praising her children and working on her series, she always had time to remind a writer that he or she had no rights to a story or even to talking about a story, the latter of which seemed to be happening with increasing frequency. To one writer, who had done a miniature volume in the Tom Swift series for the Syndicate, she displayed an almost paranoiac obsession with the issue: "We feel we should recall to your mind the idea of your work for us being a confidential matter," she wrote to him. "For this reason, in the future will you please not write on post cards data which might better be kept in a sealed envelope."

And while it was true that the Syndicate's properties, especially Nancy Drew, were taking on more and more value as they were considered for radio shows, movies, and other merchandise—one agent thought she could get far more than the $10,000 Harriet was requesting for the movie rights to the Rover Boys series, while another thought that advertisers would pay from $1,500 to $1,750 a week for a Nancy Drew radio show—Harriet's impression of the Syndicate's standing in the world at large frequently leaned toward the overblown. This resulted in often comically conflicted letters to interested parties who wrote in to the Syndicate, regardless of how harmless their requests were. One such note went out to the secretary of the University of Arkansas Public Information Bureau in the winter of 1936: "Your letter of January 2 to Grosset and Dunlap, Publishers, requesting information about Miss Carolyn Keene and her book, 'The Password to Larkspur Lane,' has been forwarded to me," it began. "In reply, I must bring to your attention the fact that there are many people in official, political, or professional life who have the urge to write books, especially for young people, but who for various reasons deem it inadvisable to attach their own names to their stories. Owing to a like situation, the real identity of Carolyn Keene must remain a mystery." This was clear enough, and it was the excuse Harriet had been giving for quite some time about why it was not possible to identify ghostwriters in the media. Never mind that no such people were actually writing for the Syndicate — from her tone, one might have thought that President Roosevelt was penning the Bobbsey Twins in his spare time.

The writer of this letter was none other than "Secretary to Miss Carolyn Keene." The absurdity of posing as the assistant to a pseudonym, and then having that assistant explain that her boss was not a real person, did not seem to occur to Harriet, who had Agnes Pearson type up the little masterpiece and send it out.

This sort of schizophrenia became the norm as more and more writers had to be kept from telling anyone about their work. No doubt as the series they ghosted became increasingly visible, and interest in them grew, the writers felt it was only fair that they be able to discuss them. They had given away their "right, title and interest" in each story they wrote, as per the release form signed for each one, but nowhere did it say anything about mentioning the books in conversation with friends or potential employers. As it had since Edward's day, it all seemed to come down to how those agreements were interpreted, a problem Harriet would set out to fix in the next few years. For the moment, all she could do was plug the leaks as they occurred.

A big part of the difficulty was that even Harriet and Edna did not have a consistent position on whether or not what the ghostwriters did was of actual creative value. They were willing to write letters to other publishers for their ghosts, praising their writing skills, but at the same time were loath to admit to the writers themselves that they were providing an invaluable part of the story by returning to the Syndicate a manuscript that could be edited. To do so would have made the release forms each author signed essentially untenable, and so they continued to behave as though the authors were nothing more than glorified stenographers.

The problem took on new dimensions in 1937, when Walter Karig reappeared. He had done no work for the Syndicate since his three Nancy Drews in the early 1930s, but he had continued to tell people about what he had done in spite of Harriet's earlier warnings. When *Publishers Weekly* printed Karig's name as the real author of the books he had, indeed, ghostwritten, Harriet wrote to the editor immediately, falsely claiming that Karig had not only not written any Nancy Drews, but any of the other books he had done for the Syndicate. While the Syndicate had provided outlines for each of his books, as usual, it was also not wholly true to say that the Syndicate had written the books. Unable to explain the complicated process that brought a Stratemeyer book into being, Harriet simply wrote Karig out of the production chain altogether.

Her fury was no doubt inflamed by the fact that Karig had done more than just talk about his role: In direct violation of his agreement with the Syndicate, he had written to the Library of Congress specifically requesting credit for the books he had written. The Library of Congress had in turn assumed he had written all of the books in the series he mentioned, a simple error of magnitude. Harriet may well have avoided telling other ghost-writers about his stunt because she feared they would copy him. "How many times the Stratemeyer Syndicate had rued the day that Walter Karig ever wrote any books for it!" she would later ex-claim in a letter to Mildred. But somehow, amazingly, she had gotten the Library of Congress on board with the Syndicate's plan. Writing to an adult fan who was requesting information after getting confused while doing research on authorship, she explained, "The matter now has been straightened out. The Library of Congress is willing that the identity of Carolyn Keene should not be known."

The Karig fiasco fell on Harriet alone. Edna was increasingly absent from the office as, at the age of forty-two (long past the age at which women were considered marriageable in those days), she had gotten married to a man named Wesley Squier. In the summer of 1937, while Harriet toiled in New Jersey, she was on her honeymoon. And she was pregnant. She gave birth to a baby girl in January of 1938 and, in spite of Harriet's having already used the name for her second daughter, named her Camilla.

Edna was back at the office by the fall of 1938, relishing her dual roles for the time being. "My lovely baby girl is now nine and one half months old and weighs twenty-two pounds," she wrote to one of the Syndicate authors. "She looks like her daddy, as girls so often do, though we both have dark hair and dark eyes. My sister's older boy is in his third year at Princeton and her three other children are most active in sports and school affairs. Between home and business we find life very exciting, with new problems to be solved every day." An admiring article that came out the following year in a local paper, the *East Orange Record*, confirmed her report, though it also made clear who was really running things over at the Hale Building:

> The two sisters now running the Stratemeyer Syndicate, Mrs. Russell V. Adams of 48 North Terrace, Maplewood, and Mrs. C. Wesley Squier of Summit, have a full working day, watching

the juvenile market, plotting stories, contacting writers, and buying and selling manuscripts. Mrs. Adams is especially well known in the local suburbs by reason of a boundless appetite for living which has made it impossible for her to follow the ordinary routine of bridges and teas which seem to comprise the daily lives of most housewives, and has instead set her feet on the road to high adventure pursued by the Rover Boys and their allies of the printed page...We don't see how she does it, but then people never could understand the inexhaustible energy of the Stratemeyer clan.

Along with the glowing press—the sisters seemed to have realized they could control it better if it was local—there was another reason to celebrate in the Adams household. Seventeen-year-old Patsy, who was touring England with a group of girls and a chaperone for the summer, received this joyful missive from her mother in mid-July: "Dear Patsy: By this time you have received the cable telling you that you are being admitted to the Freshman class at Wellesley College. Hurrah! Your worries are over." Harriet was almost as excited about her daughter's entry to Wellesley as she had been about her own. "Your course of study must reach the Dean's office by August 20. I notice that English Composition and Hygiene are the only two subjects required. You decided, did you not, that you would take Mediaeval History and French. We spoke of Speech as the extra elective. I notice from the catalog that the course which is given three hours a week comes only the second semester."

Thrilled as she was about her daughter's future, Harriet was living happily in her own present, too busy with work and the ongoing pleasure she took in her marriage to Russell to pine for her college days. "Aunt Edna is still at the shore, and I am busy not only with book matters, but with remodelling the office. By the

time she will have returned, I expect to have most of the old furniture sold and the place looking modern and attractive. I am
hoping that she will not cut me up into small pieces for my bravery!" she continued in her note to Patsy. "We trust you are having a splendid vacation, and are awaiting eagerly your first letter.
Lots of love."

Dear Carolin Keene. I am 4 and a half yrs. old and I liced your
fasson [crossed out] fasin [crossed out] fastinate [crossed out]
wonderful book about the haunted bridge. it was a corker, ex-
peshly the mistery parts. My daddy sez to never cross yor bridges
untill you come to them, but I notis he is allways in a stoo about
bizness. Wen I get big my mama sez I can rite stores like you rite
Carolin Keen. I rote a story for teacher last Wensdy that she said
it was exslent... Pleze rite more books soon, my mama and daddy
will by them for me rite away when they cum out down to Katzes
drug store wer they hav A library and mama sets and smokes
buts and reeds all the gunk they have there. With all my luve,
Virginia Cook

Thanks to the ongoing enthusiasm—fan mail for Nancy and
her creator continued to pour in—Harriet had been able to
make a deal with Warner Brothers to do a series of Nancy Drew
pictures. She had sold them the rights for $6,000, and in addi-
tion to high hopes for exposure for the series and more money,
the deal had given her the opportunity to change the release
forms that Mildred and other writers signed. Now, instead of just
right, title, and interest, the writers released their rights to all possible further use and resale of the stories and confirmed, once
again, that the signee had done them "from complete working
outlines." Because the Nancy Drew stories had an actual buyer,

as opposed to just a theoretical one, Mildred had to sign a special letter worked up by Warner Brothers, giving up her right to any royalties and assuring the company that she would not sue. This she did, happily, and in late 1938, *Nancy Drew: Detective* hit theaters around the country.

With scripts written by Warner Brothers employees, all of the films starred saucy fifteen-year-old Bonita Granville as Nancy and Frankie Thomas as "trusted friend" Ted Nickerson (a name change that appears to have been completely superfluous). *Nancy Drew: Detective*, which took some of its plot from *The Password to Larkspur Lane*, was a flimsy kidnapping story involving a wealthy elderly woman, secret messages delivered by carrier pigeon, and a bogus nursing home. In it, Nancy comes off as both bossier and yet somehow more traditionally feminine than she does in her books. She has none of the gracious elegance that defines her in print and often makes faces to get a point across. She's mean to Ted, who enters the picture by destroying her flower beds during a practice football tackle, and spouts endless maxims about women's intuition and being strong that don't quite add up with her behavior. In one of the early scenes of the movie, which takes place at the Brinwood School for Young Ladies — Nancy is a student there despite the fact that she never sets foot in its building again — she announces, "I think every intelligent woman should have a career." But every time she gets excited, she talks so quickly, and with such babyish breathlessness, that it's hard to take her seriously.

Her supporting cast doesn't help much. Carson Drew, who figures much more prominently in the film than he ever does in a Nancy Drew Mystery Story, spends a lot of time trying to convince her to get off the kidnapping case, telling her at one point:

"These men are not going to stand for Nancy Drew poking her little nose into their affairs." In general, almost everyone talks down to Nancy, from the police chief who refers to her constantly as "little girl," earning some very un-Nancy-like scowls, to Ted, who sighs "Just like all women, aren't you? No one can convince you of anything." After getting back at him by pointing out that "statistics prove from 15 to 20 a woman is five years mentally older than a man of the same age" and telling him he's about as "chivalrous as an oyster" (to which Ted responds, "Okay, then, I'm an oyster"), Nancy makes him dress up in drag as a nurse to break into the fake nursing home and, ultimately, save Miss Eldridge. In one of the most inventive, and least plausible, scenes in the film, Ted finds an old X-ray machine in the basement where he and Nancy are being held captive and uses it to broadcast interference in Morse code to the River Heights radio station, which leads to their rescue. It all takes place in sixty-six action-packed minutes, and by the end, even Police Chief Tweedy agrees Nancy is brave, in spite of her fainting at the sight of his very large gun.

Nancy Drew: Detective was followed, in short order, by three more films, *Nancy Drew: Reporter* and *Nancy Drew: Trouble Shooter*, neither of which had any relation to the plots of Syndicate books, and *Nancy Drew and the Hidden Staircase*, which drew on the book of that title. Unlike the books, however, which continued to shy away from any violence that went beyond a good conk on the head, the movies featured shoot-outs using a wide variety of guns, no doubt a ploy to get in older audiences, who were becoming accustomed to brassier women in their favorite movies. Though the Nancy Drew films were ostensibly for children, Warner Brothers was clearly trying to maximize their potential — or at least make the parents of their child audience interested enough to go to the theater along with them. The publicity for the films tried to pitch Nancy as a slightly edgier character than she was in print. "One side, flatfeet…let a real sleuth show you how it's done!" shouted the posters. "She may be just sixteen, but she's got something you guys never had…feminine intuition!" "Meet the toughest sleuth who ever captured…your heart! It's none other than that master man hunter, that champ criminologist…Nancy Drew Detective," ran another. "Nancy's through playing with dolls!…she'd rather play with danger!" The Warner Brothers publicity machine also tried to make her seem a little racier by playing up her association with men and playing down her intelligence. "She may get the answers wrong in school…but she gets the right men…in jail!" one ad teased. "What chance has a crook with Nancy Drew on his trail?" another asked. "Her homework may not be so hot…but her policework is 100%!" In her silver-screen incarnation, Nancy was a kind of junior version of the current reigning female archetype in movies—the feisty dame. Women like Hildy Johnson—the tough, newly divorced reporter played by Rosalind Russell opposite Cary Grant in *His Girl Friday* (1940)—were in the spotlight as Hollywood churned out picture after picture featuring the gutsy woman who, "at the end of the movie…has established herself as a smart, savvy professional who can do a 'man's job.'"

Two other such women had become acquainted in person at last in the summer of 1938, when a vacation brought Mildred east and she paid a visit to the Syndicate, her first since meeting Edward in his New York offices more than a decade earlier. She and her boss hit it off, however briefly. "I enjoyed having you drop in to the office but regret that you could not stay longer," Harriet wrote to Mildred after the meeting. "After you had left I thought of many things I should have liked to have talked over

with you." Mildred responded with equal appreciation: "I enjoyed my little chat with you a great deal and was sorry to have
missed Mrs. Squire [sic]." When the Nancy Drew movies were
released, Mildred wrote to Harriet and Edna to say that she had
seen *Nancy Drew: Detective,* liked it very much, and was eagerly
awaiting the arrival of the other films in Toledo. "I am glad that
you enjoyed the moving picture and wonder if by this time you
have seen others," Harriet wrote to her in the summer of 1939.
She also appeared to have enjoyed the films, though she confessed to Mildred that her hopes had not been fulfilled in one
rather important way. "I have seen only the first two, although
three have been shown in this area, and I have just heard that a
fifth is in production. Up to date we have not found that having
Nancy Drew on the screen has increased the sale of the books
any, but perhaps it takes a while to get those things started." Even
special editions of *The Password to Larkspur Lane* and *The Hidden Staircase* with jackets that said, "This is the book from which
the Warner Bros. photoplay...was made," didn't have much of
an effect.

In fact, that fifth film was never made, for audiences did not
seem to like Hollywood's interpretation of their favorite detective.
She was something of a vixen, perhaps too womanly for her loyal
fans, or too boy-crazy. She was too old for the kids and too young
for adults, and, in truth, the films themselves were simply not
very good. Though they were deemed somewhat appealing for
"occasional holiday nights when the youngsters are on the loose,"
they had very little else to recommend them. "Yarn so implausible it's virtually a satire on newspaper pictures," complained
a reviewer about *Nancy Drew: Reporter.* "Plot is so shaky it is
entirely unclear why the chauffeur of the two maiden ladies is
shot and killed" was the verdict on *Hidden Staircase.* It was no

matter, however. For even though book sales did not get the hoped-for shot of adrenaline, Nancy Drew did not need the help of Warner Brothers or anyone else.

By the late 1930s, her adventures had permeated American culture so deeply that they were being put into Braille by the American Red Cross Services for the Blind. By the end of 1940, on the tenth anniversary of publication, the Nancy Drew Mystery Stories had sold roughly two and a half million copies. Her most recent title, *The Mystery at the Moss-Covered Mansion*, had sold forty thousand copies in the first six months after it was published in January of 1941. As one article noted, the slender detective had transformed the conventional wisdom about girl readers. "Nancy Drew...has caused publishers to readjust their ideas, and now they reason that a growing number of outside activities is causing a drop among their boy readers, whereas the increasing quality of books in the girl's field is recruiting a growing army of readers." Having at last given girls what they had been clamoring for since the turn of the century—adventures of their own—and selling them with the new marketing tools that were available, like radio advertising and tie-ins with movies, publishers should not have been surprised by this turn of events. But they had underestimated the allure of Nancy Drew, which was about to grow even stronger as America, and its women, emerged from another world war more powerful than ever.

10

"They Are Nancy"

"When you receive your copy of the next Nancy Drew book you will probably wonder what in the world happened to it after it left your hands," Harriet wrote to Mildred toward the end of 1939. She was referring to *The Mystery of the Brass Bound Trunk*. The story took Nancy on a fabulous journey to England—or at least it had when Mildred handed it in. As always, the Syndicate had undertaken the final edit of the manuscript. This time, however, the revisions had been extreme, and not because of Harriet's or Edna's whims. "The story is this: At the time the manuscript was being corrected war news was particularly bad," Harriet explained, "and it looked as if the situation in England might become steadily worse: For this reason we had a conference with the publishers and decided it would be far better to transfer Nancy's trip to Buenos Aires." For the first time in its thirty-four-year history, the Stratemeyer Syndicate had run up against a reality it couldn't ignore.

Hitler had been in power in Germany since 1933, and he had ordered a massive book-burning campaign to "purify" German culture, as well as the opening of the Dachau concentration camp that same year. In November of 1938 the Kristallnacht attack on Germany's Jews had signaled the start of the Holocaust, and by the end of 1939 the Nazis had annexed Austria to Germany and taken Poland and Czechoslovakia as well, provoking Britain, France, Australia, and New Zealand into declaring war officially. Though America was still mired in its traditional isolationism after the disaster of World War I, her citizens followed the news from Europe watchfully, wondering how long it would be before their men in uniform were called to duty.

But even after Roosevelt instituted the first peacetime draft in the country's history in September of 1940, he continued to run for president on a platform of neutrality. More than sixteen million Americans turned up to register for duty on the first day of the draft as their leader pledged to keep them out of harm's way: "And while I am talking to you mothers and fathers, I give you one more assurance," he told nervous parents. "I have said this before, but I shall say it again and again and again: Your boys are not going to be sent into any foreign wars." Though he was not sending any troops, Roosevelt was providing unprecedented arms and aid to America's friends abroad. In a fireside chat in December of 1940, the president told his citizens, "The people of Europe who are defending themselves do not ask us to do their fighting. They ask us for the implements of war, the planes, the tanks, the guns, the freighters, which will enable them to fight for their liberty and for our security...We must be the great arsenal of democracy."

As Hitler's forces invaded France, Belgium, the Netherlands, and Luxembourg in 1940, isolationists at home, including the Congress, still believed the United States should only fight if directly threatened. Though Britain was America's closest ally, the country stood by and did nothing during the London Blitz, which ran from September 1940 through May 1941, destroying entire residential neighborhoods and killing thousands. In just one week in mid-October, more than 1,300 Londoners perished. By August of 1941 Germany had taken over most of Europe and the British were fighting for their lives every day. Nevertheless, when Roosevelt wanted to extend the draft term, his proposal passed in the House of Representatives by only one vote.

Among the young men called to duty was Harriet's older son, Sunny, who had become a pilot and was training military flyers down in Florida. Though his service made Harriet nervous — she referred to her affliction as "patriotic discomfort" — she also felt herself caught up in the sweep of history. "These are stirring times and I agree with you that it is a privilege to be part of this great effort to make our country safe again," she wrote to one of her ghostwriters, whose son was becoming a doctor. "I think we shall be proud of our young people and the wonderful spirit they are showing. All America is with them, surely." Still, her maternal instinct was stronger than her patriotism at certain moments, and she relied on her work to get her though, confessing in another letter to the same ghostwriter. "Wouldn't it be nice if we could have made miracle children out of these sons and kept them ageless like the Bobbseys!"

Under such conditions, certain literary concessions were necessary, even if Harriet tried to make them as innocuous as possible. Writing to Leslie McFarlane, who was at work on a Hardy Boys story called *The Melted Coins*, Harriet explained the Syndicate's somewhat tortuous efforts to have things both ways. "We are trying to play along with the War effort by not using gasoline, etc., in the stories. This need not be mentioned in the books, as we trust these stories will be read long after the War is over. We merely are trying to avoid criticism for the duration, so we are having our heroes do more walking, or going by bicycle. Here and there where a car is used, it might be termed 'essential driving.'" As the average person in America was entitled to only four gallons of gas a week, it would not do to have Frank and Joe tootling around their hometown of Bayport on pleasure trips.

Even Nancy Drew was not immune to world events. In Norway, the first foreign country to publish the Nancy Drew Mystery Stories in translation, the Nazis had stopped production of the books after six volumes. And girls were writing in to say they wanted Syndicate characters, including Nancy, to have husbands or steady boyfriends, a trend that troubled Harriet until she concluded that it was all about the war. On December 7, 1941, the Japanese had attacked Pearl Harbor, forcing the United States into the action at last. Wrapped up in the plight of their boys overseas, children longed for the presence of able-bodied men in their fiction to make up for the ones who were missing from dinner tables and movie houses everywhere.

In light of all this, the Syndicate had to come up with a better way to acknowledge the events unfolding across the ocean than simply having characters ride their bikes more frequently. "As you no doubt know from your own series, it is difficult to know what to do with certain characters in war time," Harriet wrote to Mildred. "We find it best to leave the war out of stories like the Nancys, but some of the readers wonder about this. Will you please, without mentioning the war, announce that Ned Nickerson is not appearing because he is in Europe. Also, note here and there that Nancy is taking an airplane lesson, and infer that this has something to do with the war effort, without mentioning the war. In future volumes it no doubt will be interesting to readers for her to acquire a pilot's license."

Mildred, however, had a good deal more to worry about than Nancy's response to current events. In late 1940 Asa Wirt had become ill, succumbing to the first of what would eventually be a long, debilitating series of strokes. Harriet's characteristic generosity and patience kicked in during what she recognized to be a rough situation — Peggy was only four years old, and Mildred was working as relentlessly as ever — but it became undeniable that Mildred's writing was suffering. Once again, Harriet and Edna tried to help her by writing extremely full outlines, so that she would, in their words, "be able to write the story with ease." When it came to Nancy Drew, especially, the sisters did not want any variation from their winning formula, which, by 1941, had been set out to the last blue frock and polite phrase.

So Mildred, unable to let her imagination run wild in the Syndicate books, invented Penny Parker, daughter of a newspaper editor, champion swimmer and diver, sophomore at Riverview High, and all-around wit. Penny would soon become Mildred's favorite of her characters, perhaps because she bore more than a little resemblance to her creator, and not just in the swimming pool, where she was an ace diver. She was more flippant than Nancy Drew, and because Mildred, not the Syndicate, was responsible for her adventures, the plots of the Penny Parker Mystery Series, which ran from 1939 to 1947, were a good deal more varied and spooky than the Nancy Drew Mystery Stories. They moved faster than Stratemeyer books and tended to be a bit more on the dark side than a Nancy Drew mystery. For one thing, reality was always hovering somewhere nearby. Not only did Penny have numerous car problems — no magical blue roadster for her—but the war was a presence as well. As one fan has noted, "Few books of that era dealt with black market sales, mine detection services, and brass and gold hoarding. Penny Parker encountered them all." When a friend of Penny's went off to war, it was stated explicitly, no fooling around.

Back in the real world, Americans were eager to do all they could to help the war effort. They gladly paid the enormous income tax increases that Roosevelt initiated in 1942 in order to help pay for the war. Until then, only about 5 percent of Americans had paid the income tax, with the highest rate, 75 percent, applying to people with wealth in excess of $5 million. Now anyone who made more than $624 a year was subject to a 5 percent "Victory Tax." In 1943 the payroll tax—or the "pay as you go" plan—was instituted for millions of middle-class Americans, who had no choice but to pay it even as they saved scrap metal and paper and did everything else their government asked of them. Even the Syndicate was forced to give up all its old book plates as scrap metal, and the Nancy Drews were printed with a new motto on the title page: "This book, while produced under wartime conditions, in full compliance with government regulations for the conservation of paper and other essential materials, is COMPLETE AND UNABRIDGED." Even if the war was not happening in River Heights, the girl sleuth, like everyone else, was making her contribution.

For the Adams family, the sacrifice was especially bitter. In early 1942 Sunny was killed in an accident that took place during a flight training mission in Florida. Harriet and the rest of the family had just been down to spend the holidays with him. The blow was devastating. The Syndicate office closed immediately, and it was Edna who took up all correspondence when it reopened, informing publishers and other work associates of the reason for the delay in replying. "Our office has been closed for several days because of the death of my sister's older son, Ensign R. V. Adams, Jr.," she wrote to one editor. "He is the first one in the family to die in the Service. Had my father been alive, he would have been exceedingly proud to have had his first grandson give his life for his country."

It was March before Harriet resumed her work at the Syndicate. Like many mothers who lost sons in World War II, she kept herself going by reminding herself of the reason for the grievous turn of events. "I appreciate very much your words of comfort sent in your note last week," she wrote to a sympathetic author. "As you suggest, we should feel proud to look upon our sacrifice as a patriotic one, and this we are trying to do. It is a tragedy beyond explanation that young men must give up their lives for a cause, when madmen are rampant in the world. Yet this has happened from time immemorial, and we can only hope that this war truly will be the last one."

As A BALM OF SORTS, Harriet spent more and more time at the Syndicate, working on her outlines and gathering what she called "source material" to burnish the authenticity of her tales. Even when her daughter Camilla decided to get married in a hurry in the fall of 1943 (her husband-to-be was an ensign in the navy), leaving Harriet to plan a wedding at home for two hundred guests, there was time to get after Mildred about her writing style. "In commenting on your manuscript, I am going to make a very unusual criticism," she wrote to Mildred about a Dana Girls story. "You worked too hard! We find the English too perfect for a little girls' book. The sentences seem to be long and full of big words. Since we intend to simplify the manuscript a good bit, we are sorry that you went to so much trouble to make it such a perfect specimen from point of view of synonyms and descriptive phraseology." Still, she was acutely aware of the pressure under which Mildred was operating, and she made a point of saying so. Asa was still very ill, and Harriet was too kindhearted not to send wishes for a brighter new year. "Thank you for getting the manuscript to us so promptly under trying conditions," she wrote in closing. "And may 1943 hold good things in store for you."

But 1943, unfortunately, marked the beginning of the period in Mildred's life she would remember forever as the most exhausting and difficult. She was taking care of Peggy and, as Asa was too ill to work, writing overtime to bring in extra money. "I had to write all the time," she remembered. "I had no choice on writing, it wasn't a leisurely thing at all. It was a hard deadline and I was usually three or four books behind on orders. I put my typewriter up beside my husband's bed and I'd take care of him at night and typewrite right by the bedside...I just wrote as long as I could write each day and night." Still, she endeavored to do her very best work under all circumstances, even when her idea of what that was clashed with Harriet's.

For a while, though, there was no time for conflict. Harriet had recently withstood another loss, the second within a year, and it had left her busier than ever. "Thank you for getting the recent manuscript to us so promptly. I am sorry about the delay in getting the check to you, but I have been working literally nights and days to keep up with our schedule," she wrote to Mildred. The main cause of her suddenly overwhelming workload was that in the fall of 1942, Edna had decamped to Florida with her husband and daughter for good, becoming a silent partner in the Syndicate. Though she would split Syndicate profits with Harriet forty/sixty, she was no longer involved in the day-to-day

Edward Stratemeyer in 1903, just before
the founding of his Syndicate.

Harriet Stratemeyer during her senior year at Wellesley (1913–1914),
in a photo taken during a family trip to Atlantic City.

Mildred Augustine executing one of
her award-winning dives into the Iowa
River, while she was a student at the
University of Iowa.

Iowa Women's Archives, University of Iowa Libraries

Mildred's 1926 Hawkeye
yearbook photo.

*University Archives,
Department of Special Collections,
University of Iowa Libraries*

"DON'T GIVE IN TO NANCY DREW!" HIS WIFE
SCREAMED

The Clue in the Diary.   *Frontispiece (Page 197)*

NANCY MADE A WILD SCRAMBLE TO SAVE HERSELF.
The Mystery at the Moss-Covered Mansion   *(Page 108)*

"Don't touch that!" Ned warned. "It's a trap."

In 1932's *The Clue in the Diary*, Nancy doesn't turn a hair when confronted with a dastardly criminal. In 1941's *Mystery at the Moss-Covered Mansion*, the sleuth's style has changed, but not her quick wits when she's in trouble. In matching athletic gear and headband in 1968's *Mystery at the Ski Jump*, Nancy's more efficient than ever hitting the slopes as Ned, finally her fashion equal, takes the lead.

Publicity materials for the 1938 movie version of *Nancy Drew: Detective.*

Mildred Wirt in her writing room at home in Toledo, in the summer of 1949. "Author's Books Almost Fill Her Middlesex Dr. Home" read the original photo caption.
The Toledo Blade

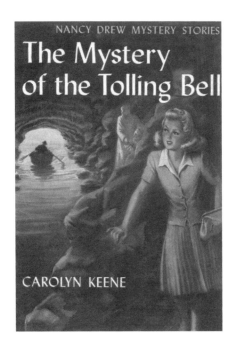

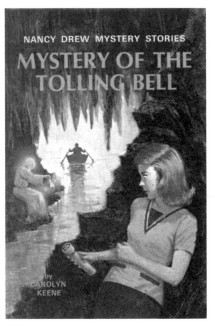

From prim 1940s pleated chic through the sporty '60s and on into the earthy '70s, Nancy has always been in vogue while on the case, unafraid of facing the unknown no matter what she's wearing.

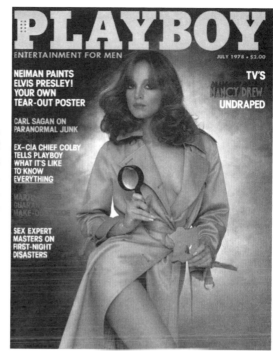

Pamela Sue Martin, wearing a trench coat and not much else, on the cover of *Playboy*, July 1978.

Harriet Stratemeyer Adams at her desk at the Syndicate in 1980, two years before her death.

Eighty-two-year-old Mildred Wirt Benson reporting for duty as the *Toledo Times*'s "Happy Landings" columnist in the spring of 1987.

business at the office. Harriet was now fully in charge of all outlines and character development, which meant, among other
things, that she had to deal on her own with changes in the juvenile book world wrought by the war.

Unlike the Syndicate, many authors and publishers had decided that children's books should address matters overseas, and
Harriet eventually felt forced to join them. She did so, in her
fashion, in *The Secret in the Old Attic*, a Nancy Drew title that
she assigned to Mildred in the spring of 1943. "Two subjects are
introduced into this story which never have been dealt with to
any great extent before," she wrote in her letter accompanying an
extremely detailed outline. "One of these is military life. We do
not wish to date our books, and therefore cannot say that characters are fighting in the present war. In order to have the story
timely, however, we have introduced a grandfather who was in
World War I, and his deceased son, who had joined the American army and had lost his life. In telling this, please do not give
the idea he was in the line of battle. Leave it indefinite enough,
so that in years to come the story will not be dated." With this
character, Harriet immortalized her hero son. When the book
came out in 1944, the fictional son, just like Sunny, had "lost his
life four years ago on a routine training mission."

The other subject, Nancy's love life, was more difficult to resolve. Certainly Harriet was not going to spill the details of her
own romantic history for use as plot fodder, so she passed to Mildred the task of trying to make modest Nancy's interest in the opposite sex a bit more overt, and rather vaguely at that. "We have
had a good bit of fan mail, asking for more romance in the Nancy
stories, so we have inculcated some in this one. Please give a modern twist to the conversation and actions which have to do with
this angle of the plot." Alas, as Mildred put it shortly thereafter,

"Romance has never been my strong point, else I should have shifted to adult writing long ago." Though Harriet was pleased with Mildred's handling of the mystery aspects of *Old Attic*, she wrote, "We are somewhat disappointed in the romantic side of Nancy's life. The treatment of this seems to belong to the ideas of a somewhat older generation than that of the modern girl." Then, admitting her own ignorance on the matter at hand, she confessed that, as in the old days, she would turn to her most trusted aides for some help. "In making some changes in this, I believe I shall have to get the assistance of my own daughters, one newly married. These youngsters are so brave and hold their heads so high these days, that it is quite a different approach to the subject of romance from that of a few years ago."

So, presumably thanks to the help of her children, the courtship of Ned and Nancy took on new and serious proportions in *Old Attic*. Nancy, who previously could not have been bothered to put anything off for Ned, spends a considerable amount of time hoping he'll invite her to the "big dance" at Emerson College, showing some uncharacteristic signs of insecurity in the process. "Maybe Ned has asked another girl," she meditated. "He has a perfect right to, of course." Though Nancy does not know it, one of River Heights' meanest girls, Diane Dight, has intercepted Ned's invitation, forcing Nancy not only to put off another suitor — "If you really can't find anyone, let me know. I'll see then what I'll do," she tells him coyly — but to wonder if her romance with Ned has gone south. When she gets the mistaken information that he has invited her nemesis Diane to the dance, "the news [comes] as a distinct shock to her." After a terrifying scene involving a spider in the attic, Nancy has a girlish moment in which she faints in Ned's "strong arms," then mystery and romance are duly resolved. "'I was pretty scared for a while, I admit, but when you came — Ned, maybe you don't know it, but you saved my life! I shall always be thankful to you'... 'It would have been my very great loss if I hadn't,' he said fervently, and again she flushed crimson." Alive and well and in love, the handsome pair dances the night away at Emerson, locked in chaste happiness.

In spite of her sympathy with Mildred's inability to write such scenes, however, Harriet was growing increasingly frustrated by trying to manage her ghostwriters. Mildred was hard to handle, she confessed in a letter to Edna the following year, and Leslie McFarlane, who was still writing the Hardy Boys books, wanted more money for his efforts. Edna, who was removed from the fray down in St. Petersburg, where she and Wesley were happily buying and selling real estate, came to both of their defenses via the post. "I believe we actually need him and Mrs. Wirt because of their particular style," she wrote to her sister, "and I couldn't vote to have the Hardy or Nancy done by any one else. Everything is too critical just now — to see what does happen at the close of the war may be an eye opener."

Harriet also harbored a soft spot for the two longtime ghost-writers, and, in a rare moment of candor, wrote to Leslie McFarlane about the general state of her life in the spring of 1944. Letting down her professional guard for a few pages, she told him of her sorrows and trials, and what it felt like to be the happily married mother of grown children who were not necessarily doing what she thought they should be doing:

> I promised to tell you something of my family, and I wish it
> might sound as happy as yours. A few years ago the story might
> have been the same. I had four children. The older boy, a Prince-
> ton graduate, became a Naval aviator but the war took his life

two years ago. I now have another boy in the service. He was only eighteen in September. He joined the Navy a little while before he became of draft age. Unfortunately he is partially color-blind and the only branch which would accept him was the Seabees. It was a great surprise to us that he was shipped out so soon after enlisting. He is now at Pearl Harbor learning more about construction. You do know, don't you, that our Seabees are the Navy Construction Battalion? It seems strange that Edward, named for my father, should have inherited his grandfather's color-blindness, but unlike him is six feet, two inches tall, and very blond. According to his sisters, he is "smooth."

Between the two boys are two daughters; one, a brunette who has been mistaken for Margaret Sullavan, and the other a platinum blond, who was on the road to being a very fine dancer and choreographer, but gave it up to marry an ensign in the Navy and keep house pro tem for him and all their school friends who pass through San Francisco.

The brunette, who graduated from my college, Wellesley, last June, is doing secret work for our Navy but is living at home. We are glad to have at least one child with us. Our big house certainly does seem empty these days.

My husband is in stocks and bonds. He is considered an authority on municipals in New Jersey and is sought hither and yon on consultation. He plays golf when he has time and fools around with his brood of chickens at our summer home. That is a delightful retreat within commuting distance of our two offices. We both love company and both our winter and summer homes are rarely without guests, especially the latter place, which possesses a large swimming pond.

For a year and a half my sister has been inactive in the syndicate. At the moment she is living in Florida, and whether or not she will make that a permanent address we do not know. She was married rather later in life than most people and has a little girl six years old. She is very bright and a live-wire. I

*think my sister felt that she ought to enjoy her as much as pos-
sible in her early years. She is already having read aloud to her
the youngest book which our syndicate produces. For years my
children were our critics, and now we are turning the job over
to the six year old.*

MIDWAY THROUGH THE WAR, the Authors Guild wrote a letter to
Carolyn Keene, asking her to become a member because "at all
times the author needs the service and protection of an organization of fellow-workers... in war time and the period of reconstruc-
tion that follows war, this need... is particularly acute." Among
the sponsors listed on the organization's letterhead were no less
than Edna Ferber, Sinclair Lewis, Thornton Wilder, and John
Dos Passos. Harriet had apparently done such a good job of keeping her trade secrets that these hilariously earnest luminaries had
no idea their letter was going out to a pseudonym. They were
not alone in their misconception. That same year, a popular teen
magazine by the name of *Calling All Girls* wrote to Ms. Keene
to request a mystery serial for their pages. "We very much want
a bang-up mystery story," they wrote to her, "and after a great deal
of consultation here and there, have come to the conclusion that
you are the best person to write one for us." Channeling the fictitious Ms. Keene, Edna promptly came up with an idea, and the
sisters assigned the tale to Mildred.

"Mystery at the Lookout" ran in the September 1942 issue of
Calling All Girls, alongside a poll of the magazine's readers, who
had become an all-important target market. Despite the rationing
of critical household items, it seemed, girls always had a bit of
pocket change to spend, and big companies wanted to know how

to get them to spend it. "Brand acceptance begins at an early age among readers of Calling All Girls," the magazine informed its advertisers. "They're today's customers…What they don't buy out of their own allowance, they ask their parents for. These sharp-witted teeners and near-to-teeners are now making up their minds about a lot of things…no advertiser can afford to 'gloss them over now and get them later.'" The girls in the poll were questioned on everything from their favorite gum (Dentyne) to their favorite cleansing cream (Pond's); deodorant (Mum's); hand lotion (Jergens); lipstick (Tangee); movie actor (John Payne, who had just returned from a tour with the army air force and would later have a role in *Miracle on 34th Street*); movie actress (Bette Davis), nail polish, radio program, radio star, record, movie, rouge, soda pop (Coca-Cola by an enormous margin over Pepsi, thank you very much), suntan lotion, soap, and just about everything else that could be identified by brand name.

Regardless of all the new products flooding the teen market, three things remained as true as ever. With their options proliferating wildly, the favorite author of teenage readers of *Calling All Girls* was still Carolyn Keene (Louisa May Alcott was second on the list, but had only half the number of votes). Their favorite book was still a Nancy Drew Mystery Story, and their favorite color, like Nancy's, was blue. As a writer interested in doing radio scripts from the series commented in a note to Harriet, "I did do some quizzing of teen agers and they were all for the dramatization of these stories—as they seem to be favorite reading for them—said they certainly would listen and love them. As you know the real angle with them is that they for the moment are doing the things themselves—they are Nancy."

But teenagers, like the rest of the country, were all too aware of the war. As one girl asked her mother, "What did the news [on the radio] have to talk about when a war was not going on?" Another wanted to know, "Has there always been war? Has there ever been other news besides war news?" Uncensored images of the dead and wounded in magazines like *Life* also brought the news to them, and for the first time, their parents—even their devoted mothers—could not shield them from it. If they went to the movies with their pals on a Saturday afternoon, there might be a cartoon before the main picture, but it could just as easily be a newsreel about the fighting overseas.

Part of the reason their mothers could not watch out for them quite as carefully as they might previously have done, of course, was because the war had sent women out to work in numbers never before seen. In 1942 military orders to factories alone totaled $100 billion, and by the end of war, the number had reached $330 billion. By 1944 the country was responsible for a staggering 40 percent of the world's arms production. When Great Britain could no longer afford to pay for its arsenal, Roosevelt created the Lend Lease program to continue supplying them, even though it was clear to many that the debt could not possibly be repaid.

With the men off in the miserable trenches of Europe, someone had to fill in for them in order to keep the factories and other workplaces going, and most of the time, that someone was female. After being discouraged from working for so long, women were now told that joining the labor force was the patriotic thing to do. "Victory Waits on *Your* Fingers—Keep 'Em Flying, Miss U.S.A," read one poster recruiting women to the civilian workforce. Sandwiched between the cheery words, a patriotic blond with a red-and-blue ribbon in her hair saluted from behind a typewriter. Over the course of the war, the female workforce would eventually grow by almost 50 percent, adding six million women to the fourteen and a half million who were already working.

"Rosie the Riveter" became a national icon, and for good reason: At one point during the war, there were some three hundred thousand women working in the aircraft industry alone. According to the Office of War Information, their ability to pick up these kinds of jobs and to do them so well "disproved the old bugaboo that women have no mechanical ability and that they are a distracting influence in industry." Still, there were some problems inherent to the new coed arrangement. As one female worker admitted: "At times it gets to be a pain in the neck when the man who is supposed to show you work stops showing it to you because you have nicely but firmly asked him to keep his hands on his own knees...Somehow we'll have to make them understand that we are not very much interested in their strapping virility." Women also took many white-collar jobs during the war years, including spots at newspapers, which, like every industry, had been virtually stripped of male employees. Among these new women in journalism was Mildred Wirt.

The first edition of *Inside the Blade*, the in-house organ of the *Toledo Blade* and *Toledo Times* newspapers, was published in October of 1943. Despite its lighthearted mission statement— "News, gossip, [and] humor going on daily in all departments"— it was a de facto war newsletter as much as anything else. In addition to amusing squibs, *Inside the Blade* ran photos and addresses of all the paper's men in the service so that staff members could write to them. Altogether, fifty men had been deployed, and many more were no doubt to follow, since, as the newsletter noted, "Draft deferments have been whittled down to a point where many of the Blade employees are now subject to call." Soon after Mildred was hired, *Inside the Blade* ran a comic interview with her under the headline "ONCE WROTE FOR CHILDREN, NOW WRITES FOR TIMES." "Married for sixteen years," it quipped, "Mildred still gets away with cooking only when she has to."

The willfully incompetent homemaker had initially started working full-time outside her home in the summer of 1944, writing to Harriet to say that she was "taking a new position as publicity writer (radio and newspaper) for the Toledo Community Chest...Mr. Wirt is in very poor health, having had five strokes, and for this reason I feel it wise to take on salary work during this period when women are so much in demand." By 1945, the year after Mildred started at the Community Chest, women made up more than a third of the civilian workforce in the country. There were also 1,000 Women's Airforce Service Pilots (WASPs)—no doubt Nancy Drew would have put her new pilot's license to use with this group—140,000 Women's Army Corps (WAC) members, and 100,000 Women Accepted for Volunteer Emergency Service in the navy (WAVES).

Mildred's job at the Community Chest was certainly less glamorous than such thrilling posts, but the real problem with it was that it was temporary. She needed work desperately if she was to continue supporting her family while Asa lay ill, so taking advantage of historic opportunity—newspaperwomen were not unheard of in the forties, but they were far from the norm—she applied for a reporting job at the *Toledo Times*. She also refused to give up writing books, continuing on with the Syndicate even as she worked full-time at the Community Chest and looked for a new job. Upon learning of all this from Harriet, Edna was amazed at Mildred's will to succeed, commenting, "Too bad about Mrs. Wirt's husband—it must be a dreadful strain. Evidently she loves to write or else would give up the work entirely."

Indeed Mildred did, so when her application at the *Times* was turned down, she simply refused to take no for an answer. She began sending stories about the Community Chest to the paper for publication. Eventually, the *Times* editors were low enough on reporters and impressed enough with her gumption and her writing to hire her. In the fall of 1944, she joined the staff of the *Toledo Times* as one of its city hall beat reporters. "It was during the war, and they were taking on women for the first time," she recalled many decades later. "[The editor] said 'As soon as the war is over, I want you to understand you will be the first one to be fired.' I ran scared for about at least 49½ years." Like many women, she wanted more than anything to keep her job after peace was declared. As an article in the *New York Times Magazine* put it, "Alma goes to work because she wants to go to work. She wants to go now and she wants to keep going when the war is over. Alma's had a taste of LIFE. She's poked her head out into the one-man's world."

But the opposite sentiment about women and work was also very much in evidence. As the country prospered and marriage and birth rates jumped, the old worry about allowing women to become too much like men cropped up again. One ominous pamphlet warned: "The war in general has given women new status, new recognition...Women are 'coming into their own' in this war...In her new independence she must not lose her humanness as a woman. She may be the woman of the moment, but she must watch her moments." Mildred's tactic in this battle was to simply work harder and longer than anyone else, and it proved to be a wise one. When the fighting finally ended, she was given a permanent spot at the *Times* because, as she put it plainly, "I could always get the story."

Working the night shift until 11:00 P.M. — though in reality she was often at the paper until 1:30 or 2:00 in the morning — Mildred often turned in six or seven stories a night as she sat amid a sea of hardscrabble male reporters who chain-smoked nonstop and listened to police scanners to pick up tidbits to publish the next day. While her mother took care of Peggy and Asa — Lillian had come from Iowa so that her daughter could work — Mildred held her ground as one of the few women working in the editorial department and the only one who was not working on the society pages. She thrived on the chance to put her excellent journalism training to good use. One of her efficiency techniques was to start her stories in her head as she walked back to the office from city hall, and often she barely had time to get them down on paper before someone ripped the sheet from her typewriter to rush it off to copyediting. Among her favorite pieces were those that covered the effects of the war on Toledo's citizens, which she filtered though her access to the various committees at city hall that regulated prices in the face of inflation caused by the rapidly expanding economy. The thriving underworld of the black market and its effect on local retailers and residents was one of her liveliest topics, and she returned to it often: "CITY'S SHOPS ON VERGE OF BARE CASES!" "EGG BLACK MARKET SWITCH REPORTED!"

After the war was over, Mildred would turn to more uplifting stories about GI brides, who were arriving in Toledo by the dozens and finding the local ways highly impressive. "The washing machines and refrigerators! Why Monday I finished a washing and ironing all in one day!" one of the British transplants exclaimed to Mildred, who added, "Many of the brides said they had found the United States a veritable promised land, and life

here much like a movie." That life in America was in stark contrast to conditions overseas could hardly have been made clearer
than it was in another story Mildred filed about a repatriated
American wife who had been living in Germany with her German husband. "I lived in Germany for 12 years and heard of only
one concentration camp,' Mrs. Frischmann said. 'The people
were kept in ignorance. Now for the first time, I think the German people are beginning to accept the truth.'"

When Mildred arrived home from a long day at the paper,
she would relieve her mother, set up her typewriter by Asa's bedside, and start her fiction work for the day. "I was a tired writer,"
she remembered. "Lots of people think that Nancy Drew just
came, but I've paid for that with blood, with real blood. I sweat
when I wrote the books and I worked hard, unbelievably hard. I
don't think very many people would ever work as hard as I
worked during the most active years of my life. I would never do
it again."

Still, she managed somehow, if only because she had no
choice. "The salary is so excellent that I cannot afford to drop it,"
she wrote to Harriet of her newspaper job, while still assuring her
that, amazingly, she could make the time to write a new Dana
Girls book. In an effort to help Mildred, Harriet had offered to
let her write her next book from an outline that was more like the
brief ones Edward had sent out. The two women had by this
time exchanged numerous letters about whose style of writing
was more suited to the work. Unable to get Mildred to see it her
way but also too busy to find another ghostwriter, Harriet decided that perhaps if she sent out just a "synopsis such as Mr.
Stratemeyer used to send," she might be able to both cut down
on her rewriting work and get a better manuscript from Mildred,

who would not be fighting the copious amounts of information and detail that Harriet had become accustomed to putting into each outline. Mildred agreed wholeheartedly with this plan, writing back, "I do feel that it would make for easier writing and a better book."

An agreement reached, however uneasily, Harriet wrote to Edna to let her know. Though Edna had not set foot in the offices of the Stratemeyer Syndicate for several years, she was still in on the profits and expected to be kept up-to-date on as well as consulted about everything. When Harriet confessed that she found Mildred increasingly hard to deal with, Edna wrote back in Mildred's defense once more: "Mrs. Wirt is certainly a go-getter," she wrote to Harriet, "and she must have a following even if you find her difficult to work with...Her style made the Nancys."

Thankfully, Harriet's new outlining methods were rewarded when Mildred handed in her next effort. "I think our plan of a less complicated outline has worked out very well," Harriet wrote to her upon receiving the Dana Girls story, reassured enough to assign Mildred the next Nancy Drew, *The Mystery of the Tolling Bell.*

Having solved her problems with Mildred, for the time being anyway, Harriet was left to face a much larger difficulty—namely, Edna. Not only were the two sisters in disagreement about some of the ghostwriters and the way the sale of various rights should be handled, but Edna's growing obsession with her royalty income had started to take the form of constant heavy criticism of Harriet's management of the business. Her letters began to take on a hectoring tone that created an awful tension between New Jersey and Florida. Disconnected from the everyday practicalities of the business, Edna had no comprehension of how it ran or just how lucky she was that Harriet was willing to put in the time to keep them wealthy. She asked constantly for numbers to show that Harriet was not making grave errors. "A convincing answer to some worries which you seem to have over the income of the Syndicate," Harriet wrote her at one point, trying to defend herself. "They [figures she had just compiled for the last fifteen years of business] prove to me that our profits have increased each year, and there is no indication the depression hit our pocketbooks."

In addition to other insults, Harriet had not had a raise since 1942, when Edna had first become a silent partner. She knew, however, that Edna was bound to be stingy about money, and her efforts when it came to getting her sister to agree to spend more were well prioritized. Instead of thinking of herself, she put the issue of a very necessary increase for the office secretaries, of whom there were now several, to her reluctant partner. Without their help, she could not run the business smoothly. The same went for ghostwriters, and so she also made a pitch for Mildred, whose work, she had discovered during her accounting blitz, had been consistent and brought the Syndicate a great deal of money over the years. "Before getting off the subject of remuneration, I think it would be a nice gesture to Mrs. Wirt to let her share in the profits of the Nancy Drew," she wrote to Edna. "Dad always gave Christmas gifts to his writers, but we have never practiced the same generosity."

Harriet could not have known just how badly Mildred needed both the money and the affirmation at that particular moment. Her bonus check for $1,000 arrived in Toledo in September of 1945, just a few months after a joyous VE Day made the end of the war official, and just weeks after America dropped the atomic bomb on Hiroshima and Nagasaki. Two hundred ninety-five thousand American lives had been lost in the fighting, but now the grief was leavened with celebration as the danger came to an end. For Mildred, however, peacetime brought new reasons to worry, as her stable job was now uncertain. Things had not improved much at home, either. "During the past four and a half years, while my husband has steadily gone down hill following a series of seven strokes, there have been times when I seriously considered giving up all writing," she admitted in her thank-you note to Harriet. "Some of the copy I turned out a year or so ago probably was not my best, but you were very patient, and I feel now that I am over the hump, so to speak...The Syndicate gift of $1,000 is more than generous, and to say I am appreciative expresses it very mildly. I trust that Nancy will go on for many years, and that she will vie with the Rover Boys in carving a lasting name for herself in popular fiction." Then, signing off contentedly, she wrote, "I have earmarked part of your gift for a new typewriter as soon as they are released to civilians! I am sure this will be good news for everyone remotely connected with my copy!"

But when Mildred handed in the next Nancy Drew, the awful pressures under which she was trying to bear up were apparent everywhere in the text. Exhausted, she had allowed her own troubles to seep into the charmed world of River Heights, most noticeably in the character of Nancy herself. Like Mildred, Nancy was no longer the strong, optimistic firebrand she had once been. One of the office secretaries wrote a mini-review of the manuscript for Harriet in which she made no effort to hide her disdain for Mildred's work: "The MS did not read like a Nancy Drew mystery at all...The characterization was outstandingly poor—everyone, from Bess to the gypsy violinist, spoke the same, and acted undistinguishably [sic]...Perhaps Nancy herself was worst of all, appearing as a sissy and a defeatist, a far cry from the girl whom the young readers have come to admire."

After reading this report, Harriet decided to take some kind of action. Nancy Drew was by this time both her favorite character and her most important asset, and she could not simply stand by and watch her be ruined. Nor did she have the time to do an extensive rewrite of every manuscript. She began to keep a list of the various criticisms she had sent Mildred over the past decade or so, presumably to create a paper trail for future reference, and she let Mildred know that her work was unsatisfactory. "Nancy does not seem like the courageous, untiring person she has always been," Harriet wrote. "She is definitely a defeatist, always weary and ready to give up. There was no differentiation between Bess and George, and the comraderie [*sic*] we had tried to build up between Mr. Drew and Nancy was lacking entirely. Nancy spoke in a very adult fashion, and it made her seem much older than in former books."

Harriet was, as always, unfailingly polite to her employee, but in a letter to Edna about the problem, she was more candid about wanting to sever ties with Mildred, and she did not hesitate to lay the blame not only on the overworked writer, but on Edna herself. "Right now we are re-writing the NANCY DREW," she wrote to her sister somewhat bitterly. "After you wrote you thought Mrs. Wirt should go on with the series I decided to try her once more. Before making any comments on the story I listened to those of three or four other people who voted it practically a washout." As usual, Edna was not ready to accept her sister's opinion. In her reply, she asked to see the outline Harriet had send to Mildred before she would agree to "drop her from the S.S." "You and I never could agree on how a Nancy should be written," she reminded her sister. "After all," she finished, jabbing at Harriet's conscience unmercifully, "her years of work mean something to her too."

Harriet put off, yet again, a decision about what to do with Mildred. But she could distract herself with other, more pleasurable pursuits, like the fact that her daughter Camilla had given birth to a baby girl. She threw herself into the role of grandmother with characteristic gaiety and pleasure. Sending congratulations on another new baby to a young man who had written an article about her in the *Herald Tribune*, she mused on the changes that had taken place since her own children had been born. He had mentioned to her that he was taking over domestic duties while his wife recovered, and the very idea brought her up short: "Recently I have reflected upon my own post-war life after World War I, when my domestic status quo was similar to yours now. I don't dare let myself think that things have retrogressed considerably, or I become wuzzy!" she wrote. "Nevertheless, my husband's situation at that time was not unlike your own, yet the country's whole economic system was so different that he never washed the dishes nor took care of the baby. Somehow you young people of today will have to straighten out the present hectic situation—and I am sure you personally will want to do it as soon as possible and get out of the dishpan!"

In the meantime, Edna had taken to getting advice from her own tax man down in Florida, no longer trusting Harriet to even present a legitimate picture of the business. Among other things, Harriet had decided in 1946 to bring out a new baseball series, and, as usual, she had consulted Edna about the contract. When Edna finally wrote back almost a year later, Harriet was as close to outraged as she could bring herself to be. "I was rather amazed at your recent reply to my letter about what you wish to do concerning the new series," she sputtered. "I wrote to you nearly a year ago about this, and again some months later, so it seems to me that you had a long time in which to get the 'expert advice' you mentioned. I had hoped to have the whole matter settled for Income Tax purposes, and also for contract with the publishers. At the end of the week I shall deliver the second baseball story to Cupples and Leon and I dislike having them bring out a series under unsettled conditions between us."

Before too long, "unsettled" was a mild way of describing relations between the sisters. When, in the middle of 1947, Harriet tried to address the issue of giving herself a raise after five years of backbreaking work at the Syndicate, Edna's response was to demand a complete and thorough accounting of all Syndicate profits and expenses before she would even consider the matter. She had pushed too hard. Harriet was both hurt and furious, and she did not mince words in her reply. "Actually, the picture from 1942 to the present is a very good one, but I have yet to hear one word of commendation from you. And despite the ever increasing amount in your pocket due to new business, you keep silent, and let me be the only one in the office who has had no raise since 1942," she wrote. "I've had all the headaches, and have given increasingly of my time and efforts, but still the sum of 37.50 a week from you that I agreed upon as a starting salary has never been changed. Frankly I cannot understand your attitude, and psychologically the effect does not make for good business... Sincerely, Harriet." A permanent rift had opened. While Harriet would continue to write letters about family news and holidays to her sister over the next decades, there was a part of her that would never forgive Edna for her mistrust and selfishness. The playful notes between "Syndicate Sisters" were a thing of the past.

In June of 1947, having decided to give her one more try, Harriet sent the plot for the next Nancy Drew, *The Ghost of Blackwood Hall*, off to Mildred in Toledo. The reply she got astonished her. As usual, Mildred had buried the lead. After four paragraphs about *Blackwood Hall,* of which the first eight chapters had been written, she wrote, rather abruptly: "On the day that the plot arrived, my husband died after a very long and hard illness. He has been a complete invalid for the past two and a half years, requiring almost constant attention. The time has been a most trying one, but I have returned to my newspaper work now and expect it to continue, as I always have enjoyed hard work." Upon hearing the news, Harriet could not have been more sympathetic, nor could she have agreed more heartily with Mildred's prescription for self-medication. "It was with surprise that I read of the passing of your husband, and I am deeply grieved that you have had this tragedy in your life," she wrote. "Such a parting is not easy, and I do send you my deepest sympathy...You are right in thinking that work is the best solace at a time of grief. Nevertheless, it must have been hard for you to have undertaken the Nancy Drew just now. I do appreciate your going ahead with it." When it came time to pay Mildred for her work, Harriet included a small bonus, and with it a kind thought: "You will notice that the check is somewhat larger than formerly. I think you certainly deserve the extra amount!"

Mildred was, indeed, grateful. Like Harriet, she was worn out. The war years and assorted family tragedies had weighed unduly on both of them, and each was ready for a new beginning. For Harriet, it would come in the form of new blood for the Syndicate; for Mildred, it would mean finding a new husband. For all their differences, the two women were alike in their determination to move forward no matter what. As Mildred wrote to Harriet during that difficult summer of 1947, "All one can do in the last analysis, is just carry on."

11

THE KIDS ARE HEP

IN THE WANING MONTHS of the war, publishers, even as they continued to print their books on low-grade paper and cut back on their orders, had kept one eye on the future. At the start of 1944, Hugh Juergens at Grosset & Dunlap wrote to Harriet: "We feel here that all of us should be alert to the changes that the end of the war will bring. That it will bring sweeping changes in the Juvenile field goes without saying…everyone seems to agree that children's books will come in for much more attention from all the publishers…We want to be ready when peace comes. We'll probably make some mistakes, but we can't afford to sit still and wait."

He couldn't have been more prophetic. By the end of the 1940s, there was no longer a doubt in anyone's mind that children's books were going to be buoyed up by America's new fortunes along with everything else. The "sweeping changes" Juergens had foreseen were not limited to his field alone, though—

if anything, the postwar transformation of the juvenile book industry from a sleepy offshoot of adult publishing to a lucrative business in its own right was simply one more symptom of the energetic makeover of American business and culture in general. Nothing would emerge from the next decade unchanged, least of all the girl detective, as everything from home ownership to the birth rate to what it meant to be teenager and a woman was transformed in the swirl of excitement and prosperity that tore across the nation after 1945. The country was full of promise and consumer goods for the first time in almost two decades, and having a family was "the ultimate symbol of security for Americans tired of depression and war."

But the expanding economy and focus on family also had a downside, and it affected women most emphatically, even as they participated in it willingly. In 1946 alone, three million women left the workforce, "eager to set up households and get on with the postwar baby boom." That same year the first edition of Dr. Benjamin Spock's *Common Sense Book of Baby and Child Care* was published, giving all these ambitious young mothers a manual that helped them but also standardized parenting in a way that made it possible to feel inadequate on a whole new level.

Just as they had resurged in the late 1920s and '30s, womanly virtues were back with a vengeance. Writing in the *Atlantic Monthly* in 1950, Agnes Meyer, an outspoken supporter of the return to what would come to be known in later generations as "family values," wrote: "What modern woman had to recapture is the wisdom that just being a woman is her central task and greatest honor…Women must boldly announce that no job is more exacting, more necessary, or more rewarding than that of housewife or mother." And though 1947 brought the number of working women higher than it had been during the war years by about three million, their average pay dropped by 26 percent as they were pushed into unskilled, unsatisfying jobs. There was little incentive to work under such conditions.

By the middle of the 1950s, 60 percent of women had dropped out of college to get married or because "they were afraid too much education would be a marriage bar." Higher education for women became merely a way station on the path to matrimony as the average marriage age dropped again to twenty and kept going down from there. As one Harvard graduate said about his wife in 1955, "She can be independent on little things but the big decisions have to go my way. The marriage must be the most important thing that ever happened to her." One of his counterparts, a 1951 Radcliffe graduate, admitted, "We married what we wanted to *be*. If we wanted to be a lawyer or a doctor we married one." Rosie the Riveter traded in her overalls and head scarf for pointy bras and big hairstyles that were worn with full scratchy skirts and petticoats. Suburbs sprung up to house all these shiny new families, who, thanks to GI benefits that made it possible to start a family before husbands were even out of college, had more children sooner. According to one study of middle-class couples, 39 percent of them wanted at least four.

It was no wonder that children's books were taking off like never before—all those babies were going to be reading soon, and someone had to serve them. Even the biggest publishers in New York couldn't deny it. "'The tail is now wagging the dog,' said Bennett Cerf, the president of Random House, in stressing the extent to which juvenile publishing has become big business," reported *Publishers Weekly* in the fall of 1949. Over the course of the 1940s, the juvenile departments of big publishers had gone from small divisions to serious business operations with bottom lines and sales quotas as inflexible as they were in other industries. As it became easier to track the tastes and preferences of young America, there was no excuse for publishing books that children didn't like.

Caught up in the whirl of postwar publishing, Harriet felt pressed like never before. "With life going along at a slower pace where you live, you probably think everybody up here is loony," she wrote to Edna at one point, trying to make her understand the new urgency of business decisions in her changed world. "Well, we probably are. Everybody is in a mad dash, feels free to change his mind at a moment's notice, but often has good ideas about which there should not be procrastination." This was by no means an endorsement of the new order of things. To Harriet, many of the changes taking place were just as much anathema as the idea of Russell doing the dishes or changing a diaper. Having taken over the Syndicate in a more genteel era, she was dismayed and irritated by the newly developed rush and tumble of New York publishing. Grosset & Dunlap had hired a new president to guide it smoothly into the Atomic Age, and she was not pleased by his attitude, an opinion she felt free to make known. He had written her a long letter trying to explain that her inability to meet their fast-paced schedule was costing everyone money, leading her to complain to one of her editors there: "I have had a feeling for some time that the new Etat Major of Grosset and Dunlap does not have the same feeling for my heroes and heroines as the former paterfamilias. It worries me to see a growing hysteria to meet printers' and mail order house demands to a point where all laughter and enjoyment is taken out of conferences." Then with a final upper-class smack that also picked up on the anti-Communist sentiment sweeping the country, she added, "In this transitional period of history, are we going to succumb to the push of the proletariat?"

Apparently, the answer was yes. As Harriet continued to turn in manuscripts late and quibble with her editors over everything from cover art to Nancy's outfits in the interior drawings, Grosset & Dunlap began to panic that she would eventually have an effect on production and sales of her very lucrative series. More and more, the company tried to exert control over the content and look of the Stratemeyer books, vetting outlines, picking art, even offering to take the burden of getting the books written off of Harriet by hiring writers themselves. This, they reasoned, would leave her free to "carry on your negotiations with the radio and movie people and perhaps to give some thought to ideas for new series. We could discuss the new titles long in advance with you, and then we could find the proper authors to write them...Our one objective *is to keep the series alive*, to keep their sales up, to make sure that they maintain their top ranking in the book trade."

Appalled by Grosset & Dunlap's suggestions, Harriet dug her heels in even further. It was true that she had made a few errors in negotiating over the years, the largest of which had been to sell all the Nancy Drew movie rights outright to Warner Brothers, rather than licensing them for a limited period of time. She was now trying to buy them back because, as she told Edna, "No prospective radio and television buyer will take the stuff with the idea that Warner can put movies on the air with a totally different cast. Since they [Warner] did not consider them money makers, it's just possible they would turn all rights back to us for a fee." Warner Brothers, naturally, would do no such thing. But even while their refusal was preventing Harriet, and Edna by association, from earning a good deal of money, in no way did Harriet consider herself unable to run her business. She did see the necessity for some changes, though, mostly to help her manage the increasing workload.

Accordingly, in 1948 she finally hired the Syndicate's first full-time nonsecretarial member, a young man named Andrew Svenson. A sportswriter for the *Newark News*, Svenson was a thirty-seven-year-old father of four. He was, Harriet wrote to Edna, "interested in the church, Sunday School, Scouts, Junior Chamber of Commerce, and very particularly sports...Mr. Svenson would be able to turn out a lot of work, including writing, and we in turn might be able to open up new fields that would bring in money after the present series begin to wane." When Edna acquiesced at last, Harriet was thrilled and couldn't help feeling that kismet had played a part in the timing of everything. "Mr. Svenson plans to come here on May 10," she told her sister. "I told him this might be a good omen, as that is the anniversary of Dad's death."

The hiring of Andy Svenson proved to be a rare concession on Edna's part. Just a year later, matters between the sisters had deteriorated again to such a degree that Harriet could barely contain herself. Edna was refusing to give Svenson a raise, and her obstinacy came at a particularly bad moment. Harriet was about to embark on a long-postponed vacation to Europe, where she and Russell would visit Patsy and her husband in England and then tour the Continent for a total of nine weeks away. Tearing along at breakneck pace as she tried to keep up, the stress had finally overwhelmed her. "My long period of good health took a nose dive about six weeks ago," she wrote to Edna in the summer of 1949. "They started pumping penicillin into me every six hours until I had the maximum they can give...I had to have my passport picture taken while I was feeling extremely punk," she laughed. "I am sure you would never recognize me. I look like dope fiend No. 1."

Her leaving was possible only because she had hired Svenson, whom she trusted implicitly. "I believe he eventually could run the SS," Harriet tried to explain to Edna while asking for his raise. "With the thought that I might suddenly drop out of the picture, I'm sure you would find him loyal and progressive." Trying, yet again, to make peace, she appealed to Edna's conscience and finances simultaneously. "Do you realize that it has been seven years that I have carried on under very trying circumstances? Any ideas you had in 1942 must have been disproved by this time about the business. The output of books has been good and your coffers have been well-filled."

It was more than Harriet could bear to think that her family was not harmonious, so even as she left the country fuming at Edna, who had not replied on the matter of the raise, once abroad she made sure to send home a raft of postcards as well as a few detailed letters about her experiences in Monte Carlo, Frankfurt, Holland, Italy, and the other places she and Russell were traveling on their grand tour.

"AUTHOR OF CHILDREN'S BOOKS WORKS OUT ENDINGS FIRST; FINDS SYSTEM PAYS OFF," ran the headline of a glowing article about Mildred in the *Toledo Times* that same summer. "NEWSPAPERWOMAN HAS HAD 126 VOLUMES PUBLISHED; NANCY DREW SERIES IN 20TH YEAR." Nowhere in the piece, which was three columns long, did the name Stratemeyer appear. "Her system may be unorthodox," the author wrote, "but it has produced such popular fiction characters as Nancy Drew, Doris Force, Honey Bunch, the Dana Girls, Dot and Dash, and Ruth Fielding. The Nancy Drew series, written for a syndicate under a pen name, was started in 1929 and is still going strong." It was not the first time Mildred had linked her name to Nancy Drew. It had been mentioned in the little profile in *Inside the Blade* back in 1944, and she had also revealed herself as Carolyn Keene in an ency-clopedic volume called *American Women, 1939–1940*, a kind of *Who's Who* that detailed her writing career thus far.

For whatever reason, perhaps because she could not spare the energy, or perhaps because all of this publicity was appearing in local sources and she was not always aware of it, Harriet did noth-ing. When Edna had wanted to have Andy Svenson sign a con-fidentiality agreement in his new contract, Harriet dismissed the idea outright, implying that the horse was already out of the barn anyway. "The only confidential matters are the names of the se-ries we control, and who the ghost writers might happen to be. As to the former point in question Mr. Garis and Mrs. Wirt pub-licized those things even though they had been told not to."

In any case, Mildred either gave false information to the *Times* reporter or simply didn't bother to correct it when she had the chance, and the idea that she was solely responsible for all of the Syndicate characters she had worked on was firmly estab-lished. Accompanying the piece was a photo of Mildred in her study at home, surrounded by the dozens of series books she had written and looking quite peppy in a striped shirt as she leaned over her typewriter to smile for the photographer.

In addition to the stacks of books testifying to a flourishing ca-reer, there was another reason for Mildred's cheery demeanor in the *Times* photo. She had fallen in love with George Benson, the recently widowed associate editor of the *Toledo Times*, and he with her. Something of a dandy, Benson was given to wearing a homburg and took Mildred dancing frequently at the Com-modore Perry Hotel in downtown Toledo. An excellent writer who had come to the *Times* from the Washington bureau of the *Minneapolis Journal*, Benson was very politically engaged. He was also known for his love of the English language. "Generally

writers, eager for their daily bread, become craven collaborators
of this cabal," wrote one admirer in a piece about the decline of
the vocabulary of the American writer. "But columnist and quid-
nunc Benson has refused to bow. From the great riches of the English language (the richest in the world) he draws such symbols
and conjures up such images as are necessary to his thoughts."
An avid reader of everything from Chekhov and Camus to Roald
Dahl and Jean Stafford, Benson was a perfect match for Mildred
in other ways as well. He was "a gregarious soul, a ready wit, a
fount of knowledge on almost any subject, a colorful speaker, an
all-round newspaperman of great excellence, and, above all else,
a very rugged individualist," as described in his own newspaper.
He and Mildred were married in the summer of 1950.

The effect of this newfound happiness was immediate and apparent to everyone. Even Harriet, who barely knew Mildred but
had recently brought her back into the Syndicate fold once again,
took note. "The new Dana book is being written by—of all
people—Mrs. Wirt," she wrote to Edna the following summer.
"After trying out some new writers and not being satisfied with
them, I began to wonder if perhaps she might be able to do it.
Knowing that she had gone back to work and that her troubles of
a few years ago were now sometime behind her, I decided to take
a chance. To my amazement, she wrote that she had married
again...The whole tone of her letter proved that she had regained her health and spirits, so I have high hopes [for] the new
story." Harriet's happy suspicions were confirmed when Mildred
and George dropped by the Syndicate office on their way to a vacation in Nantucket. "I like him very much," Harriet told Edna,
"and she is so completely changed I would never have recognized her. You recall when she dropped in here before how thin
and wan and listless she was in her plain black dress? Last week

she was dressed in a very becoming blue frock and a large hat. She had taken on some weight and looks very well. Furthermore she was very talkative and full of fun."

Mildred had been transferred to the courthouse beat at the paper, and she and George coexisted happily at the *Times*, working, as one colleague recalled, "only ten feet away [from each other]. He was the editor of the editorial page. So she would stay until the first edition, until around 7:00 P.M., and her husband was responsible for closing his page. They were entirely separate— that was church-and-state separation!" George was also a great help with Peggy, who adored him. An inspired cook, he was often the one who went home and made her dinner while Mildred, ever the hard-bitten reporter, stayed late at the office. With George to help out, Lillian Augustine had gone back to Ladora, where she would live until her death in 1971. Unlike many housewives of the time, who were finding that their reliance on motherhood as a means of self-fulfillment was not working out quite the way they had imagined it would—"I feel quite stale as though I don't use my mind enough," one of them told a researcher—Mildred was managing to have it all.

But though she had been assigned more work by Harriet, what was to be her final tenure with the Stratemeyer Syndicate was short-lived. Harriet's wrangles with Grosset & Dunlap intensified throughout the early 1950s. "They expect us to hop around, but on their side they do things just like any other corporation," she wrote to Edna. "If you argue too much, there's always someone to take your place...The old spirit is gone. Everything is just for money." Slowly she was become aware that the party losing out the most in the new world of big business was the Stratemeyer Syndicate, which was still earning the old five-cents-a-copy royalty on its books even as rising prices helped Grosset earn more and more. "Last fall I took up with Mr. O'Connor the matter of increased royalty after our books had sold over a large sum. He refused...All other publishers pay on a gradually increasing scale, and I do not see why G&D cannot follow suit. Ever since the new regime came in there, they have gone the way of big business—asking for as much as possible, and giving us as little as possible," she wrote at one point, continuing her train of thought in another letter later that month: "The attitude over at G&D's is certainly a most undiplomatic one. They take the position all the time of doing us a great favor. This morning when Mr. Juergens recommended that the Syndicate not kill the goose that lays the golden egg, I reminded him that after all it's the Syndicate who is supplying them with the golden eggs."

In response, she developed a new model for getting manuscripts written, one that she hoped would give her the best possible chance of meeting Grosset's deadlines. "We have had so much trouble with writers that I am trying out a new plan—that of doing more of the work in the office," she wrote to Edna in the fall of 1952. For the rest of her life, almost all the writing would be done in-house, with Harriet taking over some of the series herself, and Andy Svenson coming up with several more new series. The rest would be done by a staff of writers whom Harriet could influence and keep an eye on when in the office. Skeptical as always, Edna was at least willing to give Harriet's method a whirl. "Apparently you expect...to speed up and ease the story telling problem. I do hope it does, but I admit I hate to see the old policy of getting talent from various states to carry on the books go. Guess we'll just have to see the results."

Among the victims of this new policy was Mildred, who had just written Nancy Drew number thirty, *The Clue of the Velvet*

Mask, for the Syndicate. Published in 1953, the manuscript traveled to New York on the same train as George Benson, who was going there to screen nominations for the Pulitzer Prize in journalism. It would be her last Nancy Drew. Apparently, Harriet never informed Mildred of her new plan — she simply stopped writing with assignments, and with that the relationship was effectively severed.

Immediately Harriet had her staff compile character sheets on all the Syndicate heroes and heroines, so that characters and the details of their adventures, which had for so long been stored in the memories of ghostwriters, would be gathered all in one place. For Harriet, who was about to take over the writing of the Nancy Drew books herself, there were reams of information about the sleuth, her various friends and family members, and her surroundings.

Though they were intended as reference sheets, these summaries often read like the résumé of a real person. "DREW, NANCY, daughter of Carson Drew, famous criminal lawyer; mother deceased; lives in River Heights, U.S.A.," one began. It then listed all the relevant information under the appropriate headings "Education"; "Career" (amateur detective, of course); "Avocations"; and "Honors." Drawing on the plots of all the Nancy Drew Mysteries, it painted a neat portrait of the girl sleuth, who by this time seemed to be practically generating her own personality. Another key piece of paper, separate from the brief summary, was entitled "DETAILED INFORMATION AND DATA ABOUT NANCY DREW HERSELF."

> She is pretty, blond, about sixteen. Has shiny, golden curls, is resourceful and alert. Enjoys all types of games, especially golf.

This shows her lively spirit, She has attended River Heights High School. Nancy is generous to a fault. Is the most popular young person in River Heights.

Nancy has that intangible something, making one never forget her face. Pretty in a distinctive way. She speaks forcefully, but never thinks of thrusting her opinions on others. In any crowd she unconsciously assumes leadership. Sometimes her father calls her "Curly Locks." She is the apple of his eye.

Nancy, a true daughter of the Middle West, takes pride in the fertility of her State, and sees beauty in a crop of waving green corn as well as in the rolling hills and the expanse of prairie land.

Carson Drew finds it necessary to maintain a certain social position, and accordingly Nancy was frequently called upon to entertain noted professional men.

In the first book of the series, Nancy has a blue roadster. Then, in "The Mysterious Letter" Nancy gets a new car—a smart maroon roadster. In "The Password to Larkspur Lane" Mr. Drew tells Nancy he is giving her a new car, which makes the third one so far. The new car [is] a beauty and handles marvelously. Powerful engine. A powerful black and green roadster. Even so, she rather hates to part with her maroon roadster.

Nancy likes to sew, and does considerable sewing, curled up on the davenport in the living room of her home.

Nancy also likes to draw, and attends art school in River Heights.

A number of times Nancy had been present at interviews which her father had had with noted detectives who desired his aid in solving perplexing mysteries, and those occasions stood out as red letter days for her.

The responsibility of the household might have weighed heavily upon Nancy, but she was the type of girl who is capable of accomplishing a great many things in a comparatively short time. She takes plenty of time, even so, for sports, clubs and parties. In school, Nancy had been very popular and boasted many friends. She had a way of taking life seriously without impressing one as being the least bit serious herself.

Nancy possesses her father's liking for a mystery, and delights in a battle of wits when championing a worthy cause. Carson Drew had often remarked that he enjoyed the detective work of his cases better than the court work. He was so busy at times with legal matters that Nancy would have to do most of the mystery work.

Since Carson Drew knew that Nancy could be trusted with confidential information, he frequently discussed his cases with her.

Nancy wears the color blue a great deal.

Mrs. Drew died when Nancy was ten [circled, with "3" written in on one draft] years old.

Nancy very much dislikes to eat squash.

Carson Drew gives Nancy a generous clothing allowance. Nancy is a very wise buyer. There was not a year in the three during which she had enjoyed the allowance but that showed a surplus.

There would be no more haggling with Mildred over her characterization or which points in a plot to emphasize. From then on, these sheets of information would be consulted exhaustively when it came to deciding where to send Nancy on her next trip and how she should be dressed for it, or what she might or might not eat in a foreign country. Nothing would be left to chance or the creative process of anyone other than Harriet.

By 1954 the new order was up and running in East Orange, and the Syndicate had moved beyond making character and data sheets for each series to promulgating an all-encompassing theory of book writing. Andy Svenson announced to a reporter from the *New Yorker* magazine: "Whether we do yarns about Ubermenschen or pigtailed Philo Vances, we subscribe to the Stratemeyer formula...A low death rate but plenty of plot. Verbs of action, and polka-dotted with exclamation points and provocative questions. No use of guns by the hero. No smooching." The reason for the reporter's visit was the debut of a new series starring Tom Swift Jr., son of Edward Stratemeyer's beloved Tom Swift, inventor extraordinaire. Upon arriving at the office to see Harriet, the writer "found her, a pert, gray-haired lady in a green dress, sitting in a pleasant office, surrounded by hundreds of books for children. Tom, Jr., books, she informed us happily, are running neck and neck with the latest titles in the two most popular current series—the Nancy Drew mysteries and the Hardy Boys, both Syndicate properties."

Though she stuck to her guns about the moral aspects of her stories, Harriet had clearly learned her lesson about relying on her own instincts for what was new and fascinating. "'In the old days,' said Mrs. Adams, 'we used to treat scientific data rather simply. Now a battery of specialists goes over everything to eradicate the slightest error.'" Her right-hand man, sitting in on the interview, confirmed the approach. "'Scientifically, the kids are hep,' Mr. Svenson boomed."

Indeed, the kids of 1950s America were a whole new breed. By the end of the decade, with allowance in their pockets and time to spare, they were spending $50 million a year on 45s of their favorite rock-and-roll songs alone. Gyrating in basements all through suburbia to the scandalous sounds of Elvis Presley, they ushered in a new age of permissiveness. What *Calling All Girls* had started, *Seventeen* magazine now perpetuated. With stories about cosmetics and fashion and boys, "the publication that virtually invented the teenage girl" had been an immediate hit when it debuted in 1944. All four hundred thousand copies of its first issue sold out in two days, and a year later its circulation had broken one million. By the 1950s it was essential reading for the bobby-soxer set, who consulted it for information on everything from their favorite crooners to how big or short or stiff to wear their skirts. In addition to magazines, there was television, which had exploded on to the family scene and replaced radio as the most popular means of entertainment. *I Love Lucy* was first broadcast to great adoration in 1951, and *The Mickey Mouse Club* and *Captain Kangaroo* both debuted in 1955, followed by *Leave It to Beaver* and *Perry Mason* in 1957. By then, forty-one million American homes had television sets, and black-and-white was fast being replaced by color. When Dick Clark took over *American Bandstand* in 1956, American teenagers were hooked immediately, helping to seal television's dominance.

They were also buying books in record numbers. "Even the proudest firms are titans leaning on tots," wrote *Time* magazine's book reporter in 1957. "At Grosset & Dunlap children's books comprise two-thirds of the firm's publishing operation; 35% of Random House's sales volume is estimated to be in juveniles; fully $13 million of Simon & Schuster's $18 million gross last year came from books for kids." In a world this receptive to children's literature, Harriet and her pet characters hit their highest sales numbers for more than a decade and even expanded into new areas. The first edition of the Nancy Drew board game appeared in 1957, complete with miniature roadsters for game pieces and a stack of cards that players drew from as they tried to solve mysteries while traveling to many of the locations named in Nancy Drew books. Nancy Drew and other Syndicate books were also being translated and sold overseas again. In Finland Nancy was known as "Paula"; in Sweden her name was changed to

"Kitty Drew." The United Kingdom and Denmark left her as Nancy, and France, where she was published under the name "Alice Roy"—possibly because the French had a difficult time pronouncing the name "Nancy Drew"—proved to be a huge market.

Harriet felt more strongly than ever that she had to protect the integrity of her characters by being the sole person to authorize their use in any way. "I am constantly made aware of the fact that the publishers, producers and manufacturers are more interested in dollars and cents than in following any established precepts or formulas which I and those working for me insist upon in order to keep the books and corollary rights up to the high ethical standards to which they have always held," she complained to Edna. "I have continual arguments along these lines with company officers, editors, and artists who are greatly swayed by present day trends toward gun play, the shading of the truth by characters, and deviations from the factual."

Nevertheless, her characters had survived, and Harriet herself had passed a milestone: the twenty-fifth anniversary as head of the Syndicate. Just how much she had relied on her own counsel when she insisted on taking over the business back in 1930 was brought home to her in a letter of congratulations from Hugh Juergens of Grosset & Dunlap. "As I sat there I couldn't help thinking what the old gentleman would have thought of the picture of that G&D mob around that festive board with his daughter picking up the check," he wrote after a celebratory party. "Just the same, I think he would have been rather proud to see how well the Syndicate he had built up was being carried on under his daughter's administration."

There was one person, however, who refused to fete Harriet. Despite the fact that royalties were higher than ever, Edna was still refusing to authorize a higher salary for her sister. Her husband had passed away recently, and her daughter was grown, leaving her with even more time to obsess over her income and to heckle Harriet over even the tiniest things. "Better watch the office expenditure," she wrote to her sister. "Last year you certainly went to town with new items—I'll not agree to any such new gadgets this year, so watch out."

Harriet tried one last time to appeal to her sister's conscience. "In your recent letter you mentioned Christmas, and the thought came to me that the best Christmas gift which you could give me would be a change in attitude towards your sister," she wrote. Then, the decades of bad blood were aired at last as she cut straight to the heart of Edna's years of suspicion and resentment.

> *Perhaps you are not aware of how you have hurt me over a long period of years, sometimes directly, sometimes indirectly. Back in 1942, soon after I had suffered a tragic sorrow [Sunny's death], you told me that in my whole life I had never done anything for you. Since in my own mind I felt that both Russell and I had done a great deal for you, I told you a few truths. The matter was entirely a personal one and had nothing to do with business, yet I heard from two relatives that you said I had forced you out of the office because I wanted to get the business away from you. That was utterly ridiculous of course. Since that time you have harassed me by suspicious remarks in letters, but even worse by asking secretaries to spy on me...You have been away from the office for fourteen years. In that time I have built up the business from an annual income of 20,000 in 1942 to 115,000 so far this year, yet no recognizance of this has been taken by you.*

She implored Edna to listen to her. "Now Edna, I bear you no malice for the rift and the hurts, and I hope you will forgive me for any hurts I have caused you. Let's make this a happy Christmas! What say?"

Edna said no. The following year, Harriet tried to buy her sister out of her share of the Syndicate for $75,000. Edna said no to that, too, and as the decade wound down, the two of them remained locked in disagreement. Harriet simply stopped consulting her unless it was absolutely necessary and focused instead on her work. But she could not hold on to her detective forever. Before long, Nancy Drew would get even further away from Harriet than the European continent, and there was nothing she could do about it.

AFTER FORTY-FIVE YEARS of dominance, series books finally began to decline in the late 1950s. Television was just on the cusp of becoming the number-one entertainment for kids, and the competition was too stiff for all of them—all of them, that is, except for Nancy Drew and the Hardy Boys. "Offhand I would say that the continuing volume of sales on your books is little short of miraculous," John O'Connor, the president of Grosset & Dunlap, wrote to Harriet in 1958. In 1959 the year's sales for the thirty-six volumes in the Nancy Drew series would be close to one and a half million, a number that was almost unfathomable considering that the trend in children's books since the end of the war had been toward realism. With new fears about communism and nuclear bombs in the air, so the theory went, fantasy had fallen by the wayside. Books had to describe "the 'here and now'...in which nothing happens except what happens every day, from alarm clock to applesauce," as one disapproving writer put it. "The fad reached some kind of climax," he groused, "when [an eminent psychiatrist] declared that in the atomic age it is wrong to teach children to believe in Santa Claus on the ground that they will refuse to 'think realistically' when they grow up." Newly attuned to the angst of their generation and worried about the future as they hid under their school desks during air-raid drills, teenagers wanted books that dealt with their most delicate and all-consuming problems.

So it was that by the mid-1960s, even Nancy and the Hardy Boys were slipping down from the juvenile Olympus atop which they had reigned for so long. Though Harriet's royalties were still pouring in, it had more to do with the higher price of her books than actual sales numbers. In addition, there was the issue of content. As far back as 1948, concerned mothers and fathers had been writing in to Grosset & Dunlap about the prejudice and racism they saw scattered throughout the Syndicate's books, in the form of uneducated dialect for all the foreign or non-Caucasian characters and villains who were invariably from these same two groups. Harriet had been infuriated by the charges at the time, writing to her latest editor at Grosset that she and her employees had gone over the Hardy Boys book in question, *The Hidden Harbor Mystery*, "very thoroughly, to see what kind of a case your 'conscientious objector' might have on the subject of race prejudice. As to the 'Jewish' angle, I am sure the woman has no case at all. The word 'Jew' is not mentioned on Page 156 nor anywhere else in the book. A 'second-hand man' who says 'Vell' instead of 'Well' could be a German, a Scandinavian, or a native of any of various other countries." Oblivious as she was to new sensitivities following the Holocaust, Harriet was even more naive when it came to racial prejudice closer to home. "On the subject of Negroes, the woman has more of a case," she admitted, "but the whole story idea revolves around 'Can't a Negro be an evil-doer in the story?'" Of course, *The Hidden Harbor Mystery* did much more than just use a black man as its villain. In an act of mis-guided self-defense, Harriet herself listed the instances that "might have a bearing on race prejudice, etc.," in a memo she mailed off with her letter. They included a "mention of a burly, thick-set Negro who puts his feet up on seat of a train car"; "mention of a young negro, badly dressed"; "more about the same Negro, Luke Jones. He is described in unfavorable terms"; "More about the nefarious colored man" and "scheming by colored folks." Still, she insisted, none of these things added up to "give any child reader the idea all colored folks are bad."

This was clearly a matter of opinion, and it was not the first time that Harriet's genteel manners failed to cover the racism so typical of her generation and class. That same year she had also hired a lawyer to prevent a vaudeville act from using the name Rover Boys in their show. While it was an issue of general in-fringement rather than who exactly was doing the infringing — as ever, she guarded the Syndicate properties fiercely — her letter to the lawyer that handled the case made plain the "soft racism" that passed for tolerance in her circles. "Thank you for your prompt and efficient handling of the case of 'The Heirs of the Rover Boys vs. The Two Colored Vaudevillians,'" she wrote. "It is pleasant not to have to worry about the matter any longer. Although I have no desire to be allied with our Southern governors, I did come out boldly agin the negroes usurping white folks rights, didn't I?"

Harriet's reference was to the creation of the southern "Dixie-crat" party, a splinter group of the Democratic Party made up of southern delegates who opposed the adoption of new protections for minorities in Truman's civil rights platform. The buildup to the civil rights movement had begun with Truman's own 1946 Committee on Civil Rights, formed to ensure that black Americans did not lose the progress they had made during the Depression and World War II. In spite of the Dixiecrats' efforts—they ran Strom Thurmond of South Carolina as their presidential candidate in 1948, and he won four southern states—by the mid-1950s the tide had turned. In 1954 the Supreme Court handed down the groundbreaking *Brown v. the Board of Education* decision. The following December in Montgomery, Alabama, Rosa Parks refused to give up her seat at the front of a bus.

When, in the fall of 1957, the Little Rock Nine integrated Central High School in their hometown, to the dismay of thousands and accompanied by the National Guard, the civil rights movement gained a public teenaged face that energized it even further. Sit-ins at lunch counters followed, as did the creation of the Student Non-Violent Coordinating Committee. Then in 1962 James Meredith became the first black student to enroll at the University of Mississippi, setting off riots that forced President Kennedy to send in federal troops. The center of the plush, postwar world was beginning to crumble, and America's young men and women were helping it along. Harriet, meanwhile, was happy in East Orange with her safe and sane stories that also happened to be riddled with racism, guns, and outmoded clothing and cars. "The Syndicate is a challenge to me to spread happiness and good principles among the young people of the world," she chirped, even as America's restless youth roamed in search of something much more earth-shattering than a new mystery.

Now complaints about prejudice in Syndicate books, laced with real anger, flowed in with greater frequency. In 1961 the very same Hardy Boys book that had prompted such a reaction in 1948 elicited another furious letter from a parent whose son had been assigned a book report on *The Hidden Harbor Mystery*. "It had never occurred to me that you might still be ingraining the old race-riot type of fear that was prevalent in the thirties," the woman fumed. "We are trying to raise our children to appreciate Negroes for their contributions; not to fear them because of their color...Temporarily we will not be buying any more of your series books. If, however, you can suggest any point in the Hardy Boys series after which this sort of prejudice does not appear, your advice would be appreciated."

Luckily for such parents, Grosset & Dunlap had already decided it was time to take matters into their own hands. In 1958 they instituted a huge revision program designed to overhaul and reissue the early books in the Nancy Drew and Hardy Boys series. Eventually the rewriting would extend to the first thirty-four Nancys and the first thirty-eight Hardys. The news sent Harriet into a tizzy. "All of a sudden Grosset & Dunlap decided that these books were to be instantly revised because the plates were worn out and the stories antiquated and not in line with acceptable reading material for today's children (heros [*sic*] and heroines carrying guns, playing tricks on the police to outwit them, a drunken character, repetition of content, etc.)," she wrote to Edna. Though Harriet did not mention race in her letter, it was no doubt one of the biggest issues for Grosset & Dunlap. While girls might tolerate Nancy wearing a dress in situations where they would wear pants, if any more parents wrote in to say they would no longer buy series books, the financial ramifications would be enormous.

Though the Syndicate did eventually try to break out of its lily-white mold with a series about a black family named the Tollivers in the late 1960s, the effort failed, perhaps because like all the Syndicate series, it was designed to avoid reality altogether. "The series will be about a family of five Negro children who have fun and adventures," explained Andy Svenson, who was writing it, to Edna (she was still marginally involved in the Syndicate's activities) in a letter. "There will be no social problem involved, the chief idea being that Negro children will be able to identify with the story characters." In the late 1960s, it was almost absurd to expect black children to be able identify with black characters who were not caught up in civil rights and the rise of black consciousness. Nevertheless, Andy Svenson would later chalk the failure up to the fact that "the publisher could find no profitable way to market the books. It is a pity but the majority of black people have not yet been educated to buy books in any great numbers."

Obviously Grosset had been wise to count on revisions of old series with brand recognition, rather than the creation of new ones, to energize their sales numbers. The publisher wanted the first four manuscripts rewritten in two weeks each. Harriet, who was sixty-seven years old by this time, took on most of the revising herself, in addition to her regular work. The rewrites were extensive, involving everything from shortening the books from twenty-five to twenty chapters, gutting entire plots when there was no way to update them—such as in *The Clue of the Broken Locket*, a 1934 Nancy Drew in which the sleuth reunites a pair of adopted babies with their real parents, an implausible scenario that was replaced by a Civil War treasure hunt—to streamlining the language so that the stories, which now had more action and less atmosphere, read even faster than they once had. The results were snappy, but they were also devoid of much of the charm that had made the series so successful. As one critic writes, "The prolonged suspense of the early volumes, where stories started slowly and excitement built steadily, evaporated. Kids were hurled from one unrelated, action-packed mini-crisis to the next. Plots in the revised editions became mechanical, and soon it became difficult to differentiate one story from the next." In order to deal with the racial aspect of the revisions, Harriet simply got rid of ethnic characters, including black ones. Though it was the easiest way to handle the situation, it was also the least appropriate, but even if Harriet had the inclination to do something else, there was simply no time.

As for Nancy, she underwent a complete transformation, beginning with her age. In the revision of *The Secret of the Old Clock*, the first title in the series, she was established as eighteen instead of sixteen, because the driving age had gone up. A girl as reliant on her car as Nancy—who now drove a snazzy blue convertible in place of her trusty roadster—had to be able to get behind the wheel at a moment's notice without worrying about her license. In fact, her whole attitude toward driving seemed to have changed along with her more mature age. Where she had gleefully zoomed away from the scene of the crime with a stolen clock in her backseat in the original story, she was now concerned about breaking the law. "The blue convertible sped along the country road. Nancy smiled grimly. 'I'm afraid I'm exceeding the speed limit,' she thought." Her eyes "sparkle" and "twinkle pleasantly" several times in the span of a few pages, then continue to do so for the rest of the book, along with every other female character's. Her run-in with the dreaded Topham sisters at the department store, once a scene in which she shrewdly assesses her enemies, is now reduced to a put-down (delivered only in her own mind, of course, since when she does talk to the girls, she does it "evenly") as 1950s as the "tan cotton suit" she's dressed in: "I pity any future husband of hers!" Poor Isabel Topham, once doomed because her mother was going to force her to marry rich, is reduced from a tragic figure being shackled in wedlock to a catty high-maintenance wife in a world where everyone gets married, some just more happily than others.

In addition to struggling with the revisions—"I think an editor should respect an author's judgment and not try to inject his own likes, dislikes and opinions into a story," she wrote sniffily to Anne Hagan, the series' current editor, about the revamped *Mystery at Lilac Inn*—Harriet was also fighting constantly with Grosset & Dunlap about the new titles they were adding to the series at a rate of one per year. Nineteen fifty-nine's title, the thirty-sixth, was *The Secret of the Golden Pavilion,* set in the new state of Hawaii, and like all the Nancys now, it was also written by Harriet. It was an enormous workload, and the strain showed. "You say Nancy is slipping just because she does not think the way you would have her," she wrote angrily to Hagan, who had suggested that the stories might be more "taken from the police files" and that Nancy should be checking in at her local precinct more often to hash out the details of a given adventure.

Though Grosset started publishing the first revisions in 1959, putting out two that year, and another four by the end of 1962, Harriet's battles began to have an effect on production. Grosset & Dunlap could not get out as many revamped books as quickly as they hoped to—none at all were published in 1963 and 1964—and as a result, people were still buying old text with new covers and becoming outraged at the outmoded stories. Harriet responded to the scheduling pressure by hiring more writers to work on revisions in-house, including one to vet all books for plots and details that needed to be changed, and generally failed to economize in spite of every indication that she should do so. "We are expanding all the time—closing our eyes to the slump-in-business reports and counting on Junior to have a dollar to spend on his favorite hero," she wrote to one of the people she was trying to bring on board. But none of those writers would ever be given the job of writing a new Nancy Drew book. On the few occasions when someone else contributed to a volume in the series, it was done only under Harriet's extremely watchful eye. Moreover, where she had once insisted that Syndicate books were a collaborative effort, she now saw herself as Nancy's sole creator. "Our company rarely accepts plots from other writers and so far as Nancy Drew goes, I am afraid I guard her jealously as my own personal property," she wrote to one interested party. As one of her editors at Grosset & Dunlap during that period recalled later on, "Harriet had her own little world—and it was a lovely one. She felt very close to Nancy."

As such, Harriet kept a close watch on everything from Nancy's clothes to her physical appearance. The books were being produced in a new format now, with bright yellow spines and up-to-date drawings of Nancy in action printed right on the board covers instead of dust jackets, and all the art was being redone to appeal to the current generation—a plan Harriet was sometimes in line with, and other times not. "My idea is to have Nancy wearing a dress with an Inca design and I am attaching some photographs from the July issue of *Vogue* magazine," she wrote to Anne Hagan at one point; "I wish you would dress Nancy in a costume more appropriate to Spring or Fall," she wrote to Grosset's art director at another. For new cover art for *The Hidden Staircase,* she requested: "Though it is not the 'new look' could her bust be slightly more full and her legs slightly more shapely?" Even as Americans were snapping up copies of *Sex and the Single Girl* (1962) and experimenting with the birth control pill, which the FDA had approved in 1962, Harriet was fighting for Nancy's modesty. "I do not like having Nancy's legs accentuated," she wrote to the art director. "I would prefer that both her knees be on the floor and her skirt a bit longer so that this feature will not date the book. I do not like Nancy's mouth. Her upper lip is too short and having her mouth so far open gives her a dull appearance. Delete the line indicating the crotch of the man's trousers which extends over the edge of the bed." The double standard that American women were grappling with was alive and well in River Heights—sex was not for nice girls, and Nancy was nothing if not nice. She no longer talked back or spoke harshly to anyone. Even George, once so defiant about the unusual origins of her name, confessed in *The Clue in the Old Stagecoach* (1960) that it was really short for Georgia.

ALL THE WHILE, the first ghostwriter of the series was paying careful attention out in Ohio. Though she had not written for the Syndicate since the early 1950s, Mildred had not left her work for Edward and Harriet entirely in the past. As the revised Nancy Drews began appearing on the market, Mildred's alma mater, the University of Iowa, decided to include her in its Iowa Authors Collection. Begun in 1945 at the university library, the collection endeavored to gather in one place all the books of authors who were either native to the state or had some long-term connection with it. Writing back to Frank Paluka, the librarian currently in charge of the project, Mildred expressed her gratitude at being included and filled him in on her recent biography: "I presently am employed as a reporter for the Toledo Times...My interests, aside from sports on which I did a great deal of writing, include archeology. In recent years, I have enjoyed numerous trips to archeological centers in Central America."

Though she did not mention it, Mildred had made each of these trips, which she then reported on for the *Toledo Blade*, by herself. She had been widowed once again in 1959, when George Benson died suddenly of a stroke just before the couple was to leave on a vacation for Puerto Rico. With Peggy long grown up, Mildred had busied herself more than ever with her newspaper work, covering everything she could in addition to her regular courthouse beat. Richard and Pat Nixon's visit to Toledo during the 1960 election campaign elicited one of her favorite pieces, which ran under the headline: "PAT WORTH WAITING FOR, STATION CROWD INDICATES." The entire article, with the exception of a few sentences, was about the vice president's wife, "vibrant, serene, a confident 115 pounds of energy." Though Nixon was in the picture that ran alongside the article, he was clearly second fiddle to this reporter. In another equally timely piece of investigative journalism of the day, the *Blade* dispatched its least kitchen-friendly employee to her home to make a meal from an emergency rations kit of the kind that were being stowed away in bomb shelters everywhere. "Radiation shelters now being in style," Mildred began jauntily, "it behooved me, I thought, to learn through trial and plenty of error how to live the simple life on dehydrated, fortified food." Like most of her adventures in cooking, the experiment had mixed results. While the cocoa and mashed potatoes were delicious, "scrambled eggs were less of a success…My hope is that if war does come, a strenuous effort will be made to spare the hens."

But in spite of all the distractions, pleasant and otherwise, she had not lost track of Nancy Drew. Frank Paluka at Iowa had sent her a book list, asking her to confirm that she had written all the titles on it. After identifying the various books she had published without the help of the Syndicate, she explained, "Much of my early work, including the Nancy Drew books, which had such wide sale, was written for the Stratemeyer Syndicate, East Orange, N.J. I note many translations. I had no part in these whatsoever. Also, the books now have gone into many revised and simplified editions, and I had no part whatsoever in the rewriting." She clearly did not approve of what had been done to the character she had pioneered, and she did not want to be associated with what she saw as inferior writing that pandered to the lowest common denominator. "When I was very young," she told Paluka, "they induced me to sign a release of all right to the pen name, title, etc. As a result, there is today no published list of authors." Irritated as she was, however, and as long as it had been since she'd written for Harriet, she kept her promise of confidentiality. "I include this for informational purposes only," she warned Paluka, "not to be used as a published statement." She then further listed which pen names were the property of the Syndicate, as opposed to her own, and signed off. Paluka promised to keep her secret, but the fact remained that Mildred had confessed her past to a someone who had reason to care — after all, she was one of Iowa's own — and who was not about to forget it.

12

Nancy in the Age of Aquarius

COULD THERE HAVE BEEN a book that described women more different from the original Nancy Drew than *The Feminine Mystique*, published in 1963? Betty Friedan's impassioned writing, which gave a voice at last to the many housewives who had lost their identities in the 1950s, spoke of a generation who had forgone, among other things, the ideals of the teen sleuth. "In 1960, the problem that has no name burst like a boil through the image of the happy American housewife," Friedan wrote. Women were bored, lonely, and, worst of all, had forgotten how to live without a man. "The year American women's discontent boiled over, it was also reported that the more than 21,000,000 American women who are single, widowed, or divorced do not cease even after fifty their frenzied search for a man...the chains that bind her in her trap are chains in her own mind and spirit. They are chains made up of mistaken ideas and misinterpreted facts, of incomplete truths and unreal choices." Nancy Drew, never to be

married, burdened with children, or distracted from her chosen
path in life—not to mention a stickler for the facts—suddenly
seemed new again.

Though total sales of *The Secret of the Old Clock* passed one
million in the spring of 1963, and sales of the series in the United
States increased by another 36 percent in the following year, it
was the sleuth's older fans, not her new ones, who were about to
usher her, with enormous fanfare, into the swinging sixties. As
the seventy million children born in the postwar baby boom
began to reach adulthood in the early and mid-1960s, a second
wave of feminism arose, fueled by intelligent, stalwart young
women who discovered that they had something in common
with their thirty- and forty-something cake-baking mothers after
all: Nancy Drew. Having hit reading age before the revised books
came out, they knew the same Nancy as the previous generation,
and they loved her just as much. Unlike their mothers, though,
they were determined not to forget what she had taught them.

She was first elevated to the status of activist icon in the summer of 1964, in the pages of *Mademoiselle* magazine, a paragon
of modern young womanhood, which devoted twelve full pages
to a nostalgic Nancy Drew fashion shoot complete with captions
from various stories and a beautiful young TV star named Joanna
Pettet as Nancy. "What better way to open MLLE's first mystery
number than by revisiting the girl girls have adored for the past
34 years?" the article asked, before turning to photos of Nancy in
everything from her trusty convertible to a tasteful nightgown,
accompanied by Bess, George, Ned, Carson Drew, and the occasional spinster in need of rescue. There were no hot pants or revealing tops in sight, and though the feature certainly had its
share of campy sensibility, it was overall a loving tribute to the girl
sleuth with a few concessions to the here and now. Ned, the text

noted, "has become an exchange student at Chung Chi College, Hong Kong, and wants to go into the U.S. Intelligence service." Coming just after the Bay of Pigs and the Kennedy assassination, there was certainly no more noble pursuit.

Harriet was thrilled to discover that Nancy's junior adorers had grown up and were now working for the media. "Again, may I say how much I enjoyed meeting you and being taken around to chat with my ex-fans?" she wrote to her contact at *Mademoiselle.* "I shall treasure particularly the comment, 'Miss Keene, you have really made a great contribution to America.'" Writing in to the Wellesley alumni magazine that same year, Harriet could not suppress her great joy at having left a mark on her country's culture: "It is my hope that the real children in my life have permanently benefited from their actual or imaginary kinship with me and my fictional characters," she wrote, taking credit for the entire series in one fell swoop.

Her Nancy was going strong, and the books Harriet wrote in the 1960s and '70s were full of the tidbits of educational information and good manners that she loved. In *The Clue of the Dancing Puppet,* published in 1962, Nancy proved that in spite of her revised self, she could still crack a case. Centered on a life-size dancing ballerina puppet that spins out, unassisted and only at night, onto the lawn of a couple who run an amateur theater group right outside River Heights—Bess, as giggly as ever, is a member—the story takes Nancy and her chums to the farm where the troupe performs. There, the husband of the frightened couple confesses, "That ghostly dancer is getting me down." Almost immediately, as per the fast-paced formula that now governed all the books, Nancy gets knocked out by a mysterious bowling ball in the attic of the house and has to be put to bed with some chicken broth to recover—not the kind of treatment she would ever have agreed to in the past. Nevertheless, she's still on the case. "You mean that someone sneaked up to the attic and deliberately knocked you out?" Bess asks her. "'I'm inclined to think so,' Nancy said. 'And I intend to find out who it was!'" Soon enough, the girls are rammed from behind while out in Nancy's convertible, which allows them to enlist the help of the local mechanic in tracking down just who it is that doesn't want them to discover the secret of the puppet. Thrown into the mix is another houseguest who walks around reciting suggestive lines from Shakespeare ("O, what may man within him hide. / Though angel on the outward side!"), all of which the girls have no trouble identifying, adding scholar to Nancy's already long list of talents; a vicious leading lady named Tammi Whitlock; a jewel theft; and several frightening episodes with masked men. "You're cool customers," one of them says to Nancy and George. "But you won't keep so cool if you stay around here." At one point Nancy is forced to take over Tammi's role in the play, which she does so brilliantly, it's suggested she give up sleuthing for acting.

But how could she? In *Dancing Puppet* alone, she gets to be "thunderstruck" and recite lines from *Henry VI*—after which she "beams" and "blushes" in a way she never would have before. She also gets to wear loafers instead of those pesky high heels— so much easier to step into when one has to run out across a dewy lawn to investigate the appearance of a creepy puppet. By story's end, the puppet has been revealed as the hiding place for a stash of stolen jewels, and the Shakespearean actor, no longer a suspect, ties up the bard with the mystery most satisfyingly by quoting some lines from *As You Like It*: "All the world's a stage, / And the men and women merely players," he tells the girls, adding, "Has it ever occurred to you that people are really puppets in this world?"

The same feeling was starting to permeate the world outside River Heights as well, which was becoming more complicated by the hour, it seemed. The sixties were transforming every aspect of American culture from music to clothes to politics, and women were at the forefront of many of the changes. In November of 1961 fifty thousand housewives had organized "Women Strike for Peace" to protest the ongoing militarism and nuclear proliferation of the cold war. The strikers were "perfectly ordinary looking women, clad in sundresses and pushing baby carriages," marveled a report in *Newsweek*. "They looked like women you would see...shopping at the village market, or attending PTA meetings." That same year, President Kennedy appointed the Commission on the Status of Women, with Eleanor Roosevelt as honorary chair, which eventually led to the Equal Pay Act of 1963. Though the group decided that an Equal Rights Amendment was not necessary for the time being, it was the first acknowledgment on the part of the government that women's issues mattered. Women, as *Harper's Magazine* noted in 1962, were "ardently determined to extend their vocation beyond the kitchen, bedroom and nursery." In 1963 a poster advertising a public appearance by Betty Friedan challenged, "What kind of woman are you?"

As the decade progressed, the culture only seemed to shift faster and faster. The percentage of married women who worked had hit 30 percent in 1960—double the number in 1940—and it kept growing. While Nancy was going on an African safari in *The Spider Sapphire Mystery* (1968), the Vietnam War raged and the student movement that cropped up to oppose it became, in the words of one historian, "the final ingredient for the rebirth of feminism." Within the movement, a kind of "macho radicalism" prevailed, and women were fed up with it. The call for revolution went out across campuses and cities nationwide, and, in the words of radical feminist Charlotte Bunch, the personal became political.

In a split that echoed the divide between feminists of the 1920s and the generation that came after them, the women's lib movement divided into two camps: the radical feminists, who wanted to dismantle what they viewed as a patriarchal class system and saw themselves as a single, politically oppressed unit; and the less militant groups, like NOW (National Organization for Women), which had been founded in 1966 by Betty Friedan and others to press for "integration, not separation, and reform, not revolution." As things heated up, protests took many forms. One of the more memorable ones occurred in 1968, when members of the Women's Liberation Front threw their bras, girdles, and other symbols of oppressive female beauty standards into a trash can outside the Miss America Pageant in Atlantic City. Despite the fact that they were being monitored by FBI anti-riot agents, they managed to get into the pageant hall and create a ruckus loud enough to be heard at home by television audiences, shouting, "No More Miss America" and "Freedom for Women." Young America ruled the culture, and it was not shy about making its myriad voices heard. The cover of the September 30, 1970, issue of *off our backs: a women's liberation biweekly* showed a woman on a motorcycle wearing a flak jacket and holding a baby in the crook of her arm.

While women in their twenties and thirties heralded the intrepid Nancy Drew of their youth, for young girls both the new books in the series and the revised old ones (of which there were nineteen by 1969) served as the antidote to everything happening off the page. Nancy's car was fashionable, her hair was now in a neat pageboy, and she had lost the gloves and hats of her early days, but she was still a steady, stable influence. "When you have to top last year's sales figures, isn't it nice to know there's a new Nancy Drew," ran the copy at the top of a 1968 Grosset & Dunlap sales pitch. The sleuth—"titian-haired, still with those twinkling, serious, interesting blue eyes...[wearing] double-knit suits, stretch pants and stacked heels"—became the subject of more and more admiring articles that marveled at how she continued to defy the counterculture with such success. "Remember how you used to thrill to the adventures of Nancy Drew?" a piece in the *Chicago Tribune* teased. "She's still around and still a best seller." Noting that Ned had managed, after all this time, only to be promoted to "special friend," the writer then pointed out that the cranky librarian she had interviewed, who disapproved of the books, was, in fact, "the only female below the age of 50 who didn't tell us: 'Of *course* I read Nancy Drew when I was little.'" Nancy had successfully made the transition from the Atomic Age to the Age of Aquarius, and she had done it her way. "The dauntless, bewitching girl detective is still happening," wrote another admirer. "In a world of gaudy exhibitionism, subteens find refuge in Nancy's enviable, secure, conservative world... Like the Land of Oz, Nancy Drew Land is in another time dimension."

Both of these articles, as well as several others in the late 1960s, identified Harriet as Carolyn Keene. She had been referring to herself that way for some time, especially when she thought it gave her more authority with her editors ("Your inference that I do not know how to construct a good mystery...is a bitter dose to ask Carolyn Keene to swallow," she wrote to Anne Hagan at one point), but only now had she consented to such a revelation in public. She had done it for the simplest reason possible: She was tired of other people trying to claim the name for themselves.

She had had another nasty round with Walter Karig, or rather the ghost of Walter Karig since he had died in 1956, when a reader who wrote in to the *Sacramento Bee* in California was erroneously told that Karig was Carolyn Keene. ("Mr. Karig never was Carolyn Keene," she wrote back, equally erroneously. "As for proof of my authorship of the books, Mr. Karig has been dead for many years!") The biggest blow, however, and the decisive one for Harriet, had been the 1966 publication of a book by Howard Garis's son, Roger Garis. Called *My Father Was Uncle Wiggily*, the book was a harmless, rather self-involved memoir, but Garis did imply that his parents had been essentially responsible for the Bobbsey Twins and that his father had written the Tom Swift books from scratch. Howard Garis himself had died in 1962, so he was not around to prove or disprove any of his son's claims for him. "Needless to say I would like to go to court about this," Harriet wrote to a friend in the business, "but our attorneys say one has to prove either libel or financial harm. They also tell us that the book probably will not have much of a sale and perhaps it would be better to let the whole thing die a natural death." But she could not help a bit of petty retaliation. "I am also enclosing a copy of material sent to Miss Elisabeth Stevens [*sic*], who is writing an article on the BOBBSEY TWINS for Life magazine," she wrote to another friend. "It may or may not get published, but if it should be, and Roger Garis sees it, I am wondering what his reaction will be. On purpose I've left out his parents as among the ghost writers." She also wrote to Grosset & Dunlap's publicity department, enclosing a complimentary article from 1966. "It will give you an idea of the kind of publicity we are permitting. For years we kept the ghost-writing angle a secret because children liked to think of an author as one individual without complications. But now, with Roger Garis's unwarranted claims for his parents, I decided we would have to break down and tell the true story."

There was another reason why Harriet threw herself into this new campaign with such zeal. The year before Roger Garis published his book, Russell Adams had died, leaving her bereft. As ever, she was determined to work through her pain. One of her employees at the time remembered that Harriet seemed to have "decided she was going to have a new life and start over. She [was] not one to...feel sorry for herself. By her behavior, it was evident that she just decided that she was not going to die because her husband died." Having lost her partner, the man who had supported her in her unorthodox decision to take over the Syndicate and for thirty-five years after, Harriet turned as much to her fictional family as her real one for comfort.

Suddenly she was everywhere as articles began to appear like wildfire. The press, which had long wanted to reveal the secrets of the Stratemeyer Syndicate, was now thrilled to get the real story behind the rising "it" girl of the 1960s women's lib movement, Nancy Drew. The opportunity to interview the woman who they thought had dreamed her up was too good to pass up. "THIS GRANNY MASTERMINDS THE THRILLS AND SPILLS," ran one headline. In a piece in the *New York Times*, Harriet, by now almost eighty, held forth about her books from a rocking chair in her Maplewood living room. "'They don't have hippies in them,' she said in an interview in her 14-room home here. 'And none of the characters have love affairs or get pregnant or take dope.' Mrs. Adams, writing under assorted male and female pseudonyms, is the mastermind of several mystery adventure series that have been thrilling and chilling children for years." Harriet, it seemed, was taking credit for everything from the Rover Boys and the Dana Girls to Nancy Drew. Never mind that many of these series had been started when she was just a child, or that she had had help in one form or another with all of them — not least from Edna. This was her moment, and she seized it.

In story after story, Harriet was portrayed as the hardest-working grandma in America. The pieces described her writing methods — primarily dictating into a Dictaphone from an outline written in a bound notebook — the ladylike atmosphere of her office, which was furnished with velvet chairs and a reproduction French desk, and the bevy of secretaries that surrounded her and Andy Svenson, who had, by this time, become a partner in the business so that he could share in the profits. He owned 25 percent of the Syndicate, which he had earned over a period of five years at 5 percent per year, while Harriet and Edna each held 37.5 percent. "One secretary spends almost full time answering the fan mail," one of the reporters noted, "which Mrs. Adams signs with different handwriting, depending on whether she is 'Carolyn Keene' or 'Laura Lee Hope.'" All at once, Harriet had declared herself single-handedly responsible for the development of several generations of America's youth. As one reporter cooed that year, "Most of us have learned to read for entertainment by reading what she has written."

While this may have been a slight exaggeration, it was perfectly true that the Syndicate's characters were by this time so familiar that they served as cultural catchwords unto themselves. Though Nancy Drew was sacred enough to avoid parody for the time being, other heroes and heroines were not. "The Bobbsey Twins in Sexville?" teased an ad for *Billy & Betty*, a new novel about a brother and sister who "live in a grotesque comic world of a futuristic American suburb where life is a series of sexual obsessions." To Harriet, who was still as conservative as ever, this must have seemed like a disgusting ploy.

Fortunately, the popularity of sexual experimentation, Eastern religions, Jimi Hendrix, Jack Kerouac, Janis Joplin, marijuana, and any number of other psychedelic 1960s by-products that seemed to emanate outward from San Francisco's Haight-Ashbury with alarming consistency had absolutely no bearing on Nancy Drew. Though the average age of her readers had gone down thanks to the newfound sophistication of America's young adults, they were as devoted to her as ever. "Apparently there is a rock-ribbed streak of conservatism in the nine-to-eleven group," summed up a 1969 article by Arthur Prager called "The Secret of Nancy Drew—Pushing Forty and Still Going Strong," which was published in the *Saturday Review*. By that time more than thirty million copies of the Nancy Drew Mystery Stories had been sold. "She is an example of the fantasy world in which prepubescent girls live in daydreams," Prager opined, and then offered a few more reasons as to her continued success, not least among them the fact that "a girl usually gets her introduction to Nancy Drew from someone else: a gift or loan from some friend or relative." As much as the sixties had changed youth culture, he observed, girls were still girls. "They will participate in outlandish fads for the sake of show, but they like things simple, basic, well organized. Just as the brashest smart aleck will still gulp down a massive lump of anguish when Amy, in *Little Women*, comes in out of the snow and says, 'Beth, the baby's dead…,' the loudest little cynic will retire to her room, curl up among the psychedelic posters and 'Legalize Pot' buttons, and devour some forty Nancy Drews in a row with deep concentration and heartfelt involvement."

WHILE NANCY DREW had been busy showing off her Shakespeare, Mildred had been learning to fly. She had been interested in it since she was a little girl, when a pilot out barnstorming on the Iowa prairie had landed his wooden-strutted "Jenny" biplane in the grass near her house in Ladora. Seized with, as she later called it, "the fever to fly," Mildred had scraped up the $15 fee for a ride, "donned a helmet and was buckled into an open cockpit for 15 minutes of joy. Off we went with a breathtaking rush," she remembered. "As we cruised over the town, I sat in a paralysis of delight, staring straight ahead until the pilot tapped me on the shoulder, pointing down." After begging to go up again and being refused by her father, who chewed her out for taking what he considered to be an enormous risk, she turned to her other passion, writing a "glorified essay on my first plane ride, greatly enlarging upon the dangers," for school. Later, in the early 1930s, she had taken it one step further, writing a juvenile series about a girl pilot named Ruth Darrow.

By the second half of the century, her interest in aviation had dovetailed perfectly with her growing curiosity about archaeology. As part of her repeated trips to visit Mayan ruins in the 1950s, she had begun to charter private planes to fly her out to remote sites. This had led, in short order, to flying lessons, and in 1964 when she was fifty-nine years old, she was awarded her pilot's license. Writing about her first solo flight for the *Toledo Times*, she admitted she had not been a natural: "Touch the throttle and it would snort with rage. Step too hard on the brakes and it would try to pitch the instructor through the windshield. Airborne, it arrogantly flew itself, tying me into a mental pretzel." Her stubbornness paid off as always, though, and when she finally got a handle on the controls, she was elated.

When flying was not adventurous enough for her, Mildred went back to Mexico for what she described as "a three-day dugout canoe trip down the crocodile-infested Usumacinta River in Mexico's most remote section of Chiapas." Even Nancy Drew could not have topped her adventures there, which included whirlpools in the river that were as large as houses, an unplanned plane crash in a swamp, a treacherous climb up a steep, mossy cliff, and having her wristwatch cut off by thieves in the middle of the night as she slept, unsuspecting, in a hammock. At sixty-two years old, Mildred was exhilarated by the whole experience, writing it up in a piece for the *Cleveland Plain Dealer*'s Sunday magazine called "A Woman Dares the Jungle." After extolling the natural beauty of the landscape ("From low, overhanging branches, huge lizards plopped into the water, barely missing the cedar log dugout. At every turn there were orchids, scarlet mushrooms, swarms of sapphire butterflies, herons, falcons, unknown exotic birds and small game"), she admitted it had been a rough ride. But not for long. "I was tired, my feet swollen, skin riddled by bites from flies, chaquistes and pulgas...The trip was worth it...I had lived in a breath-taking, enchanted world."

But despite her widening horizons, Nancy Drew was still on them. Soon after the "The Secret of Nancy Drew" was published in the *Saturday Review* in 1969, its author, Arthur Prager, received a letter from Toledo, Ohio. In his article, he had attributed all forty-three existing Nancy Drews to Harriet, and Mildred was both curious as to where he'd gotten his information and wanted to set the record straight. Prager had no way to know better, but Mildred, of course, did, and by this time she could no longer bear the machinations of the publicity machine that had put Harriet on high as Carolyn Keene. Though she was wary of going truly public, she felt compelled to correct errors on an individual basis whenever it was possible.

She had some help from a young man named Geoffrey S. Lapin, who had read the Nancy Drew books as a bored boy on summer vacation in Atlantic City in the 1950s ("the quaint world of roadster, running boards, and touring cars stayed with me into my adult years"). Something of a detective himself, he had discovered Mildred's Carolyn Keene identity several years earlier through a little research at the Baltimore library where he was employed. He had also discovered that, to his great delight, "Carolyn Keene was alive and well and living in Toledo!" After reading Prager's piece, he wrote Mildred a letter and, at her request, paid her a visit at her desk at the *Toledo Blade*. Over the course of years, he would devote countless hours to writing letters to the various publications that printed mangled versions of the history of the Syndicate and Nancy Drew.

With his one well-timed visit, Lapin set into motion a competing narrative about who the real Carolyn Keene was that made it into newspapers by the early 1970s. "The Artful Ways of Millie — Nancy Drew was her brainchild," exclaimed one of the articles. In it, Mildred was described as not only the true creator of Nancy, but as "paranoic. She's afraid that any publicity will get her in Dutch with the Stratemeyer Syndicate... 'You say anything that hurts sales, and they'll be right...on...my...neck!' Millie agonized." In spite of her own efforts to get the truth on the record, and angry as she had become about missing out on the profits from the character she considered to be her own just as much as Harriet did, she was still unwilling to cross her former employer.

But Nancy Drew was just a sideshow in Mildred's life, unlike Harriet's. It was flying that remained her best love, and by 1970 she was writing an aviation column for the *Toledo Times* called "Happy Landings." In addition to chronicling her own flight experiences, including a test run in an "acrobatic airplane designed for the sporty businessman" that left her waiting "for my bifocals to track normally again," she wrote frequently about the goings-on at Toledo's Wagon Wheel Airport and the local aviators who used it as home base. Among them, increasingly, were women. "Women these days wear coveralls, tear airplanes apart, and put them together again just to gain experience," she wrote in a 1968 "Happy Landings" column. "For proof that aerospace mechanics no longer is entirely a man's field, drop in at adult airframe class at Macomber Vocational High School any Wednesday or Thursday night. There, Mrs. Ione Shelton, a Bowling Green nurse... more than holds her own with a dozen men...Mrs. Shelton explains that her goal is not to become a certified mechanic. Instead, she seeks knowledge which will assure work being done properly on her own plane when she authorizes it." In the same column, Mildred also mentioned that a series of competitive events were being planned by the Ohio chapter of the Ninety-Nines, Amelia Earhart's original women-only flying group. "We hope men will enter," said a Toledo member of the organization, "but may the best woman win."

Independent women were not just living in Ohio, either. The women's lib movement was in full swing by now, with NOW fighting relentlessly for the Equal Rights Amendment, which finally passed in Congress in March of 1972 (but has yet to be ratified by every state in America). When Gloria Steinem and others published *Ms.*, the first national feminist magazine in 1971, the first three hundred thousand copies sold out in eight days. By the mid-1970s women's applications to law school and medical school had risen 550 percent since the start of the decade, while the number planning to teach elementary school or be nurses went from 31 percent to 10 percent. Women were on the move at last.

Mildred, a self-avowed conservative when it came to the social issues involved with feminism ("I believe in freedom," she
would tell an NPR interviewer in the early 1990s. "I don't believe
in license, which many [women] have interpreted freedom to
mean"), nonetheless covered women's lib for the *Toledo Times*
on more than one occasion. "She's Studying to Be Aggressive:
NOW Generation Surveyed for Clues to Success," published in
the summer of 1969, discussed the travails of people who, like
Mildred herself, were not quite with the times. Not only was it
impossible to tell the sexes apart thanks to the fad for long hair,
she groused, but girls had become, in her opinion, almost uncon-
scionably forward. "'A man can't get a good night's rest any more,'
complained a long-suffering father. He told me that his phone
rang the other night at 2 A.M. 'Is Georgie there?' inquired the
voice of a sweet chick. 'He's in bed,' the father answered. 'Why
the hell aren't you?'"

On the eve of the massive Women's Strike for Equality, which
took place on the fiftieth anniversary of the passage of the woman
suffrage amendment, August 26, 1970, and brought thousands of
women to the streets in protest all over the country—fifty thousand in New York City alone—Mildred's coverage of her gender's
plight took on a more serious aspect. In an article about whether
or not Toledo women were militant feminists, she found that
much like their counterparts around the country, "Women of
Toledo are less concerned with loss of small male courtesies than
with equal job and pay opportunities." For all her nay-saying,
Mildred was a feminist at heart, even if she preferred not to be
labeled one. "MALE PSYCHES SHAKEN, MILLIE REPORTS AS SHE
LANDS NEW BROADSIDE," screamed a headline on one of her
pieces. She had written a column the week before criticizing "the

unfairness of the male sex to women." Now she was experiencing what was fast becoming a by-product of feminism in America. "If there's one thing the Women's Lib Movement has done, it's to make me increasingly unpopular with men."

Though she had a different perspective than most reporters, even other women, due to her age, Mildred was hardly alone in her reporting on women's lib. It was hard to pick up a magazine or a newspaper without finding some kind of coverage. While *Ms.* was specifically devoted to issues of feminism and equality, even old standbys like *Family Circle*, once a haven for cookie recipes and harmless fiction, took up the cause. "Are you hurting your daughter without knowing it?" it asked its anxious, newly liberated readers in February 1971. "Are you—like many of our schools—teaching your daughter to have fewer aspirations than the boys in her class?" By two and a half columns into this piece, the author had gotten, as usual, to the evils of series books. Once again, however, the girl detective emerged not only unscathed, but revered as an icon of the new female order: "Of course there are books in which girls figure as principal characters: Cherry Ames is a student nurse, Vicki Barr a flight stewardess, and Peggy Lane an aspiring actress. But these girls seem somewhat pallid beside Tom Swift, budding scientist, and Tom Corbett, space explorer," the author wrote. "The one exception, the girl who outsells them all—more than a million copies a year as compared with 40,000 for Cherry Ames—is Nancy Drew, who tootles about the country in her roadster, solving mysteries and living a life of freedom. Interestingly, a psychoanalyst...discovered...that Nancy Drew's image satisfies the young girl's daydream that 'maybe I can be a boy.'"

As pop psychology took off, the language of self-awareness and self-fulfillment that came to be a hallmark of the 1970s permeated the ever-proliferating examinations of Nancy, many of

which were injected with pseudo-Freudian theories to boot.
Even the Syndicate got on the bandwagon. "Psychologists say
that Nancy Drew provides a perfect release for pre-teen girls,"
Andy Svenson told one reporter cheerfully. A sociologist at UC
San Francisco thought that her success was due to the fact that
"she's an atypical girl, an adventurous girl who could somehow
compete with a boy and not upset the sexual role definitions." He
also thought, however, that no small amount of nostalgia was fu-
eling her revival. "We sense things are changing very quickly," he
told *McCall's* magazine, "and traditional values are being challenged. When this happens, one looks inward to anchoring
points for some kind of stability." Nancy as anchor: It must have
made sense to the group of Nancy Drew–loving adults who answered an ad in a California newspaper and met for a "Nancy
Drew Circle" to discuss their favorite sleuth. In addition to husbands who were dragged to the event by their "N.D. Freak"
wives, there was a woman who worked for the local telephone
company who confessed to the *San Francisco Sunday Examiner
and Chronicle*: "You can really get into her character. I traveled
through Canada on a vacation, signing myself Nancy Drew."
There was also a more sobering story about the power of the girl
detective. "'In Hungary, I was in the resistance to the war,' Gisele
Chobaji told the group. 'We couldn't endure all we had to if we
couldn't read something beyond realism. Our two favorites were
Nancy Drew and the Agatha Christie books, we read one a day
in the bomb shelters.'" In another article, yet one more former
obsessive gushed: "Is it possible that there breathes somewhere a
female between the ages of nine and 49 who doesn't know Nancy
Drew?" Nancy was like the cool girl next door, and she was just
modern enough to get away with it. "I wasn't thinking about
women's liberation when I wrote the books," Harriet told this

same reporter. "I've never thought of myself as a women's libber but I do believe that women have brains. Nothing makes me angrier than to have my intelligence insulted."

Given this statement and the nature of the press coverage of Nancy, the Syndicate's big idea for 1973 seemed woefully out of step with the times. *The Nancy Drew Cookbook: Clues to Good Cooking* was full of quaint recipes with a secret included in each one ("A DETECTIVE NEEDS ENERGY: Add more protein to your cake by mixing ½ cup of finely chopped pecans to the maple sugar mixture") seemed like a thing of the past before it even hit bookshelves. With page after page of kitschy dishes named after Nancy's various mysteries, like Crumbling Wall Coffee Cake, Tolling Bell Tuna Rolls, Mysterious Letter Chili, and a host of others, it almost seemed designed to infuriate feminists who had taken up the sleuth with a vengeance. Young fans bought the book, but press reactions ran the gamut from politely amused to outright enraged. Fortunately for Grosset and the Syndicate, as one reviewer noted, "There are some books that need no reviews to insure their success. This is one of them. If only one per cent of Miss Keene's readers buy this book, she'll sell millions of copies."

Other pieces were less kind, harping on the throwback nature of a cookbook for girls in a time of social change for woman. "People are always asking me if Nancy is a 'women's libber' [Mrs. Adams] confided, sounding a little weary of the notion," the *New York Daily News* reported. "'I suppose,' and here she brightened, 'that Nancy was ahead of her time.' In the same breath, though, Mrs. Adams refuses to concede that Nancy might lose any analytical powers by putting on an apron." No doubt when she received her copy of the article, Harriet also refused to admit the implications of the fact that it ran on the same page of the *Daily*

News as a story about women at MIT demanding that the prestigious university admit even more women.

And then there was *Ms.*, which ran a first-person essay about Nancy Drew and her culinary adventures that not only established her—in her original form—even more firmly in the feminist pantheon, but took Grosset & Dunlap to task for its "recent innovations." The writer did not like the revisions, and she liked the cookbook even less. "Even though Nancy Drew was sixteen and I was only nine, I knew she and I were kindred spirits," the writer rhapsodized as she looked back on her childhood sleuthing exploits investigating a suspicious geography teacher. "I remember Nancy the intelligent, go-getting detective." Distressed about *Clues to Good Cooking*, which she believed threatened Nancy's "feminist value," the author went straight to the source, whom she referred to, of course, as "Ms." Adams. There, she learned that "Harriet Adams says she would much rather write a Nancy Drew detective guide."

This was, in no uncertain terms, untrue. Though Harriet had balked at a sewing book and one other offshoot of the cookbook, original plans for the *Clues to Good Cooking* had included further volumes "on cookies and candies, then perhaps on other specialties." It was only after years of effort on the part of others, and, perhaps, the subtle force of a friendly memo from a bookseller in Charlotte, North Carolina, that she decided to put Nancy Drew in the kind of book she had previously associated only with the Hardy Boys. "I think the NANCY DREW COOKBOOK is a cute idea and we are selling them here in Charlotte," the writer, who was a man, no less, began. "But I also think, from women's liberation point of view, that we may be relegating the famous girl detective to the kitchen."

> *I feel that a better selling book would be a Nancy Drew Detective Handbook type of project. I mention this because of the great increase in women in police work. In the future this country may have as many women as men in police departments. Such a Nancy Drew Handbook could be different from the Hardy Boys' Handbook because you could use world-wide situations. In fact a chapter on Interpol would be highly interesting.*
>
> *Some people might argue that girls who read the Hardys would buy the* HARDY BOYS' DETECTIVE HANDBOOK, *but the overwhelming number of girls who peruse the Nancy Drew section of my bookshop indicate to me that a Nancy Drew Detective Manual could sell equally as well, and maybe better than the Hardys.*
>
> *If you can excuse me for making a title suggestion how about* "How To Become A Girl Detective."

Though a second version of *The Hardy Boys Detective Handbook* had gone to press at the same time as *The Nancy Drew Cookbook*, it would take until 1979 for Harriet and the Syndicate staff to realize the wisdom of this suggestion. *The Nancy Drew Sleuth Book: Clues to Good Sleuthing* was finally released that year, and on the back cover, the real appeal of Nancy Drew was acknowledged at last: "Every reader of the NANCY DREW MYSTERY STORIES has wished at some time that she, too, could solve a mystery. This is now possible."

13

BECOMING
THE GIRL DETECTIVE

BY THE LATE 1970s, Harriet had taken to referring to Nancy
Drew as her daughter in interviews, and the sleuth had become
Harriet's way of communicating her values to the world at large.
She was as protective of Nancy's image as she was of her own,
whether it was in new titles or a revision that was still being
worked over. "I feel you overstepped your position in trying to revamp Nancy's character," she wrote to her old nemesis at Grosset, Anne Hagan, in 1972. "She is not all those dreadful things
you accuse her of and in many instances you have actually
wanted to make her negative." The following year, she was in-
censed on her "child's" behalf yet again: "Anne, are your remarks
intended to mend story holes or do you get some sadistic fun out
of downgrading and offending me? It will take me a long time to
live down the remark 'Nancy sounds like a nasty female.'" She
was even more distressed about the revisions to *The Clue in the
Crumbling Wall*: "I must tell you quite frankly that you cause me

a great deal of unnecessary work, which brings my creation of a new story to an abrupt halt. There are hundreds of unwarranted word changes which are apparently whims on your part, like 'peer out' to 'look out.' What bothers me even more is your supposition that you, not I, know what Nancy, Mr. Drew, et al. would say or do, like deleting Nancy's lovely gesture of putting an arm around an elderly woman who has just done the young detective a great favor. In the future will you please stick to the functions of an editor and not try steering my fictional family into a non–Carolyn Keene direction."

But if Harriet thought Nancy's treatment by Grosset & Dunlap was rough, she was in for a big surprise. By allowing her beloved detective to move into the cultural mainstream as a symbol to girls and women everywhere, Harriet had unwittingly opened her up to the so-called highest praise of all: imitation — or, rather, parody. It's not difficult to imagine how Harriet must have felt in the summer of 1974, when that bastion of foulmouthed humor, *National Lampoon* magazine, decided to set its sights on Nancy in the June "Pubescence" issue. Along with ads for "I am not a crook" Nixon watches ($19.95 apiece) and features ranging from "VD Comics" to "Masturbation Foto Funnies" appeared "The Case of the Missing Heiress," in which Nancy Drew and Patty Hearst meet up. Hearst, still on the run with the Symbionese Liberation Army after her kidnapping some months before and a spectacular robbery at a Sacramento bank, had recently made headlines yet again by participating in a shootout at a sporting goods store. In the *Lampoon* version, Nancy was called in to deduce the identity of Hearst's kidnapper, who turned out to be not the SLA but her own newspaper magnate father. The SLA got involved in the plot regardless, trying to kill Nancy along the way by giving her an overdose of Midol, the

over-the-counter remedy for menstrual cramps. Full of racial ep-
ithets and outrageous situations, the story wound down with a
gentle mockery of the teen sleuth's propensity for emerging unscathed from any situation.

> "There's still one thing I don't understand," Bess Marvin called
> from the rumble seat as they motored east for River Heights...
> "When the SLA gave you that fatal overdose of Midol, how
> come you still could set the fire and escape without being
> knocked out?" "That's still a real puzzler," Nancy laughed
> pertly. "I still haven't been able to figure that out for myself!"
> With a chorus of appreciative chuckles, Nancy and her chums
> sped merrily into the darkening landscape, little knowing that
> Nancy's next adventure, *The Secret of the Fatal Motoring
> Mishap*, would solve more than a few mysteries.

Depending on how you thought of it, Nancy had either
scraped rock bottom or reached the very height of popular culture. But when the *New York Times Magazine* ran another parody, "The Real Nancy Drew," in October of the following year,
Harriet could not keep quiet. The piece, which ran as a mock interview with an aged Nancy, did everything from imply that the
sleuth had grown up to be a lonely old maid ("Old age has its
compensations and royalties," she answers jauntily to that question) to state outright that George was a lesbian. "George didn't
come clean with me, pretending she was a tomboy, when actually she was a... Q: She didn't come out of the closet? A: Kept it
locked and threw away the key." It was too much for Harriet to
bear. She wrote a letter to the *Times*, berating them for violating
their own standards as well as hers, and for "belittling and reversing the principal characters in this famous series (which I write
under the name Caroline [*sic*] Keene) with innuendoes of sex

and pornography. Surely the millions of loyal Nancy Drew fans of all ages will find this travesty most distasteful." In her reply, the parody's author simply piled on more. "I did not tell all," she wrote. "Now that my back is up against the haunted house, I feel it is my duty to set the record straight... it was Nancy Drew who backed Calvin Coolidge all the way, who was the first woman to wear a tube dress in the jungle in order to be more feminine, who photographed Bomba the Jungle Boy for *Life* magazine (making him an overnight sensation), who personally slapped Bertrand Russell to teach him that infidelity doesn't pay." Nancy had officially gone from private to public property.

As much as the besmirching of her prized "daughter" bothered Harriet, it was good for business. By 1976 sales of the series had been increasing steadily for four years, reversing the gradual drop-off that had been happening since the late 1950s. "Nobody's sure why," one reporter wrote. "Except mothers who grew up with the books now seem to be buying them for their daughters." Often these mothers were unaware that the books had been revised, but in any case the new Nancy seemed to be exciting enough for the younger set. The nostalgia factor was still running high, too, as women's libbers fell more in love with Nancy than ever. "In the Drew books, there were mysteries to be solved and she solved them," the president of NOW told the *Philadelphia Inquirer.* "[Most juvenile heroines] never did anything. I think the idea that she may have had a lot to do with liberating women is probably the case." A former staffer at *Ms.* opined that "Nancy Drew, whose exploits have filled the contents of 50 books, is one heroine who qualifies in many ways as a role model for young feminists," leaving the reporter on the story to conclude that "her daring, self-confident, competent personality may be increasingly attractive to today's 'new woman'—and today's children."

Part of her appeal, it seemed, was that she didn't make a big fuss about her independence. "Their impact on me was simply that I read every one I could get my hands on," explained one fan, now twenty-six years old. "I was excited by what she was doing. I didn't realize how feminist they were because I sort of figured that's the way the world was." Taking her passion to the extreme, another woman wrote, "I can foresee the day when Nancy Drew stories will be transmitted via satellite to colonies on the moon... She'll be 19, wear a space helmet, and drive her own space ship. And if the space ship runs short of atomic energy... Nancy will say: 'Don't worry... only one rocket is out.'"

Nancy had become such a familiar, accepted presence in the cultural landscape that she had even breached the stratosphere of groovy music. Twenty-four-year-old folk singer Janis Ian, one of the country's hottest stars at the moment thanks to her hit single "At Seventeen," called her up as a reference point in a 1976 interview. "Janis Ian is proud to be arrogant. She figures she's earned it. 'Arrogance means to me that you know what you're doing, and you're not polite or humble about it... It's like self-confidence, but self-confidence is like Nancy Drew. Nancy Drew was self-confident and if anybody said to her "Nancy, you suck," Nancy would say "Okay," and walk away. Now if Nancy had been arrogant, she would have said "Fuck you." That's the difference between arrogance and self-confidence to me.'"

By the time Janis Ian made her declaration, Harriet was the sole remaining guarder of Nancy's integrity. In March 1974 Edna had died, after years of very little communication between the sisters. Harriet noted the event in her diary as if her sister was someone she had been vaguely acquainted with: "Edna Squier passed away." After taking only three days off of work to fly down to St. Petersburg for the funeral and offering her condolences to

Edna's daughter, Camilla, whom she did not know well, she went right back to work. Edna's 37.5 percent of the Syndicate, which she had hung on to until the bitter end, reverted back to Harriet. Her death, which might once have had a major effect on the Syndicate, came and went. Harriet had long ago written her out of the history of the company, anyway. Occasionally she would tell a reporter that her sister had helped out for "a few years" before becoming inactive, but that was the most press Edna received, so her years of work on the Nancy Drew books and other series went virtually unheralded at her death.

It was Andy Svenson who had taken over Edna's role, so it came as a much larger blow to Harriet when he died the following year, at the age of sixty-five, from bone cancer. Harriet bought back his 25 percent of the company from his widow for the price of $174,508.34 and assigned her the rights to the Happy Hollisters series (1953–70), one of Svenson's projects, which he had based on the experiences of his own family. Then she was alone but for the three assistants she had hired over the past decade. Together, they continued to turn out books in the four surviving series, the Dana Girls, Hardy Boys, Bobbsey Twins, and, of course, Nancy Drew. In 1974 Nancy had solved the *Mystery of the Glowing Eye*. In 1975 it was *The Secret of the Forgotten City*. In 1976 her adventure was called *The Sky Phantom*, and it took Nancy to flight school in the Midwest, where she unraveled mysteries involving a hijacked plane and a horse thief. In spite of her efforts to make Nancy Drew more up-to-date, however, Harriet was only willing to go so far. When *Rolling Stone* ran a little piece about the Hardy Boys in the fall of 1976, it couldn't help but mention that "Mrs. Adams originally agreed to be interviewed for this article, although she had never heard of *Rolling Stone*. Her secretary went out and bought her a copy, which happened to be last fall's 'men's issue' and included articles and illustrations on sexual themes. Mrs. Adams cancelled the interview."

Part of the reason for the magazine's interest was that after Harriet's years of arguing with Warner Brothers, and several more years of negotiating with Universal Studios and ABC, she had finally gotten the rights to make television shows out of the Hardy Boys and Nancy Drew. In 1969 there had been a Hardy Boys Saturday morning cartoon, but it had lasted only two years. Now the real thing was about to hit the airwaves. Both shows were produced by, as one article described them, "two extremely bright and pretty young women, who, like millions of others, survived adolescence with the help of Carolyn Keene's Nancy Drew books." Both "30ish" ("With an accent on the ish," one said. "Not too much accent—we're not 35ish"), they had worked their way up from secretaries to associate producers. The Syndicate television series were their big chance to break through the glass ceiling. "We're not card carrying feminists but things are opening up," one of them told a reporter. "I could see myself being an associate producer for the next 50 years if I didn't do something."

After casting teen heartthrobs Shaun Cassidy and Parker Stevenson to play the Hardy brothers and actress Pamela Sue Martin to play Nancy, the shows began shooting. Each was an hour long, slated to broadcast on alternate Sunday nights in the newly conceived "family" slot designed to appeal to—and not offend—an audience of all ages. The viewing public, critics included, waited impatiently to see their favorite detectives brought to the small screen at last, and they knew the reason for the delay. "It has taken Nancy Drew and the Hardy Boys a long time to make it to television," one anticipatory article explained. "This is because Harriet S. Adams, who as Carolyn Keene is responsible for the 'Nancy Drew' mysteries and as Franklin W. Dixon is the author of the 'Hardy Boys' stories, wanted assurance that the characters would be depicted as they are shown in the books. Now, with the coming of the Family Hour concept in viewing, Mrs. Adams's requirements have been met."

Harriet was not the only person with a vested interest in the series. In 1975 Mildred had written to NBC—the station she thought, incorrectly, was airing the program—upon first hearing mention of the show. The letter she received in return, which threatened legal action if she so much as attempted to get in touch with the Syndicate, went so far as to accuse her of potential libel. Mildred was irate. Writing back, she sputtered: "For more than 45 years I have faithfully abided by the terms, making no claim whatsoever to story material, the pen name Carolyn Keene, titles, or any share of the profits. I do feel I have inherent right with respect to the character, and to say otherwise would be a denial of birthright." Though it was not entirely true that she had made no claim to the series, having by now told her friends at the University of Iowa and several newspapers about her role, she had never tried to make any money off it. Believing she might have a stake in a television show, she saw what she thought might be her chance to do so legally and had simply written to inquire as such. Now she was furious. "Without reason, you have threatened and accused me of untrue and false statements, and of contract violation, demanding that I brand myself as a liar. This, I resent, as my character long has been established as the opposite—an honest and honorable person. Likewise, I believe in fairness and justice. I intend to abide by an agreement I have made."

Soon thereafter Geoff Lapin, who was still making it his business to tell everyone he could about Mildred's participation in the series, dropped her a line to see if she was getting anything out of Nancy's appearance on network television. She wrote back appreciatively: "Dear Mr. Lapin: Indeed, I do remember you, and also I knew of your fine defense [of me] as the unknown author of Nancy Drew...Intended to write you about it, but I've been on an exciting fly-your-own plane trip—the Louisiana Air Tour, and hadn't managed it." She was seventy-three years old. Then, summing up the incident with the lawyer with characteristic pragmatism, she finished: "When series hit TV I tried to assert TV rights. The Syndicate, network and produter [*sic*] all came down on me, threatening lawsuit. According to my contract, they insist I don't exist." Her temper was on the rise, and she couldn't resist a quick postscript in which she felt compelled to tell her young friend, "Mrs. Adams, so far as I know, never made a success of any books that she started from scratch. Her fortune and success rests almost entirely upon Nancy Drew and the Hardy Boys."

Whether this was true or simply her opinion, it's hard to imagine she wasn't a little bit satisfied when the show did not turn out to be the great success everyone involved had hoped for. While Harriet was very pleased with it, having won her various battles over sex, drugs, and violence, no one else seemed to be. A few months earlier, ABC had started airing *Charlie's Angels*, a much racier show about not one but three female detectives, and though no explicit comparison was made, Nancy's clean, wholesome adventures must have paled in contrast. In addition, TV viewers were just coming off of seven years of the *Mary Tyler Moore Show*, which much more accurately depicted the feminist ideals of the day, and *Wonder Woman*, a literally strong character, was on the air as well. The producers also ran into the same problem that had plagued the 1930s Nancy movies: No one wanted to accept another person's idea of what Nancy looked like or how she behaved. The show had made her a brunette, a huge mistake that was only one of many. "How could they take an untalented little snip who looks frighteningly like Patty Hearst and cast her as the 'red-haired' detective of my youth?" snarled one embittered critic. She was equally harsh on George: "The television series only gives us George, but has provided her with Bess' timid personality." Bess was added in during the next season, and the actress playing George cut her long brown hair to satisfy outraged fans who demanded the proper boyish style, but it was too late. As for Ned, they had gotten him wrong, too, and for all the worst reasons: "He was the strong, silent type, a far cry from the whimpering bumbler who appears in the television series. This, of course, is producer Glen Larson's nod to women's lib. But he's missed the point. You don't make a female character strong by playing her opposite a buffoon. You just make her strong... Changing Nancy Drew makes about as much sense as giving Superman a mustache."

In short order, poor Nancy Drew was voted a total failure. "Ratings for Pamela Sue Martin's 'Nancy Drew' series started off with lovely promise, but then, week by week, began to lose a point or so until, finally, the ratings were below the 30 percent share of audience which is classified as minimum success," wrote one paper. "Why? We conducted a fast phone survey in an effort to find out. The answer seems to be that the shallow level of the youthful mystery detective stories managed to attract initial interest from all-family viewers, but it could not hold that audience. Virtually all of those who had watched the series said they would have continued if the shows had been more adult, offered more meaningful plots and more in-depth characterizations." Harriet's plan to keep the show clean had backfired—her requirements had hamstrung the show's writers and producers. For several generations of women and girls who had by this time internalized Nancy, seeing her and her chums portrayed in such a clumsy manner was a huge disappointment. As one sad fan put it in an essay she wrote upon finding an old flashlight she had bought as a child: "At a younger age I thought that I'd be another Nancy Drew. (I had even thought that I'd one day be dating a Ned Nickerson, Nancy's college beau.)...Anyway, whatever the reason for the drop in ratings, I personally hope that the series makes it. Nancy, you see, is a friend of mine. I grew up with her."

But devotion, no matter how pure, was not enough to save the girl detective. When the Nancy Drew series did not do well enough on its own, her character was folded into the Hardy Boys show. Pamela Sue Martin quit immediately, unwilling to share star billing, and went straight to the tabloids, which ate up her story. "Pamela Sue Martin: TV's Virginal Nancy Drew Is Super-Sexy Lover in Real Life!" Two weeks later she offered the *National Enquirer* a choice quote: "I'm not gearing my career to the people who watch Nancy Drew. Playing a hooker or a really different kind of character would be great. If I did it well, it wouldn't hurt me with the audience at all."

Harriet, who no doubt never imagined she would read the word "hooker" in the same paragraph as the name of her beloved fictional daughter, must surely have thought things could only get better from there. A new Nancy Drew was hired, and the combined Nancy Drew/Hardy Boys hour continued airing, but by the fall of 1978 Nancy Drew was removed entirely after being eclipsed by Shaun Cassidy and Parker Stevenson's teen idol status. Nancy's television sojourn may have been over, but Pamela Sue Martin was not finished with her yet. There was one place that every ambitious young actress who was willing to do certain things for her career ended up in the 1970s, and that was where

Martin went next. In July of 1978 she appeared, barely trench-coated and holding a magnifying glass, on the cover of *Playboy*. "TV's Nancy Drew Undraped," read the cover line. Inside the magazine, Martin was photographed in everything from a transparent teddy to a strategically placed swath of red velvet to practically nothing at all. Interspersed with the racy shots were a photo of her with Parker Stevenson, aka Frank Hardy, and one of her in a prissy suit drinking milk. "Pamela's tired of the assumption she's as bland as a glass of milk," read the caption. "Someone recently said to me, 'Gee, you're dispelling all my illusions about Nancy Drew.' I said, 'What the hell do you think? You think I'm Nancy Drew?'" In the full-page interview that came next, she bashed her former role with abandon. "Nancy Drew never cried or experienced an inordinate amount of pain. There was never any tragedy or extreme emotion. Never a kissing scene or any sign that she would indulge with the opposite sex. A big moment for her was coming across an old skeleton in a dungeon and screaming. Or being attacked by a bat in Transylvania."

Harriet, as one of her writers put it, was "fit to be tied." Ready to sue, she was advised by a lawyer to let the whole thing blow over or risk even more publicity. Instead, she fought back by running ads, at great cost, in *Playboy* and elsewhere denouncing the piece. Then she simply refused to acknowledge what had happened in public in anything but the most oblique terms. "Can the reputation of an 18-year-old sleuth — ingenious, alert, the darling of generations of preadolescent girls — survive the Seventies unsullied by sex and violence?" questioned one newspaper she talked to. "Harriet S. Adams is battling to see that it does. 'I fight publishers, scriptwriters, and magazines constantly. It's gotten to be one confrontation after another...They want to put in not just violence, but profanity, politics, and sex.'" Though she had only recently said she thought women's libbers took their politics "too far," when another interviewer asked Harriet about her difficulties, she "confessed to having a hard time fighting for what she believes in, not just with the TV studio, but also within the syndicate, of which she is a senior partner. 'Why? Because of men,' she said. 'They don't like women who disagree, and they don't like women to have their own ideas.'"

14

WILL THE REAL
CAROLYN KEENE
PLEASE STAND UP?

"WE'RE EXTRAORDINARILY HAPPY—and we always have been—about our association with the syndicate, and with Harriet Adams in particular," Harold Roth, the president of Grosset & Dunlap told the *New York Times* in 1977. In addition to being "the youngest lady her age I've ever met"—she was eighty-four—and "a terrific human being as well as a business associate," he continued, Harriet's "royalties would rank, I am sure, with the absolute top of any author, including best-selling authors on the fiction and nonfiction lists. I'm certain of that."

There was seemingly no end of love to spread around between the Syndicate and Grosset & Dunlap, which by then had been publishing Stratemeyer books for more than seventy years. What the company's president did not say, however, was that even though Harriet's royalties were substantial, well over half a million dollars in 1977 in today's terms, they were still a tiny percentage of the overall earnings of her books. Despite repeated efforts,

Harriet had never had any success in getting Grosset to raise her royalty rate. An attempt in 1969, when she wrote a letter trying to make her case, was typical of her methods. "It occurred to me recently that when my father signed a contract with your company some forty years ago re Nancy Drew and the Hardy Boys the books sold for fifty cents and he received a royalty of two cents; in other words four per cent. Since that time the rate has never changed, which makes a unique situation in publishing." Harriet knew what was wrong—standard publishing contracts now included a graduated royalty rate that increased according to the number of copies that were sold, and Grosset refused to give the Syndicate that deal—but she didn't know how to assert herself in order to fix it. So she employed her usual method of passive aggression papered over with false cheerfulness. "Don't you agree that it is high time we update our thinking in line with the present day practices and increase the percentage or royalty to world renowned Carolyn Keene, Franklin W. Dixon and Laura Lee Hope?"

Her challenge went unanswered, and as she had many times before, she let it drop. Frustrated as she may have been, Harriet was also intensely loyal to Grosset & Dunlap, not least because she was still grateful that back in 1930 they had accepted her, a woman with no business training, as a legitimate replacement for her father at the time of his death. But the other Syndicate employees held no such illusions about what was happening. In the late 1970s, Harriet had brought her three assistants into the Syndicate as what she called "junior partners," giving them each a percentage in the company. Though Harriet did not seem to realize it, this new blood knew that something had to change if the company was going to survive. The younger women sent Harriet back to the negotiating table, and when she failed once again, she finally listened to their arguments about switching to another publisher who would offer the company a more lucrative contract.

They found it in Simon & Schuster. Bolstered by a promise of higher royalties, the Syndicate signed with their new partner to publish all future books in the Bobbsey Twins, Hardy Boys, and Nancy Drew series (the Dana Girls series ended in 1979). S&S also wanted to host a blowout celebration for Nancy Drew's fiftieth anniversary, which was coming up in 1980, a wise appeal to Harriet, who had been extremely disappointed that the seventy-fifth anniversary of the Bobbsey Twins had come and gone in 1979 without much fanfare. Though the change was critical to the company's continuation, according to one of the junior partners, "Harriet just absolutely held out for the longest time. She really did not want to make that move to Simon & Schuster or anybody else for that matter, because of this intense feeling of loyalty. Even as we were losing money." Though Harriet planned to leave the books Grosset had already published with them, she failed to mention to her longtime publisher that she had sold the rights to all future titles to somebody else. When they heard the news, Grosset was furious with her. In a panic over the loss of their lucrative series, they filed a lawsuit for breach of contract and copyright infringement, eventually asking for $300 million in damages. In an article in *Publishers Weekly*, Harold Roth "said he regretted the necessity of the action in view of his company's 75-year relationship with Stratemeyer and with Harriet Adams, one of the Syndicate's partners. 'The relationship has probably established a record of its kind in terms of durability in book publishing,' Roth declared." In public, Harriet announced that the Syndicate found Grosset's behavior "shocking," while Simon & Schuster called it "frivolously vindictive." Privately, she was less stalwart.

"I think in some way she just felt betrayed," one of Harriet's junior partners remembered. Still, "the fact of the matter was it [the arrangement with Grosset] was a bad deal and she had been taken advantage of." *Publishers Weekly* agreed, noting that "in spite of multi-million dollar sales of Stratemeyer books, the Syndicate was never treated like best-selling authors by Grosset & Dunlap."

The court case was to go to trial in May of 1980, but until then the media would be treated to a steady diet of all Nancy Drew, all the time. With their massive marketing and sales departments ever more finely calibrated to the tastes and whims of young America, Simon & Schuster would be able to capitalize on the Nancy Drew name in a way that a smaller company like Grosset had never done, and they intended to start as soon as possible. If there was anyone in the country who hadn't yet heard of the girl detective — admittedly an unlikely occurrence — the situation was about to be remedied. By the end of 1979, in addition to a commemorative boxed set of Bobbsey Twins books, Simon & Schuster had brought out new Nancy Drew and Hardy Boys titles in paperback for the first time ever. The first Nancy Drew, *The Triple Hoax*, was set in New York and Mexico, and its bright blue cover featured a Nancy as modern as the turquoise miniskirt she wore during her adventures. In addition to the new books, word of a "large party" on Nancy's fiftieth birthday and press interviews with Harriet for the occasion percolated through the publishing world like rumors of a juicy affair.

Starting in February of 1980, a veritable landslide of press about the anniversary hit newsstands everywhere. Much of it continued along the same lines as the feminist-slanted coverage of the 1960s and '70s, further cementing Nancy as the thinking woman's detective. "A model of women's liberation long before the time for that particular idea had come, blue-eyed, titian-haired Nancy is independent, resourceful, a leader not only of men but of women, girls, and boys, too," said *Good Housekeeping*. "She is, in fact, much like her creator—an 87-year-old great-grandmother, writer, world traveler—and astute businesswoman—named Harriet Adams." Many of the pieces invoked the story of an eleven-year-old girl who had been kidnapped and molested several years earlier and escaped through the large taillight opening of her attacker's trunk after removing the light itself. The officer on the case had told reporters, "She's read something like 45 Nancy Drew books. That seems to have prepared her mind to deal with the situation and to escape." They noted that first daughter Amy Carter and bright, peppy Mary Tyler Moore were fans of the series and quoted a modest Harriet: "I think my father would be absolutely amazed at what's happened. I doubt that he thought anyone would carry on." By now Harriet's standard story was that Edward had died leaving behind only drafts of the first three Nancy Drews, and that she had taken on the series—as well as the whole company—single-handedly from there, rewriting those rudimentary manuscripts, "making Nancy a bit more polite and respectful," and never once looking back.

Out in Iowa City, notice of the publicity free-for-all was being taken. "I thought you might be interested in this AP story," a woman in the University of Iowa's office of public information wrote in a memo to Frank Paluka, the librarian from the Iowa Authors Collection who had first contacted Mildred in the 1960s. "I don't see how Adams can get away with these blatant lies. What can be done? Have you heard from OUR Carolyn Keene lately?" Paluka sent a copy of the article on to Mildred, who wrote back with a bit of interesting news. "Many thanks for the Nancy Drew publicity shot on Mrs. Adams. This was the Syndicate's latest blanketing of the country with a syndicated article, seemingly to establish in the minds of readers that Mrs. Adams is the author of the Nancy Drew books. Immediately thereafter, she was put under oath in connection with Grosset's litigation, and, at least as I was notified by phone from New York, acknowledged that I, not she, wrote all of the early books. She was especially tripped up by the first three, which for a time, she claimed were written by her father, Edward Stratemeyer...I understand I am the only remaining ghost still alive, as the author who wrote the Hardy Boys for her died last year." The case, she went on, was to come to trial in a few months, and she had supplied Grosset's lawyers with some letters between her and Harriet and a few other Syndicate-related materials she had to help bolster their story.

But before the trial came the anniversary. Nancy Drew turned fifty with as much glitz and glamour as a film actress at a premiere. In spite of Judy Blume books, video games, MTV, and all the other distractions that had cropped up over the course of her existence, she was still a star. On April 16, 1980, Simon & Schuster threw a party fit for fictional royalty at New York City's chichi Harkness House on Fifth Avenue, "with honored guest Harriet Adams (Carolyn Keene)." In addition to "some terribly serious contemporary writers," the five hundred guests included Mayor Ed Koch, Bette Davis, Barbara Walters ("Seems to me I read all of them"); Joan Mondale ("I was crazy about them"); Fran Lebowitz ("she, for one, said she still reads Nancy Drew"); Beverly Sills ("I loved them. She had a car and she was pretty and to us kids in Brooklyn, that was sophisticated"); and Ruth Bader Ginsburg ("I liked Nancy Drew, yes. She was adventuresome, daring, and her boyfriend was a much more passive type than she was").

After passing the blue roadster parked out front, attendees had to enter the party via a "cave of chilling, pre-recorded screams. The only defense was a mini-flashlight, given to each cave stroller as a party favor." A full cast of characters, including a 1930 Nancy and a 1980 Nancy, Ned Nickerson, Bess, George, Hannah, and a dastardly assortment of criminals, decoys, police, and mystics roamed the four-floor party. "For of course," the writer for the *Washington Post* deadpanned, "the party had a plot. Every hour a loudspeaker broadcast a clue... around midnight, the butler offered the bass player a crème de menthe, and when he declined; the butler brushed the band member's lapels, and in so doing, removed his emerald stick pin and dropped it into the liqueur. Then the butler sort of pussyfooted across the floor. Halfway, Nancy Drew and Ned Nickerson surrounded him and cried, 'The Butler did it.'"

Harriet was in mystery heaven. When a reporter asked her about the impending lawsuit, she simply shrugged it off: "I don't see any reason for it," she said. "It's taken a fabulous amount of time, which interrupts my writing."

But a few weeks later, reality hit, and she found herself in the Federal Courthouse in downtown Manhattan. The preceding days of deposition had already taken a toll on her—she was eighty-seven and not in the best of health—and on May 27, 1980, the opening day of what would be a five-day trial, she got another jolt. Seventy-four-year-old Mildred Wirt Benson, whom she had not seen for almost thirty years, appeared in the courtroom to testify. She had been brought in from Ohio—in what turned out to be a self-defeating move by Grosset—to explain that she had written the Nancy Drew Mystery Stories and other Syndicate titles from 1929 to 1953. Upon seeing Mildred, whom she was not expecting and did not recognize without an introduction, Harriet uttered a single, amazed sentence: "I thought you were dead."

HARRIET'S REACTION was not, perhaps, as catty as it sounded. After all, the era of the first Nancy Drew books was as bygone as the cloche hats and kid gloves that had accompanied her fashionable entry into the world. Benson must have seemed like a ghost to her former employer, an envoy from Harriet Adams's early years in business. Furthermore, Mildred's presence was far from the vengeful act it might have seemed. Just by chance, around the time that the lawsuit had been filed, a small old-time publisher called Platt & Munk, which now owned the rights to Mildred's Penny Parker series from the 1930s and '40s, had been bought by Grosset & Dunlap. An editor at Grosset wrote to Mildred to see if she was interested in revising Penny Parker for reissue, no doubt looking for a way to fill the gap if Grosset lost Nancy Drew. When Mildred wrote back to say yes (though the project never came to fruition), she had mentioned something of her interest in the pending lawsuit. "As you no doubt know, I wrote all of the early Nancy originals, continuing until they were established as big sellers at which time Mrs. Adams took them over completely. I sincerely hope that Grosset wins in any litigation and that the Syndicate finally pays for the privilege of benefiting from others' work, without giving credit." As she was clearly willing to talk by this time, rights and releases be damned, Grosset decided to call her in to testify, hoping she would somehow be able to help their case by talking about her work on Nancy Drew and other series, thereby proving that Harriet had not written them all and thus did not really own them.

As the trial dragged on, the story of the Syndicate's ambiguous writing process and both Mildred's and Harriet's attachment to Nancy Drew came out. Though she had admitted in earlier questioning that Mildred had written many of the manuscripts for the early Nancy Drew series, Harriet had become so identified with the sleuth in her own and the public's minds that she was unable to square her previous statements with her emotions. "In the early books, I did not care for the way she treated her housekeeper, and so I made her and the housekeeper different," she told the examining lawyer. "Was that during the time that Mrs. Wirt was doing the ghost writing for the Nancy Drew series?" he asked. "She was filling in from my outlines that I did," Harriet answered, splitting hairs and conveniently forgetting that Edna had also written some of the first Nancy Drew outlines.

"I wanted to know whether or not this change vis-à-vis her relationship with the housekeeper had occurred while Mrs. Wirt was doing writing on the series," the lawyer explained. "Not the way Mrs. Wirt wrote them. But I edited them," Harriet equivocated, admitting that Mildred had written the books even as she tried to take full responsibility for them. "I also felt that she was too bossy, too positive...there are places in early books where Nancy spoke to people too sharply...So I changed her." Arguing for a legacy as much as creation rights, she then added, "I think after I changed her is the way she has been thought of for years and years."

Mildred claimed just as passionately during her own testimony that she had created the Nancy that so many women loved and remembered. "In the course of writing the first seven books, did you attempt to develop the character of Nancy?" an attorney asked her. "Yes, it came naturally, I think. In each book it developed a little more...It's just like life, a character is always evolving. So long as you're writing, you're contributing to your character." Finally, Mildred admitted that perhaps she cared a bit more about old Nancy than she had previously been willing to let on. "I didn't intend…to come until just a few days ago," she announced to the judge. "After all that wave of publicity I decided to come." She was referring to the stories that had come out on Nancy Drew's fiftieth anniversary, the ones, as she put it, "about the fact that someone was a writer of those books." Even the editor of her own newspaper had left a copy on her desk without comment, humiliating her and making her feel as though he took her for a liar when he read that Harriet Adams, not Mildred Benson, was Carolyn Keene. The story, she said, "just flooded the whole countryside…My friends are sending them to me and scribbling on them 'How come?' That's the time I thought if I'm ever going to tell the story of Nancy Drew, this is it."

Tell it, she did. But rather than trying to take full credit for anything, she tried to explain that just as there had been two Carolyn Keenes (and a few interlopers like Karig along the way), there had simply been two Nancys. "Mrs. Adams's style of writing Nancy is not the style I had, and I imagine that things I wrote in there did not hit her as Nancy. I mean, the Nancy that I created is a different Nancy from what Mrs. Adams has carried on," she said. "There was a beginning conflict in what is Nancy. My Nancy would not be Mrs. Adams's Nancy. Mrs. Adams was an entirely different person; she was more cultured and she was more refined. I was probably a rough and tumble newspaper person who had to earn a living, and I was out in the world. That was my type of Nancy. Nancy was making her way in life and trying to compete and have fun. We just had two different kinds of Nancys." All she wanted was credit where it was due. "No, I'm not angry at them [the Syndicate]," she told the judge, falling back on the tenets of journalism that had served her so well. "I don't resent anything. I think if there are misstatements of fact, they should be corrected. Because when a statement is made wrong and is repeated over and over and over again, it becomes firmly entrenched in the mind of the reading public as truth."

When it was all over, the judge, as Mildred had suspected, found in favor of the Syndicate and Simon & Schuster, which walked away with the very lucrative rights to take three of America's bestselling series into the rapidly expanding global marketplace. (Grosset & Dunlap was given the rights to publish only the hardcover versions of the pre-1979 Nancy Drews, Bobbsey Twins, Hardy Boys, and Dana Girls, a sorry consolation prize in a world full of inexpensive paperbacks.) Mildred was satisfied, writing to Geoff Lapin: "Even if I didn't get it across to the court, I know who wrote those books and set up the form which made them top sellers. I judge that the trial just about nailed the coffin lid in future sales, so perhaps we finally have heard the last of Nancy Drew."

It was wishful thinking on her part. "SKYROCKETING SALES PROMPT ACCELERATED EXPANSION OF NANCY DREW AND HARDY BOYS SERIES," boomed a press release from Simon & Schuster in January of 1981. Over one million copies of the new paperback additions to the series had been sold in less than a year, and as a result, the publisher was planning to add four more Nancys and four more Hardys to its list in upcoming seasons. Nostalgia had also created high prices for first editions and other memorabilia, like lunch boxes and Halloween costumes that had come out around the time of the failed TV series.

ON March 27, 1982, while watching *The Wizard of Oz* on television at her farm, Harriet Adams died, very swiftly, of heart failure.

The response was immediate and overwhelming. On and on went the obituaries: "THE NANCY DREW LEGACY"; "GROWING UP FEMALE WITH NANCY DREW"; "FAREWELL TO THE WOMAN BEHIND NANCY DREW"; "HARRIET ADAMS, CREATOR OF NANCY DREW." Many of them also noted her devotion to educating her readers—as per all the Shakespeare in *The Clue of the Dancing Puppet*—and her great zest for life. Above and beyond anything else, the obituaries made it clear that regardless of the two different Nancys Mildred had brought to light at the trial, the sleuth would never have survived in any form without Harriet's devoted guardianship. Simon & Schuster ran perhaps the most poignant ad of all, which said, simply: "We mourn the passing of a great lady."

They did not mourn her so much, however, that they did not keep their eye on the bottom line. In 1984 the Stratemeyer Syndicate was bought outright by Simon & Schuster. The little company had been damaged financially by the cost of the lawsuit and other mishaps—like the *Playboy* ads—and was now running at a loss. At Harriet's death, it had been split fifty-fifty between her three remaining children, who were inactive partners much as Edna had been, and her three junior partners. When the children realized that no one in the family was in a position to take over, they agreed, at last, to sell. On July 31 of that year, Simon & Schuster paid $4,710,000 for the honor and privilege of publishing, forever more, the century's most famous young detectives. They now had total control over the future of the original series and any spin-offs they could come up with.

"Juvenile publishing is a key area for expansion and development," said the company's chairman, "and I cannot think of a more auspicious way to grow than by acquiring Stratemeyer—a remarkable company...These books are true pieces of Americana, and I'm proud to bring them to the company. We'll help ensure that future generations of children can lose themselves in the adventures of these characters just as we did." The vice president and publisher of Simon & Schuster was less dewy-eyed about his new series. "We have to breathe new life into them," he told a reporter for the *Wilson Library Bulletin*. "The characters are showing signs of age and need updating. Nancy, for example, doesn't reflect the reality of 1980s girlhood."

By the time S&S launched the new Nancy Drew Files series two years later, they found it "necessary to give her a complete makeover," one more time. Now, however, Harriet was not around to control the changes, and so they included many things she would no doubt have disapproved of, like a flashy car, designer jeans, credit cards, and even the occasional foray to a rock concert—though only for the purposes of solving a mystery involving record piracy. "Nancy Drew," predicted one writer, "will now skillfully maneuver a Mustang into another exciting adventure— and another generation of readers' hearts."

The first volume of the Nancy Drew Files, titled *Secrets Can Kill*, was published on June 1, 1986. Clocking in at 153 pages, its cover showed a distinctly eighties Nancy with feathered hair and tight jeans, and its format was what Simon & Schuster called "rack-size"—larger than the "digest size" paperbacks it had been publishing since 1979—to appeal to older readers. The smaller books were geared toward ages eight to eleven, whereas the new Files series would "reflect the interests and concerns of today's teens." From the very first pages of *Secrets Can Kill*—the plot involved Nancy going undercover at Bedford High to investigate a series of crimes—it was clear that not only Nancy, but Bess and George, had arrived in the present, and that S&S had identified "the interests and concerns of today's teens" primarily as boys and clothes and the kind of superficial issues that the Nancy of old would never have considered:

> Nancy studied herself in the mirror. She liked what she saw. The tight jeans looked great on her long, slim legs and the green sweater complemented her strawberry-blond hair. Her eyes flashed with the excitement of a new case. She was counting on solving the little mystery fairly easily. In fact, Nancy thought it would probably be fun! "Right now," she said to her two friends, "the hardest part of this case is deciding what to wear."
>
> "That outfit, definitely," Bess said, sighing with envy at Nancy's slender figure. "You'll make the guys absolutely drool."
>
> "That's all she needs," George joked. "A bunch of freshmen following her around like underage puppies."
>
> "Oh, yeah? Have you seen the captain of the Bedford football team?" Bess rolled her eyes. "They don't call him 'Hunk' Hogan for nothing!"
>
> Bess and George were Nancy's best friends, and they were cousins, but that was about all they had in common. Blond-haired Bess was bubbly and easygoing, and always on the lookout for two things: a good diet and a great date. So far she hadn't found either. She was constantly trying to lose five pounds, and she fell in and out of love every other month.
>
> George, with curly dark hair and a shy smile, was quiet, with a dry sense of humor and the beautifully toned body of an athlete. George liked boys as much as Bess did, but she was more serious about love. "When I fall," she'd say, "it's going to be for real."

By the end of the story, Nancy has solved the thefts, but she has also "thrilled to the touch" of another boy. Though the vice president and publisher of Simon & Schuster's juvenile department claimed that the company had "extrapolated the new Nancy Drew out of the old," it was clear that a new era had begun.

Gone were the chaste picnics, the worry about being invited to the Emerson College dance. The tension between Nancy's sleuthing and her boyfriend was now front and center. The back cover copy for Nancy Drew Files number eight, *Two Points to Murder*, pitted them directly against each other: "All Nancy has to do is catch the practical joker who's terrorizing the Emerson College basketball team—the team Ned plays for. But then the joke turns deadly—and Nancy's main suspect is Ned's best friend!... But if she solves this case, can she hold onto the boy she loves?" As one reviewer of the new series put it, "It is the 1980s. Men can wear jewelry. Women can run for vice-president. And Nancy Drew can finally feel tingly when she gets kissed."

And this time there were plans for more than just the books, which already had a hefty budget behind them. The vice president and director of marketing at Simon & Schuster told *Publishers Weekly*: "We're trying to promote a lifestyle." It would include the offering of "clothing, accessory and cosmetics licenses to manufacturers. The fashion collections, called Nancy Drew's River Heights, USA, will be aimed at 12- to 18-year-old girls."

But even as Nancy Drew made her way into the 1980s, Mustang convertible and all, a question was looming ever larger in the minds of fans everywhere. Now that Harriet Adams was gone, who was Carolyn Keene?

"THE DAY THE OBITUARY of Harriet Stratemeyer Adams appeared, Millie Wirt Benson rubbed her wrinkled forehead and frowned.

A slight woman with graying hair, Mrs. Benson knew history would come bubbling up again and there wasn't much she could do about it." Less than a month after Harriet's death, an intrepid reporter with a mind to getting the truth on the public record had found Mildred out, and she was none too happy about it. "She fears publicity," his piece continued. "Mrs. Benson turns down most interviewers and agreed to talk to the Associated Press 'just to set the record straight.'" (She had already nixed a profile in *Life* magazine.) Much to her chagrin, it was only the beginning. Thanks to the efforts of Geoff Lapin, the Iowa Authors Collection, and a group of other devoted fans, Mildred Benson was becoming a star as big as Harriet had been—as big as Nancy Drew herself. Eventually, she gave in to it. First came a short notice in *Ohio* magazine, then a few more newspaper pieces. By 1985 the *Iowa Alumni Review* ran a tribute that left no doubt as to who was the new reigning Carolyn Keene: "Before Geraldine Ferraro, before Gloria Steinem, before Jane Fonda—there was Nancy Drew...And before Nancy Drew, there was Mildred Wirt Benson...creator of the Nancy Drew series."

Two years earlier she had breathed a sigh of relief to Frank Paluka about the end of the trial and its aftermath—"this should mark the end of my Nancy Drew tribulations"—and assumed, perhaps because she understood the power neither of modern marketing nor the name Nancy Drew, that once Grosset and Simon & Schuster sold out of their current stock, Nancy would be gone for good. Now she was more than happy to hold forth about her newly acknowledged creation: "It seems to me that Nancy was popular, and remains so, primarily because she personifies the dream image which exists within most teenagers," she told an interviewer in 1985.

"She never lost an athletic contest and was far smarter than adults with whom she associated. Leisure time was spent living dangerously. She avoided all household tasks, and indeed, might rate as a pioneer of Women's Lib. In a way, she started a movement." But, perhaps because the word wasn't coined until decades after she wrote the Nancy Drew series, Benson said she doesn't consider herself a feminist. "But I do believe in equality," she says emphatically. "Which, by the way, women still do not have!"

Good-bye, Harriet; hello, Mildred.

Before long, reporters desperate to fill the Carolyn Keene void opened up by Harriet's death pounced on Mildred. Nobody seemed to care that she was not currently writing the series. It only mattered that she had been there back at the beginning. After all, the women reading magazines and newspapers in the 1980s knew the old Nancy, not the one in Jordache jeans and eyeliner. When the story about Mildred being the true, original Carolyn Keene had finally been reported to death—the only thing better than being able to report on Harriet as Keene was being able to report on the idea that she had lied about it—the press looked over the events of Mildred's life again and began to proclaim her not just the real Carolyn Keene, but the real Nancy Drew. In 1991 the Smithsonian made it official when it asked Mildred for some of her papers and her fabled Underwood typewriter, which it planned to include in its Americana collection along with Judy Garland's red shoes from *The Wizard of Oz*. She had been elected to the Iowa School of Journalism Hall of Fame and wrote repeatedly to Geoff Lapin to thank him for his efforts on her behalf. "If I am not able to tell you later on, please remember that I always will be grateful to you for taking the lead in establishing that I was the original writer of Nancy Drew. To have won against such great odds...was indeed amazing."

But a strange thing was starting to happen. Just as Mildred had once been written out of history, Harriet was now being sidelined in favor of the spunky newspaperwoman from Iowa. Even when a reporter understood the complicated story of who had authored what and when, Harriet still lost out, thanks to what a writer for the *Atlantic Monthly* referred to, in a 1991 article, as "the Great Purge." Where she had once been heralded for keeping Nancy alive, Harriet, when she was included at all in the story of Nancy Drew, was now there only to play the villain. "She directed that all the books in the company's...Nancy Drew series (whose author of record is Carolyn Keene—initially Adams herself, it once was thought, but in reality a woman named Mildred A. Wirt [Benson], who is now eighty-six and lives in the Midwest) be thoroughly revised," the *Atlantic Monthly* piece fumed. Nevermind that the author was not aware of Grosset's role in the revisions. As Mildred herself had acknowledged in court, once the public reads something in print enough times, even if it is wrong, it becomes the truth. In the media at least, the Mildred camp began to take the lead.

The occasion for this article was the reissue, by a small Massachusetts press called Applewood Books, of what would come to be known as the "original text" Hardy Boys and Nancy Drew books in facsimile editions. "Antiques though these novels be, they deserve a second look," the *Atlantic* writer opined, "because they're richer than the versions of the same books now in print." He was not alone. "Nancy is no longer the intrepid, independent detective of the original novels," pitched in that old standby *Ms.* in 1992. "The teenage detective who was once a symbol of spunky female independence has slowly been replaced by an image of prolonged childhood, currently evolving toward a Barbie doll detective." In the opinion of the writer, Nancy's latest update was simply more of the same. *Ms.* had been disappointed in the revisions of the 1950s and '60s, too, and the magazine's writers had not forgotten the earlier betrayal. Though Harriet was congratulated for removing the guns and racial prejudices that were so unpalatable, she was taken to task for, as this writer put it, "constricting Nancy's independence." As far as critics were concerned, Simon & Schuster's efforts to modernize her had only made her worse.

The renewed interest in the 1930s and '40s rendition of Nancy overwhelmed Mildred, who, while she was glad to have been acknowledged at last, thought too much was being made of the issue she had once testified about so passionately. "Mildred Wirt Benson, arguably the person most responsible for Nancy Drew's success, couldn't care less about the hoopla surrounding the reissuing of the early Nancy Drew books," the *Los Angeles Times* reported in 1991. By then she was, according to another article, "bemused at this group of grown-ups who were...spending their time and tremendous sums of money tracking down her old books, who were wasting their time when they could be out there DOING something, instead of paying homage to a dusty relic like Nancy Drew."

Then in 1993 the University of Iowa organized a Nancy Drew conference. A three-day extravaganza devoted to the girl sleuth and to Mildred, it was held in Iowa City that April. The media went wild—as Mildred remarked wryly in a letter to Geoff Lapin, having learned her lesson by this time, "Anything about Nancy Drew sells instantly." Peter Jennings and ABC News chose her as their "Person of the Week." "Recognition for this woman we choose was a very long time in coming," Jennings said at the start of the broadcast. Then Mildred appeared, every inch the hard-boiled author: "I didn't analyze things," she informed Jennings pertly. "I just sat down at my typewriter and put a piece of paper in there and let 'er roll." Also on the show were interviews with a series of girls who were devoted to Nancy: "She gets into a lot of trouble, but always gets out of it. I wish I could do that," sighed one. "When my mother was very little, my grandma used to buy her all the Nancy Drew books, so it like...it runs through the family," said another.

At the conference itself—which featured academic panels with names like "The Crack in the Cannon: The Nancy Drew Novels as Subversive Reading"; "Lesbian Code in the Nancy Drew Stories" (which outraged Mildred); and "Can This Relationship Be Saved" (about Nancy and Ned, of course)—the adult fans were no less doting. "One woman...said she had joined a police department, after drawing on Nancy Drew for inner strength to overcome her innate shyness, and later was able to investigate the mess left behind after a triple murder," the *Chicago Tribune* reported. "Another said that, after a bad marriage, she had withdrawn to her bedroom 'with all my old Nancy Drew mysteries and brought myself back together.'" The conference's keynote speaker, feminist literary scholar and mystery author Carolyn Heilbrun—who, the *Tribune* noted, "last year took early retirement as a professor of English at Columbia University to protest her department's treatment of women"—was less emotional about the sleuth but just as affecting. "Everybody perks up at her name, though few remember the plots or many of the details," she said. "The pleasure comes from her autonomy, her taking events into her own hands."

At a press conference with Mildred, the star of the show, the venerated author refused to take the bait on a question about Harriet — "I think she took some of the spice out of them. But I don't think...never mind, that's enough" — and then denied that Nancy Drew had influenced her life in the way she had influenced so many other girls'. "No, I was the same. You can't change me — that's what they say at the office. They try. They've tried for a whole generation to change me and I am impossible. There's only two things I believe in — well, a few more things than that — but I believe in absolute honesty and honesty in journalism... and I believe in integrity."

Perhaps that was why, stranded in Chicago's O'Hare Airport on her way to Iowa City, "carrying a red leather pocket book and wearing a crinkly plastic rain bonnet," she had snapped, "I'm so sick of Nancy Drew I could vomit," at the *New York Times* reporter who was traveling with her. True to form, she then tried to get the facts on the record correctly yet again, telling her captive audience, a woman "49 years her junior who spent her childhood addicted to Nancy Drew," that she had never been bothered by giving up her rights to the stories. "The only thing that did [bother her], she said, 'was a period when doubt was expressed that I'd written them.'" Then, in spite of her irritation — she was later annoyed that the reporter had included the vomit comment as well — she offered some helpful advice about writing a good story: "To the woman who has written more than 120 tales, today's plot was obvious," the reporter recounted. "'I'd tie this into being stranded here,' she said, 'if you want some advice from an old hack.'"

Still writing for the *Blade* every week, Mildred was hardly a hack. Her column was called "On the Go," and it covered the doings of elderly people who, like Mildred, had more going on in their lives than just golf and card games. There were also many pieces on how outraged she was when people suggested to her that she, too, might be old. Her resistance to joining the senior set was so ingrained that one day in 1998, when she was ninety-three years old, she dropped by the desk of a much younger fellow reporter and announced, "Well, I'll see you later. I gotta go interview some old fogey."

The year after the Iowa conference, Simon & Schuster made the next big push in expanding the Nancy Drew brand when it launched a spin-off series for girls from five to eight years old called the Nancy Drew Notebooks. In them Nancy, Bess, and George are in third grade, and Nancy has already developed the habits of good sleuthing. She keeps track of the details of her mysteries in a blue notebook in between hobbies like playing on the school soccer team and solves important crimes like *The Slumber Party Secret,* in which she must find out what has happened to her friend Rebecca's stolen invitations. At eight years old, she already has an inquisitive mind, as her opening lines make adorably clear: "'But how can party invitations just disappear?' Nancy Drew asked. She stopped right in the middle of the sidewalk and looked at her friend. 'Don't ask me,' Rebecca Ramirez moaned. 'All I know is my birthday party is ruined. Now no one will come!' She stuck out her lower lip and pouted."

The following year, Simon & Schuster gave the girl detective yet another push forward, but in an entirely different direction. The first title in the Nancy Drew on Campus series, in which Nancy leaves the cocoon of River Heights for Wilder University, told practically the whole story in four short words: *New Lives, New Loves.* The first press release left no doubt as to where the books were headed. "It's 65 years later... Will Nancy Drew finally break up with Ned Nickerson? Stay tuned..." On the back of *New Lives, New Loves,* was a special hotline number that readers could call "to vote on Nancy and Ned's love life." The books were less concerned with mystery than they were with college life. As one critic has written, "The classic Nancy Drew sleuth became Nancy Drew co-ed... Nancy's baffling mysteries of yesteryear became the baffling mystery of living life on her own away from the comfort of home and far away from the comfort of Ned." The series took up everything from date rape to college loans and, in doing so, portrayed Nancy as an average girl who was more in search of a good time than an engrossing mystery.

No matter what Simon & Schuster did, though, everyone still seemed to prefer the version of the sleuth they had known as children, as a Washington, D.C., rock band called Tuscadero made clear in a 1995 song called "Nancy Drew." Its lyrics recounted "the horror of discovering that your mom threw out your collection of the teenage sleuth's books." "You write about what you know the best," said the band's female guitarist and vocalist, "and I happen to know a lot about Nancy Drew books and jerky guys that I've dated."

"Like hamburgers and Disney cartoons," the *Boston Globe* pronounced, "Nancy Drew has entered global culture." By the mid-nineties, it was more apparent than ever that Nancy Drew represented a certain eternal something to everyone who knew about her, and she remained reassuringly the same in the eyes of her fans. Referring to what it called "her quintessential '*Drewness*,'" the in-house guide to a Nancy television show filmed in Paris and broadcast in the United States in 1995 tried to pin down just what that something about Nancy was. "This quality is expressed in her wardrobe. She chooses clear, saturated colors that reflect her moral certainty. When Nancy wears green, it's not olive green or sea foam or celadon. It's *green*." Even the furnishings in her TV apartment, the guide explained, would radiate "a feeling of security; they have a timeless quality that is impossible to date…a sofa is a sofa…It has a pure design that reflects a sofa's essence, its truth. Visually, Nancy's world will make sense." The outside world, on the other hand, "is a world of unsolved mysteries, a place filled with cold glaring light and turbulent disorder." In short, the description finished off, "it can be described as a world without Drewness."

None of the later versions of Nancy, either in print or on television, captured the popular imagination the way the original sleuth had. The Nancy Drew on Campus series lasted only three years, and the "lifestyle" that Simon & Schuster had hoped to promote under the River Heights, USA, label back in 1986 never took off. The *Nancy Drew Files* lasted for ten years, a respectable run but one that nonetheless didn't even come close to the first Nancy's more-than-fifty-year reign. Simon & Schuster's only enduring line was the Nancy Drew Notebooks for little girls, which were written, by necessity, without the loud, flashy plots and clothing and crushes that so marred their other attempts to revamp the sleuth. It was, and still is, the Stratemeyer Syndicate's Nancy who lives in the public imagination, in both her original and revised versions—the Nancy of moral certainty and neat, elegant actions. The one written by women who understood, in ways nobody else could, who she really was.

ON THE AFTERNOON of May 29, 2002, after handing in her column at the *Blade*, Mildred left the office by taxi for her home. Several hours later she was taken to Toledo Hospital, where she died that evening at the age of ninety-six. All across the country, obituaries heralded her—as they had heralded Harriet years earlier—as Carolyn Keene, the author of the Nancy Drew books.

"Nancy Drew, girl sleuth extraordinaire: We loved her, we wanted to be her, we couldn't put her books down," the *Washington Post's* tribute began. "The original Carolyn Keene—the first, and best, of the ghostwriters, the one who gave Nancy her personality and her keenness, her independence and her spunk—is exactly what we'd hope to find. Her name was Mildred Wirt Benson, and she died Tuesday night in Toledo."

By the time she passed away, Mildred had confessed to Geoff Lapin, "Nancy Drew demands have about put me under." She had been inundated with fan mail for the better part of a decade, and, having lost her eyesight, had resorted to signing a printed form thanking readers. (She had also taken to using a very large magnifying glass to read the text on her computer screen at work, a Nancy-like turn of events if ever there was one.) "It reached the point where, whenever we saw some hapless cameraman setting up light in the newsroom," one of her colleagues recalled after she died, "we wondered only which network was here to interview her this time."

In the end, her past with the Stratemeyer Syndicate became a burden, but Mildred never forgot why she had started writing children's books in the first place. Her final column, posthumously published, was about her love of reading and her admiration of public libraries, the very institutions that had both provided her with the detail and atmosphere that made many of her books so magical and provided so many young readers the chance to read to them.

⊶∞∞⊷

"It's HARD TO ACCEPT that Nancy Drew is dead," mourned one obituary writer. But she had it wrong. Though Mildred and Harriet are both gone, Nancy is anything but. She turned seventy-five in April of 2005, and in preparation Simon & Schuster launched her into the world yet again. Written in the first person—Nancy talks more directly to us than ever—the new Nancy Drew Girl Detective series nonetheless harkens back to the old Nancy, the Nancy of Harriet and Mildred. "Long before *Charlie's Angels, Murder She Wrote's* Jessica Fletcher, and *CSI's* Catherine Willows, super-sleuth Nancy Drew was fighting crime and keeping the streets of River Heights safe," the press materials that went out with the first book began. Though she now drives a hybrid car and solves crimes while doing things like competing in a bike race for charity, the sleuth has regained some of the spark she lost in the 1980s and '90s. "My friends tell me I'm always looking for trouble, but that's not really true," she announces in *Without a Trace*, the first title in the new series. "It just seems to have a way of finding me." She may be using a global positioning system, but she's still our Nancy. In her first new outing, she's late for a movie date with Ned while out on a case, and later she confides in us: "Ned's not into mysteries in the same way I am, but he's more than smart enough to follow along when I'm in full hypothesizing mode." After the wild college years and the boy-crazy moments, Nancy's got her feet back on the ground again.

The cover design of the new books pays a respectful nod to the past, too—a cutout of Nancy's inquisitive eyes that runs across the top of each book comes from the cover of the 1950s edition of *The Secret of the Old Clock*, the revision of the title that started everything back in 1930. On Nancy's seventy-fifth anniversary, both the original version of *Old Clock* (in its Applewood Books edition) and the revised version are still selling well. In 2002 about 150,000 copies of Harriet's 1959 *Secret of the Old Clock* were sold, which put it—outdated fashions, lingo, and all—among the top fifty children's books.

Vintage Nancy Drew books are not the only things that linger on from the past. Women today continue to face the same problems that Harriet and Mildred dealt with as they made their way through the twentieth century. The balance of home and work feels more off-kilter than ever, adequate child care is still unavailable, office culture has barely given an inch to women who want to have families without falling behind professionally, and it seems like rarely a year goes by without someone publishing a tome lamenting the lack of progress. Women still earn less than men, and they still feel—for the most part, anyway—that it's their job, not their husbands', to give up their careers in order to hold a family together.

Fortunately, Nancy Drew is still here, too, a guide for the ages. She and the rich, tumultuous lives of the women who created her remind us of the rewards of perseverance and the value of confidence. Thanks to Mildred and Harriet and the generations of women and girls who glimpsed in Nancy Drew a vision of what they might be someday, it doesn't look like the sleuth is going away anytime soon, which is a good thing. There are fighting days still ahead of us, and we're going to need her.

ACKNOWLEDGMENTS

I AM DEEPLY GRATEFUL to The Dorothy and Lewis B. Cullman Center for Scholars and Writers at the New York Public Library, and to Mel and Lois Tukman, without whose support my fellowship there would not have been possible. Many thanks to Pamela Leo, Amy Azzarito and Rebecca Federman, and to Peter Gay and Jean Strouse. Also at the library, thanks to Bill Stingone, Wayne Furman, and the entire staff of the Rare Books Reading Room. Janet Weaver and Karen Mason at the University of Iowa Women's Archives have been endlessly generous, as have David McCartney and the staff of the University of Iowa University Archives. In Marengo, Iowa, Eva Schmidt and the staff at the Iowa County Genealogy Society tracked down information that I could not have gotten anywhere else. At Wellesley, Jean Berry was immensely helpful, as were Nancy Hawkins and Mary Mackzum at the *Toledo Blade*. Thanks also to John Robinson Block, who graciously granted me permission to access the *Toledo Blade* Library.

I am grateful to Sally Vallongo for permission to use her long interview with Mildred Benson, and to Richard Gallagher for sharing both his impressions of Harriet Adams and his interview with her from the 1970s. Carolyn Stewart Dyer was my host in Iowa City and a wonderful source of stories about Mildred Benson.

I was taken in without a second thought and with great kindness by a group of people who knew, and no doubt still know, far more than I do about various aspects of the Stratemeyer Syndicate and Nancy Drew, and who generously shared material with me: James Keeline, Deidre Johnson, Ilana Nash, and Geoff Lapin all added immensely to my research and my understanding of my subject. Jennifer Fisher, president of the Nancy Drew Sleuths, has been helpful in more ways than I can count.

Thanks to Ben Winters, transcriber and playwright extraordinaire, and to Libby Gills, who saved me from logging more hours in front of the microfilm reader.

Thanks also to Sarah Chalfant and Jin Auh, and to Jennifer Gilmore, Michelle Blankenship, David Hough, Sara Branch, and Lydia D'moch at Harcourt, the kind of publishing house at which every author should be so fortunate to land.

Brad McKee has read just about every word I've produced over the last decade, and his boundless support along with his candid, perceptive comments have made me a better writer. The thoughtful criticism of MacKenzie Bezos, who read this manuscript more than once with both enthusiasm and a very keen eye, has been indispensable. The (relatively) successful management of my literary neuroses can be attributed almost exclusively to my fellow neurotic, Patrick Keefe, whose formidable work ethic spurred me on, and whose friendship is an endless source of pleasure and good conversation.

The incomparable Andrea Schulz saw what this book might be the very first time she read the proposal and then she made it her business to get me to see it, too. Her talent and dedication are the stuff of which only the very best editors are made.

In August 2002, in the face of great skepticism from me, Noah Isenberg put me on a plane to Iowa, fully believing that I would come home with a book in my head. Over the course of three years his unshakable faith in me with regard to this project and so much else has been the reason many improbable things became possible. Living with a writer—this writer, at least—can be maddening; he does it with grace, compassion, humor, and the enviable good sense of a man who knows what really matters.

NOTES

INTRODUCTION

"**Eighteen and attractive**": All excerpts from *Mystery of the Tolling Bell* in this section come from Carolyn Keene, *Mystery of the Tolling Bell* (New York: Grosset & Dunlap, 1976), pp. 1, 164, 181.

"**I was such a Nancy Drew fan**": Dick Pothier, "Nancy Drew: First Libber?" *Boston Globe*, January 6, 1976.

"**If there is a woman**": unsigned editorial, "Harriet S. Adams," *Springfield (MA) Daily News*, March 31, 1982.

"**'Keeping Nancy Drew Alive'**": Sara Paretsky, "Keeping Nancy Drew Alive," introduction to the facsimile edition of Carolyn Keene, *The Secret of the Old Clock* (Bedford, MA: Applewood Books, 1992).

"**'I Owe It All to Nancy Drew'**": Nancy Pickard, "I Owe It All to Nancy Drew," introduction to the facsimile edition of Carolyn Keene, *The Hidden Staircase* (Bedford, MA: Applewood Books, 1991).

"**Novelist Bobbie Ann Mason**": Bobbie Ann Mason, *The Girl Sleuth: On the Trail of Nancy Drew, Judy Bolton, and Cherry Ames* (Athens: University of Georgia Press, 1995), p. x.

"**Writing in the *New York Times***": Maureen Dowd, "Our New No-Can-Do Nation," *New York Times*, April 11, 2004.

"**At odds with**": Mildred Benson, "The Nancy I Knew," introduction to the facsimile edition of Carolyn Keene, *The Mystery at Lilac Inn* (Bedford, MA: Applewood Books, 1994) (hereafter cited as *Lilac Inn* intro).

"A tangle of white curls": Christopher Borrelli, "The Storied Life of Millie Benson," *Ohio* magazine, December/January 1991, p. 62.

"As a 9-year-old": Fredda Sacharow, "When Nancy Drew's Mother Revealed the Secret of Cooking Up a Mystery Plot," *New York Times*, April 11, 1982.

CHAPTER ONE: THE STRATEMEYER CLAN

"These suggestions are for": Edward Stratemeyer to Grosset & Dunlap, September 20, 1929, Stratemeyer Syndicate Records, 1832–1984, New York Public Library, box 320 (hereafter cited as SSR/NYPL).

"'Victor Horton's Idea'": *Golden Days*, November 2–9, 16–23, 30, 1889, SSR/NYPL, box 310.

"A scholarly appearance": "Mr. Stratemeyer, a Writer for Boys," *Newark Sunday News*, March 9, 1902.

"A tranquil-faced man": "Newarker Whose Name Is Best Known," *Newark Sunday Call*, December 19, 1917 (hereafter cited as "Newarker Whose Name...").

"His initial long story": "Newarker Who Writes for Most Critical of All Readers Has Far Exceeded Standard His Mother Set," *Newark Evening News*, June 4, 1927 (hereafter cited as "Newarker Who Writes...").

"I think you would become": *Golden Days* to Edward Stratemeyer, January 29, 1889, cited in Trudi Johanna Abel, "A Man of Letters; a Man of Business. Edward Stratemeyer and the Adolescent Reader: 1880–1930" (Ph.D. diss., Rutgers University, 1993), p. 29 (hereafter cited as Abel).

"Wholesale and retail": Abel, p. 18.

"You ask when": Edward Stratemeyer to Richard A. Bird, September 15, 1919, SSR/NYPL, box 24.

"Two chapbooks": These were shown to me by James Keeline, who has copies in his private collection in San Diego, CA.

"I had quite a library": "Newarker Who Writes..."

"Only 1 percent": Nancy Woloch, "Women's Education," *Houghton Mifflin Reader's Companion to American History* (New York: Houghton Mifflin, 1991), p. 326.

"He continued to combine": James D. Keeline, "Edward Stratemeyer, Author and Literary Agent, 1876–1906" (paper presented at the annual meeting of the Popular Culture Association, San Diego, CA, 1999).

"No sermonizing": Selma G. Lanes, "Who Killed St. Nicholas," *Down the Rabbit Hole* (New York: Atheneum Books, 1976), p. 18.

"Mark Twain, Rudyard Kipling": Nancy Milford, *Savage Beauty: The Life of Edna St. Vincent Millay* (New York: Random House, 2001), p. 7.

"The gap between": Frank Luther Mott, *A History of American Magazines*, 5 vols. (Cambridge, MA: Harvard University Press, 1930–86), cited in Deidre Johnson, *Edward Stratemeyer and the Stratemeyer Syndicate*, Twayne's United States Authors Series, ed. Ruth MacDonald (New York: Twayne's Publishers, 1993), p. 34 (hereafter cited as Johnson).

"M is for millions": "Newarker Who Writes..."

"By 1926": Arthur Prager, "Edward Stratemeyer and His Book Machine," *Saturday Review*, July 10, 1971.

"As one hometown": "Newarker Who Writes…"

"The only great act": Cynthia Adams Lum, "Nancy Drew's Mother" (paper presented at the Nancy Drew Sleuths conference, New York, NY, May 3, 2003) (hereafter cited as Adams Lum).

"The best wife": Adams Lum.

"Mrs. S has read": Edward Stratemeyer to Evelyn Raymond, November 17, 1906, SSR/NYPL, box 20.

"Altogether too much": Street & Smith to Edward Stratemeyer, March 15, 1890, cited in Abel, p. 39.

"As one dazzled reporter": Edward Bok, "Literary Factories," *Publishers Weekly*, August 13, 1892, cited in Abel, pp. 41–42.

"In 1890 roughly 60 percent": Karen Manners Smith, "New Paths to Power: 1890–1920," in *No Small Courage: A History of Women in the United States*, ed. Nancy F. Cott (New York: Oxford University Press, 2000), p. 359 (hereafter cited as Manners Smith).

"A brand new": Edward T. LeBlanc, *Street & Smith Dime Novel Bibliography Part I: Black and White Era 1889–1897* (privately published, n.d.), p. 85, cited in Abel, p. 43.

"The 'Literary Account Book of Edward Stratemeyer'": SSR/NYPL, box 317 (hereafter cited as Literary Account Book).

"This week, I sold a book": Adams Lum.

"I grew up in a story-book house": *The Secret of Nancy Drew*, 16mm, 32 min., Protean Productions, Inc., New York, 1982 (hereafter cited as *Secret of Nancy Drew*).

"My recollection of him as a child": Harriet Adams interview by Richard Gallagher, East Orange, NJ, January 23, 1973.

"I was fortunate": Brenda Woods, "Goody Goody Gumshoe," *New York Daily News*, May 13, 1980.

"I am afraid I shall have to": Edward Stratemeyer to J. F. Flood, 1907 (letter is incorrectly dated 2/46/07), SSR/NYPL, box 20.

"Don't take the heart out of a fellow": Edward Stratemeyer to W. F. Gregory, December 29, 1906, SSR/NYPL, box 20.

"The Newark neighborhood of Roseville": "Roseville Days—A View of Newark Boyhood in 1888, by One of the Boys," *Proceedings of the New Jersey Historical Society*, vol. XII (Newark: New Jersey Historical Society, 1927), pp. 445–51 (hereafter cited as "Roseville Days").

"The city had been purchased": Edward S. Rankin, "The Purchase of Newark from the Indians," *Proceedings of the New Jersey Historical Society*, vol. XII (Newark: New Jersey Historical Society, 1927), pp. 442–45.

"By 1897": John T. Cunningham, *Newark* (Newark: New Jersey Historical Society, 1966), p. 201.

"Streets had been cut through/the pleasure of city": "Roseville Days."

"**Games and recreation/Rare was the girl**": Victoria Bissell Brown, "Golden Girls: Female Socialization Among the Middle Class of Los Angeles," in *Small Worlds: Children and Adolescents in America, 1850–1950*, ed. Elliott West and Paula Petrik (Lawrence: University Press of Kansas, 1992), p. 244 (hereafter cited as Bissell Brown).

"**After the age of thirteen**": Anna Kohler Barnes, "Children's Ideas of Lady and Gentleman," *Studies in Education* 2 (June 1, 1902), p. 147, cited in Bissell Brown, p. 253.

"**The best one-handed fence vaulter**": Carlette Winslow, "Alias Carolyn Keene," *Suburban Life*, February 1968.

"**The inculcation of respect**": Bissell Brown, p. 233.

"**Among the boys**": Karen DeWitt, "The Case of the Hidden Author," *Newsday*, August 8, 1977 (hereafter cited as DeWitt).

"**When her grandmother gave her the gift**": Adams Lum.

"**Born without a middle name**": song lyrics from Harriet Adams's eighty-third birthday party, December 1975, SSR/NYPL, box 50.

"**She was enamored**": Susan Sherman Fadiman, "The Mystery of Carolyn Keene," *St. Louis Globe Democrat*, December 21–22, 1974.

"**What I would like to have been**": Linda Abrahams, "Mystery Writing a Family Tradition," *South Middlesex (NJ) Sunday News*, March 12, 1978.

"**A couple of hours**": DeWitt.

"**One day in second grade**": Harriet Adams, notes for luncheon speech delivered at the Wellesley Club, May 10, 1973, Stratemeyer Syndicate Papers, Beinecke Rare Book and Manuscript Library, Yale University, box 8 (hereafter cited as SSP/Beinecke).

"**The author had hoped**": Edward Stratemeyer, preface to the revised edition of *Richard Dare's Venture; or, Striking Out for Himself* (Boston: Lee & Shepard, 1902), p. iv.

"**Difficult task**": "Newarker Whose Name…"

"**But the depression of the 1890s**": Douglas Steeples and David O. Whitten, *Democracy in Desperation: The Depression of 1893* (Westport, CT: Greenwood Press, 1998), p. 50.

"**Of all the deadly schemes**": Frank A. Munsey, *The Story of the Founding and Development of the Munsey Publishing-House* (New York: Devine Press, 1901), pp. 21–22, cited in Abel, p. 84.

"**An enterprising man**": Ralph D. Gardner, *Horatio Alger; or, The American Hero Era* (Mendota, IL: Wayside Press, 1964), p. 292, cited in Richard Gallagher, "Edward Stratemeyer: A Study in Cultural History," spring 1974, Western Connecticut State College, p. 1 (unpublished).

"**An experiment**": Abel, p. 102.

"**The people do not seem**": Mershon Company to Edward Stratemeyer, April 10, 1898, cited in Abel, p. 107.

"**Lost overboard while on a trip**": Edward Stratemeyer to Lee & Shepard, June 13, 1898, cited in Abel, p. 108.

"**Almost before the smoke of battle**": Ayers Brinser, "For It Was Indeed He," *Fortune*, April 1934, p. 206 (hereafter cited as "For It Was Indeed He").

"The Rover Boys broke out": "For It Was Indeed He," p. 208.

"Motivations were of the essence": "He Invented the Rover Boys," *Christian Science Monitor*, December 5, 1942, p. 19 (hereafter cited as "He Invented...")

"Were never embarrassed": "He Invented...," p. 7.

"Although many of the incidents": Edward Stratemeyer to Luther Danner, February 2, 1917, SSR/NYPL, box 24.

"Mr. Stratemeyer thoroughly deserves": Waldo G. Browne, "Sketches of Writers, XVII—Edward Stratemeyer," *Writer*, March 1902, p. 41.

"Nan was a tall and slender girl": Laura Lee Hope, *The Bobbsey Twins; or, Merry Days Indoors and Out* (New York: Grosset & Dunlap, 1904), p. 2.

"Almost as many girls write to me": Edward Stratemeyer to Rowland Stalter, April 2, 1906, SSR/NYPL, box 20.

"The little girl begins": "Newarker Whose Name..."

"I have two little girls": Edward Stratemeyer to Grace LeBaron Upham, September 23, 1901, cited in Abel, p. 257.

"The plots and outlines": "Newark Author Great Favorite with Young Folks, Talk of Stories for Boys," *Newark Sunday News*, June 16, 1903, cited in Johnson, p. 6.

"A book brought out": Edward Stratemeyer to W. L. Alison Co., October 12, 1898, SSR/NYPL, box 20.

"Neck deep": Edward Stratemeyer to James Logan, February 28, 1905, SSR/NYPL, box 20.

"All right, title and interest": Stratemeyer Syndicate Books author release form, 8/29/1930, SSP/Beinecke, box 1.

"In 1905, the first year of its existence": Literary Account Book.

"The syndicate idea is booming": Edward Stratemeyer to Mershon & Co., March 21, 1905, SSR/NYPL, box 20.

"The father of": "For It Was Indeed He," p. 87.

"Did you ever use": Edward Stratemeyer to Weldon Cobb, September 15, 1906, SSR/NYPL, box 20.

"A sunshiny room": Harriet Adams to Frederick Chase, September 26, 1941, SSR/NYPL, box 29.

"The exciting stories": Bissell Brown, p. 253.

"He thought I should": DeWitt.

"As a result": Adams Lum.

"At the turn of the century": Gail Collins, *America's Women: 400 Years of Dolls, Drudges, Helpmates, and Heroines* (New York: William Morrow, 2003), p. 259 (hereafter cited as Collins); Manners Smith, p. 360.

"The average marriage age": "Estimated Median Age at First Marriage, by Sex, 1890–present" (U.S. Bureau of the Census, 2004), p. 2.

"A strong religious undercurrent": "College Set on Many Hills," *New York Sun*, February 26, 1911.

"$175 annual tuition": *Wellesley College Calendar, 1910–1911*, Wellesley College Archives, Wellesley College, p. 145 (hereafter cited as WCA).

"In addition to making a flurry": Edward Stratemeyer to Ellen Fitz Pendleton, June 7, 1910, SSR/NYPL, box 21.

"Like any teenager": Edward Stratemeyer to Mrs. H. B. Lawrence, May 1910, SSR/NYPL box 21.

"A 'combination' course": Edward Stratemeyer to Jonathan Meeker, September 3, 1909, SSR/NYPL, box 21.

"Appears to like the school": Edward Stratemeyer to Jonathan Meeker, October 19, 1909, SSR/NYPL, box 21.

"Yesterday Mrs. S and myself": Edward Stratemeyer to Jonathan Meeker, October 27, 1909, SSR/NYPL, box 21.

"Why is Nancy Drew so good": Margo Miller, "Nancy Drew Follows the Wellesley Motto," *Boston Globe*, March 4, 1978.

CHAPTER TWO: MILDRED

"A most extensive": "Dr. J. L. Augustine Dies at His Home," *Williamsburg (IA) Shopper*, November 11, 1937.

"The little town of Ladora": "The First 100 Years, Being a Historical Outline of the First Century of Ladora, Iowa," published by the Ladora Centennial Committee, August 17, 1968.

"Though some mistook it": "Music Teacher Names Ladora from Music Syllable," *Marengo (IA) Pioneer Republican*, October 1, 1931.

"My mother was quite": Mildred Benson interview by Sally Vallongo, May 8–10, 2001, Toledo, OH (hereafter cited as Vallongo).

"Into a traditional person": Mildred Benson press conference, University of Iowa Nancy Drew Conference, Iowa City, IA, April 17, 1993.

"A center for rather/typically American": "A Very Brief History of the Chautauqua Movement," Colorado Chautauqua Association, www.chautauqua.com/aboutus_ movement.html (hereafter cited as CCA).

"Chautauqua functioned for many": CCA.

"Instead of presenting her": Melanie Rehak interview with Kay Morgan, Ladora, IA, August 26, 2003.

"There was an awful lot of work": Vallongo.

"Ladora Presbyterian Ladies' Aid Society": *Favorite Quotations* (Ladora, IA: Ladora Presbyterian Ladies' Aid Society, 1902), Iowa Genealogical Society, Marengo, IA.

"In the spring": Mildred Benson, "Simple Grand: Not Just Anybody Can Be a Grandparent," *Toledo Blade*, September 6, 1991.

"Watched the firey beast": Mildred Benson, "Comet Sighting Still Memorable After 75 Years," *Toledo Blade*, December 20, 1985.

"I had an affair": Vallongo.

"Coming upon a shelf": *Lilac Inn* intro.

"I read everything": Vallongo.

"I craved to read/a single glass case": *Lilac Inn* intro.

"[They] weren't very readable/according to their rules/We had a hut": Vallongo.

324 NOTES

"In general, I preferred": *Lilac Inn* intro.

"She was always trying": Vallongo.

"I...wanted": John Seewer, "Nancy Drew Author Still Working at 96," *Worcester (MA) Telegram & Gazette*, January 3, 2002.

"My mother always encouraged me": Vallongo.

"The page announcing": *St. Nicholas* XLVI, no. 8 (June 1919), p. 756.

"'The Courtesy'": Mildred Augustine, "The Courtesy," *St. Nicholas* XLVI, no. 8 (June 1919), p. 762.

"Her first big sale": *Lilac Inn* intro.

"Like her creator": Mildred Augustine, "The Cross of Valor," *St. Nicholas* LIII, no. 8 (June 1926), pp. 797–833.

"Luck was it": Mildred Augustine, "Wishbone Luck," *Youth's Comrade* 13, no. 52 (December 29, 1923), pp. 6–7.

"Code of a 'Good Sport'/You have a rather/A child born on this day": memory book of Mildred Augustine, 1922–1928, Mildred Augustine Wirt Benson Papers, 1915–1994, Iowa Women's Archives, University of Iowa, box 2 (hereafter cited as MAWB/IWA).

"Senior activities were dismal/a fantastic document/I tried to speak": Mildred Benson, "Latest Graduation Gets a Top Grade," *Toledo Blade*, May 15, 1999.

"Their numbers had doubled": Sarah Jane Deutsch, "From Ballots to Breadlines: 1920–1940," in *No Small Courage: A History of Women in the United States*, ed. Nancy F. Cott (New York: Oxford University Press, 2000), p. 429 (hereafter cited as Deutsch).

CHAPTER THREE: ALMA MATER

"The Higher Education of Women": Katherine C. Balderston, *Wellesley College, 1875–1975: A Century of Women*, gen. ed. Jean Glasscock (Wellesley, MA: Wellesley College, 1975), p. 1 (hereafter cited as Balderston).

"Woman's brain was too delicate": Balderston, p. 8.

"Robert Hallowell Richards": diary of Robert Hallowell Richards, May 1873, Robert Hallowell Richards Papers, Institute Archives and Special Collections, MIT Libraries, Cambridge, MA, collection MC116.

"The so-called learned professions": Helen Lefkowitz Horowitz, "The Great Debate on the Education of Women: President Eliot of Harvard and President Thomas of Bryn Mawr" (paper presented at the "Gender at the Gates: New Perspectives on Harvard and Radcliffe History" conference at Harvard and Radcliffe, Cambridge, MA, November 1998).

"Wellesley did not": Wellesley College, *President's Report*, 1912, p. 9, WCA.

"Nearly a third": Collins, p. 292.

"Thought that homemaking was too complex": Manners Smith, p. 365.

"314 students were admitted": Balderston, p. 14.

"I am glad to report": Edward Stratemeyer to W. F. Gregory, September 29, 1910, SSR/NYPL, box 21.

"In the new code of laws": L. H. Butterfield, Marc Friedlander, and Mary-Jo Kline, eds., *The Book of Abigail and John: Selected Letters of the Adams Family, 1762–1784* (Cambridge, MA: Harvard University Press, 1975), pp. 121–22.

"By 1848": S. B. Anthony, M. J. Gage, and E. C. Stanton, eds., *History of Woman Suffrage*, vol. 1 (New York: Fowler & Wells, 1881), p. 67.

"We will remain out of the union": Collins, p. 235.

"But this initial burst": Much of the information in this chapter and in this section, while not quoted directly, is taken from Nancy F. Cott, ed., *No Small Courage: A History of Women in the United States* (New York: Oxford University Press, 2000).

"Harriet May Mills": Select Committee on Woman Suffrage, Hearing on the Joint Resolution Proposing an Amendment to the Constitution of the United States Extending the Right of Suffrage to Women, February 18, 1902 (Washington, DC: Government Printing Office, 1902).

"I ask you to consider": "Inauguration of President Pendleton at Wellesley," *Boston Evening Transcript*, October 19, 1911, WCA.

"Lack of knowledge": "Results of the Suffrage Vote," *Wellesley College News*, February 15, 1911, WCA.

"But by 1912": Balderston, p. 412.

"White buckskin golf shoes": Alice Payne Hackett, *Wellesley: Part of the American Story* (New York: E. P. Dutton, 1949), pp. 192–93 (hereafter cited as Hackett).

"Can you dance the Boston": "Modern Dancing," *Wellesley College News*, November 27, 1913, WCA.

"Be alive, be awake": "Editorial," *Wellesley College News*, October 5, 1910, WCA.

"They were not allowed to go": *Official Circular of Information: For the Use of Students, 1910–1911* (Wellesley, MA: Wellesley College, 1910), WCA.

"The precincts of any men's": *Official Circular of Information: For the Use of Students, 1911–1912* (Wellesley, MA: Wellesley College, 1911), p. 7, WCA.

"Standing about": *Student's Handbook*, presented by the Christian Association, 1910–1911 (Wellesley, MA: Wellesley Christian Association, 1910), p. 51, WCA (hereafter cited as *Student's Handbook*).

"An activity referred to": *Student's Handbook*, p. 196.

"To Boston, where": *Student's Handbook*, pp. 193–96.

"One day to Boston I did go": "On the Sights of Boston," *Wellesley College News*, December 18, 1913, WCA.

"The department of Hygiene": *Wellesley College Annual Reports, President and Treasurer, 1910* (Wellesley, MA: Wellesley College, 1910), p. 9, WCA.

"If one strips each of the great religions": Harriet Adams, notes for luncheon speech delivered at the Wellesley Club, May 10, 1973, SSP/Beinecke, box 8.

"An average student": Sidney Fields, "What Ever Happened to...?" *New York Daily News*, April 4, 1968.

"In any non-military country": "The Fifth Woman-Suffrage State," *Wellesley College News*, November 30, 1910, WCA.

"Let us...be glad for them": "Suffragists!" *Wellesley College News*, March 29, 1912, WCA.

"Are you a suffragette": Edna Stratemeyer to Harriet Stratemeyer, n.d. (spring 1913), private collection of Cynthia Adams Lum.

"**Scheduled to arrive**": Much of the information in this section comes from Sheridan
 Harvey, "Marching for the Vote: Remembering the Woman Suffrage Parade of
 1913," adapted from *American Women: A Library of Congress Guide for the Study of
 Women's History and Culture in the United States* (Washington, DC: Library of Congress, 2001) (hereafter cited as Harvey).

"**Next Wednesday morning**": Edna Stratemeyer to Harriet Stratemeyer, n.d., private
 collection of Cynthia Adams Lum.

"**Those ideals toward which**": Official program of the Woman March for Suffrage, pp.
 14, 16, cited in Harvey.

"**Suffragists are**": Nellie Bly, "Suffragists Are Men's Superiors," *New York Evening Journal*, March 3, 1913, cited in Harvey.

"**Where are your skirts**": Harvey.

"**There would be nothing like this**": Harvey.

"**As for Wilson**": Officers of the National Woman Suffrage Association to the Honorable Woodrow Wilson, February 12, 1913, National Woman's Party Records, Group
 I, box 2, cited in Harvey.

"**As it was at all**": "The Wellesley College Press Board," *Wellesley College News*, April
 17, 1913, WCA (hereafter cited as "Press Board").

"**The disconnected work**": "Press Board."

"**Wellesley girl who ran**": "Press Board."

"**When her first payment**": Adams Lum.

"**At that time Wellesley**": The whole anecdote about the photographers is taken from
 Harriet Adams, notes for luncheon speech delivered at the Wellesley Club, May 10,
 1973, SSP/Beinecke, box 8.

"**Don't kiss each other**": "New List of Don'ts for Wellesley Girls," *Boston World*, n.d.,
 scrapbook of Helene Fischer/Class of 1914 Collection, WCA.

"**On Sundays**": *Official Circular of Information, 1912–1913* (Wellesley, MA: Wellesley College, 1912), WCA.

"**Tomorrow night is the Glee Club Concert**": Mary Rosa to her mother, February 6,
 1913, Mary Rosa Papers, Correspondence 1912–1913/Class of 1914 Collection, WCA.

"**Preventive of the 'turkey trot'**": "Wellesley Girls Decree That All Dancers Must Keep
 3 Inches Apart," *New York Herald*, n.d., Clippings on Wellesley, 1890–1919, WCA.

"**Young men who call on**": "Beaux Must Go to Church," *Boston World*, n.d., scrapbook of Helene Fischer/Class of 1914 Collection, WCA.

"**In the earliest hours**": Much of the account of the Wellesley fire of 1914 comes from
 Hackett, pp. 167–81.

"**What few words can picture**": Hackett, p. 169.

"**Miss Harriet Stratemeyer**": *Newark Evening News*, March 18, 1914.

"**No one thought of Self**": *Wellesley College Bulletin Annual Reports, President and
 Treasurer 1913–1914* (Wellesley, MA: Wellesley College, 1915), p. 16, WCA.

"**One cheery soul**": Adams Lum.

"**Attired in costumes**": "Tells of Dash from Wellesley Flames," *New York Herald*,
 March 17, 1914.

"This heroine": "Girls Flee $1,500,000 Wellesley Fire," *Boston Traveler and Evening Herald*, March 17, 1914, College Hall Fire Collection, WCA.

"Not one girl": Adams Lum.

"Some style to Billie": unknown to Harriet Stratemeyer, March 23, 1914, private collection of Cynthia Adams Lum.

"Edward gave": Edward Stratemeyer to Dorothy Clark, April 3, 1914, SSR/NYPL, box 23.

"Whoever you inherited": Magdalene Stratemeyer to Harriet Stratemeyer, May 15, 1914, private collection of Cynthia Adams Lum.

"Commencement week": *Wellesley College Bulletin Annual Reports, Dean, 1913–1914* (Wellesley, MA: Wellesley College, 1915), p. 22, WCA.

"I am just back from Wellesley": Edward Stratemeyer to F. S. Grow, June 22, 1914, SSR/NYPL, box 23.

"Everything in Newark is War": Edward Stratemeyer to Will Vroom, August 7, 1914, SSR/NYPL, box 23.

"He felt that as long as": *Secret of Nancy Drew*.

"Instead, written at the top": *Secret of Nancy Drew*.

"On another": Sandy Rovner, "Growing Up with Sensible Nancy," *Washington Post*, March 30, 1982.

"On the 20th, my older daughter": Edward Stratemeyer to St. George Rathbone, October 11, 1915, SSR/NYPL, box 23.

"An elaborate dress": "Adams-Stratemeyer," unnamed newspaper clipping, October 20, 1915, Harriet Stratemeyer Adams Collection, WCA.

CHAPTER FOUR: HAWKEYE DAYS

"Frosh Women": All headlines from the *Daily Iowan*, fall 1922, memory book of Mildred Augustine, 1922–1928, MAWB/IWA, box 2.

"Perhaps the most prominent": *Hawkeye*, 1924, University Archives, University of Iowa, p. 259 (hereafter cited as UA/UI).

"The feature event": "Hawkeye Swimmers Give Exhibitions at the Big Dipper," *Daily Iowan*, n.d., memory book of Mildred Augustine, 1922–1928, MAWB/IWA, box 2.

"Swimsuits themselves/Ederle": Collins, pp. 345–46.

"The University of Iowa": Much of the information about U of I in this chapter comes from the *University of Iowa Handbook*, vol. XXXIII, 1922–1923, UA/UI.

"Above all in the 1920s": Deutsch, p. 413.

"Women who were daring": Collins, p. 300.

"At one point during the fighting": Manners Smith, pp. 406–7.

"In New York, where many women": Deutsch, pp. 416–17.

"Margaret Sanger": Manners Smith, pp. 402–3.

"What was the point": Collins, p. 312.

"I always voted": Vallongo.

"Popular magazines": Deutsch, pp. 419–20.

"**Modern new Currier Hall**": Florence Livingston Joy, "In and Around and About Currier Hall," *Iowa Alumnus* XI, no. 6 (March 1914), pp. 10–12, UA/UI.

"**Today's woman gets what she wants**": Collins, p. 335.

"**I see in your books**": Edward Stratemeyer to Howard Garis, April 17, 1919, SSR/NYPL, box 24.

"**The president of Mount Holyoke College**": "Young People Less Superficial Than Twenty Years Ago," n.d., *Daily Iowan*, memory book of Helen Andrews Brown, Helen Andrews Brown Papers, 1924–1927, IWA, box 1.

"**The National Woman's Party**": Deutsch, p. 422.

"**In a *Harper's Magazine* article**": Deutsch, p. 424.

"**An impudent**": Vallongo.

"**Hawkeyes Beat Yale**": This and all other *Daily Iowan* quotes in this section are from the memory book of Mildred Augustine, 1922–1928, MAWB/IWA, box 2.

"**Athena Literary Society**": Mildred Chant, "History of the Literary Societies of the State University of Iowa" (Ph.D diss., University of Iowa, 1944), p. 144, UA/UI.

"**I always had one or two**": Vallongo.

"**Among the offerings**": *State University of Iowa News Letter* 3, no. 57 (December 19, 1918), p. 2, UA/UI.

"**We Never Sleep**": *Iowa Journalist*, February 1926, p. 16, UA/UI.

"**The most gory**": Mildred Benson press conference, University of Iowa Nancy Drew Conference, Iowa City, IA, April 17, 1993.

"**Our Sardines**": unsigned editorial, "Our Sardines," n.d., *Daily Iowan*, MAWB/IWA, box 2.

"**Faults in Expression**": *Iowa Journalist*, October 1925, p. 13, UA/UI.

"**Advice to the Young Reporter**": *Iowa Journalist*, July 1925, pp. 10–11, UA/UI.

"'**Wanted—An Idea**'": Mildred Augustine, "Wanted—An Idea," *Youth's Companion* 20, no. 23 (June 9, 1923).

"**I think you need**": Vallongo.

"**Echoed the enormously**": Deutsch, pp. 435–36.

"**I enjoin**": Arthur F. Allen, "On the Need of Being Exact," *Iowa Journalist*, September 1925, p. 1, UA/UI.

"**I came from the town of**": Mildred Benson press conference, University of Iowa Nancy Drew Conference, Iowa City, IA, April 17, 1993.

"**The Stratemeyer Syndicate**": advertisement in the *Editor*, April 10, 1926, SSR/NYPL, box 15.

CHAPTER FIVE: NELL CODY, HELEN HALE, DIANA DARE

"**I wish it understood**": Edward Stratemeyer to John Rhidabeck, April 19, 1914, SSR/NYPL, box 23.

"**This is my machine**": All excerpts from the Motor Girls in this section come from Margaret Penrose, *The Motor Girls; or, A Mystery of the Road* (New York: Cupples & Leon, 1910).

"Forty-six new girls' series": Carol Billman, *The Secret of the Stratemeyer Syndicate: Nancy Drew, the Hardy Boys and the Million Dollar Fiction Factory* (New York: Ungar, 1986), p. 57 (hereafter cited as Billman).

"Comes of my ignorance": Edward Stratemeyer to Gabrielle Jackson, October 26, 1906, SSR/NYPL, box 20.

"Among other things, we want": Edward Stratemeyer to Gabrielle Jackson, October 18, 1906, SSR/NYPL, box 20.

"Dorothy Dale": Margaret Penrose, *Dorothy Dale, a Girl of Today* (New York: Cupples & Leon, 1908), p. 3.

"I have too much good sense": Margaret Penrose, *Dorothy Dale's Engagement* (New York: Cupples & Leon, 1917), p. 161.

"Must appeal to children": Harriet Stratemeyer Adams, "Hint on Procedure for Writing Children's Books," n.d., Harriet Stratemeyer Adams file, Class of 1914 Collection, WCA.

"To get good books written for girls": Edward Stratemeyer, advertising copy, n.d. (early 1900s), SSR/NYPL, box 329.

"I have never permitted a murder": Edward Stratemeyer to Lillian Garis, November 7, 1911, SSR/NYPL, box 21.

"It is the Century of the Child": Ernestine Evans, "Trends in Children's Books," *New Republic*, November 10, 1926.

"By 1927 nearly two-thirds": Collins, p. 335.

"One middle-class woman": Deutsch, p. 138.

"A large part of this": For much of the information in this section, I am indebted to Paul Deane, *Mirrors of American Culture: Children's Fiction Series in the Twentieth Century* (Metuchen, NJ: Scarecrow Press, 1991); and Cornelia Meigs et al., eds., *A Critical History of Children's Literature* (New York: Macmillan, 1953).

"A well-known child psychologist": G. Stanley Hall, "What Children Do Read and What They Ought to Read," cited in Gwen Athene Tarbox, *The Clubwomen's Daughters: Collectivist Impulses in Progressive Era Girls' Fiction, 1890–1940* (New York: Garland, 2000), p. 46 (hereafter cited as Tarbox).

"Much of the contempt for": Walter Taylor Field, *The Guide to Literature for Children, 1915* (Boston: Ginn and Company, 1928), cited in Tarbox, p. 46.

"127,000": A Virtual Boy Scout Museum, www.boyscoutstuff.com.

"'Blowing Out the Boys' Brains'": Franklin K. Mathiews, "Blowing Out the Boys' Brains," *Outlook*, November 16, 1914.

"Personally, it does not matter much to me": Edward Stratemeyer to chairman, Book Committee, Newark Public Library, November 11, 1901, cited in Abel, p. 294.

"Maybe I'll scare her into something": Edward Stratemeyer to Magdalene Stratemeyer, May 16, 1921, cited in Abel, p. 295.

"Indeed, the following year": Tarbox, p. 45.

"He has probably influenced": Corey Ford, "The Father of the Rover Boys," *Reader's Digest*, May 1928, p. 58.

"Boys had paper routes": David Nasaw, "Children and Commercial Culture," in *Small Worlds: Children and Adolescents in America, 1850–1950*, ed. Elliott West and Paula Petrik (Lawrence: University Press of Kansas, 1992), p. 18.

"The names and Addresses": "Best Books for Boys and Girls," Cupples & Leon catalog, 1923, private collection of Geoffrey S. Lapin.

"Too busy shooting marbles/an insidious narcotic": "For It Was Indeed He," pp. 89, 193.

"No matter where you are": Bobby Miles to Stratemeyer Syndicate, n.d., SSR/NYPL, box 56.

"If I had enough money": Maurice Brasel to Stratemeyer Syndicate, March 29, 1933, SSR/NYPL, box 56.

"During adolescence": Leslie McFarlane, *Ghost of the Hardy Boys* (New York: Methuen/Two Continents, 1976), p. 13 (hereafter cited as *GHB*).

"Write a mystery about": unknown to Stratemeyer Syndicate, n.d., SSR/NYPL, box 56.

"You will perhaps be interested": Edward Stratemeyer to Cupples & Leon, May 14, 1926, SSR/NYPL, box 26.

"Dear Sirs": Mildred Augustine to Stratemeyer Syndicate, April 17, 1926, SSR/NYPL, box 14.

"I have looked over these stories": Edward Stratemeyer to Mildred Augustine, May 10, 1926, SSR/NYPL, box 26.

"A bitter rival": Edward Stratemeyer, advertising matter for *Ruth Fielding and Her Great Scenario; or, Striving for the Motion Picture Prize*, February 16, 1927, SSR/NYPL, box 258.

"Through all her": All excerpts from *Ruth Fielding and Her Great Scenario* in this section come from Alice B. Emerson, *Ruth Fielding and Her Great Scenario; or, Striving for the Motion Picture Prize* (New York: Cupples & Leon, 1927).

"Many Americans had begun to fear": This quote, plus much of the other information in this paragraph, comes from Deutsch, pp. 428, 435–36, 438, 453.

"What do the neighbors think": Deutsch, p. 438.

"The number of women who never/Most college women": Deutsch, p. 439.

"Vassar College": Deutsch, p. 441.

"Can the devoted wife and mother": *Ladies' Home Journal*, March 1929, p. 247.

"What had looked": Deutsch, pp. 441, 447.

"Fought her on": Mildred Wirt Benson, "The Ghost of Ladora," *Books at Iowa* 19, November 1973.

"Dear Mr. Stratemeyer": Mildred Augustine to Edward Stratemeyer, October 6, 1926, SSR/NYPL, box 14.

"I think you can": Edward Stratemeyer to Mildred Augustine, September 29, 1926, SSR/NYPL, box 26.

"Two brothers of high school age": *GHB*, p. 62.

"As McFarlane later joked": introduction to *GHB*.

"By mid-1929": Marvin Heiferman and Carole Kismaric, *The Mysterious Case of*

Nancy Drew and The Hardy Boys (New York: Simon & Schuster, 1998), p. 20 (here-after cited as Heiferman/Kismaric).

"For this series I have in mind": Edward Stratemeyer to Barse & Hopkins, June 27, 1927, SSR/NYPL, box 27.

CHAPTER SIX: NANCY DREW LAND

"Stratemeyer thought her accomplishment": Edward Stratemeyer to Mildred Augustine, June 8, 1927, SSR/NYPL, box 27.

"Attempt[ing] to improve": Mildred Augustine to Edward Stratemeyer, June 6, 1927, SSR/NYPL, box 27.

"A few months ago": Mildred Wirt to Edward Stratemeyer, May 16, 1928, SSR/NYPL, box 117.

"As perhaps you know": Edward Stratemeyer to L. F. Reed, July 19, 1929, SSR/NYPL, box 27.

"Suggestions for a new series of girls books": Edward Stratemeyer to Grosset & Dunlap, September 20, 1929, SSR/NYPL, box 320.

"If the titles are acceptable": L. F. Reed to Edward Stratemeyer, September 26, 1929, SSR/NYPL, box 27.

"I have just succeeded": Edward Stratemeyer to Mildred Wirt, September 29, 1929, SSR/NYPL, box 27.

"I trust that you will give": Edward Stratemeyer to Mildred Wirt, October 3, 1929, SSR/NYPL, box 27.

"Between 1929 and 1933": Collins, p. 313.

"Ten million women": Eunice Fuller Barnard, "And After All, It Is Still a Man's World," *New York Times*, November 23, 1930.

"Seven out of ten": R. L. Duffus, "Women Who Work Increase in Numbers and Influence," *New York Times*, September 14, 1930.

"From 1930 to 1940": Deutsch, p. 453.

"I know now": Deutsch, p. 454.

"A party frock": All excerpts from *The Secret of the Old Clock* in this section come from Carolyn Keene, *The Secret of the Old Clock* (New York: Grosset & Dunlap, 1930).

"Even as Eleanor Roosevelt": Collins, p. 359.

"Dear Mrs. Wirt": Edward Stratemeyer to Mildred Wirt, December 11, 1929, SSR/NYPL, box 27.

"At the end of *The Bungalow Mystery*": Carolyn Keene, *The Bungalow Mystery* (New York: Grosset & Dunlap, 1930), pp. 137, 204.

"Selling like hot cakes": Henry Altemus to Harriet Adams, March 21, 1931, SSR/NYPL, box 17.

"We expect to publish a few juveniles": Laura Harris to Harriet Adams, May 8, 1931, SSR/NYPL, box 18.

"By Christmas of 1933": "For It Was Indeed He," p. 88.

"Dear Miss Stratemeyer": Harriet Otis Smith to Edna Stratemeyer, January 28, 1930, SSR/NYPL, box 28.

"This is all Dad has to say": Edna Stratemeyer to Harriet Otis Smith, January 27, 1930, SSR/NYPL, box 17.

"It is a question": Harriet Otis Smith to Henry Altemus Jr., May 8, 1930, SSR/NYPL, box 28.

"Your Husband and Father": George Sully to Magdalene Stratemeyer and daughters, May 25, 1930, cited in Abel, p. 296.

"Now Mr. Stratemeyer": "Passing of an Epoch," *New York Times*, May 13, 1930.

"He was the 'grand old man'": Alexander Grosset to Magdalene Stratemeyer, May 14, 1930, cited in Abel, p. 297.

"Although I had never met him": Leslie McFarlane to Harriet Otis Smith, May 15, 1930, SSR/NYPL, box 28.

"Dear Miss Smith": Mildred Wirt to Harriet Otis Smith, May 15, 1930, SSR/NYPL, box 17.

"Edward had made provisions in his will": Last Will and Testament of Edward Stratemeyer, February 19, 1920, private collection of Geoffrey S. Lapin.

"His one complaint": Edna Squier to Harriet Adams, November 6, 1961, SSR/NYPL, box 46.

CHAPTER SEVEN: SYNDICATE FOR SALE

"Author, Juvenile": advertisement in *Publishers Weekly*, July 5, 1930.

"I never dreamed": Edna Stratemeyer to Harriet Otis Smith, May 16, 1930, SSR/NYPL, box 46.

"Mr. Stratemeyer was far too kind": Harriet Otis Smith to Edna Stratemeyer, May 16, 1930, SSR/NYPL, box 28.

"If these publishers suddenly lose": Harriet Otis Smith to August M. Hoch, June 14, 1930, SSR/NYPL, box 28.

"My dear Miss Smith": Harriet Adams to Harriet Otis Smith, May 18, 1930, SSR/NYPL, box 17.

"Were it not for": "The Rover Boys Carry On," *East Orange (NJ) Record*, June 1939.

"The only person": Harriet Otis Smith to Edna Stratemeyer, July 11, 1930, SSR/NYPL, box 28.

"If you are interested": Harriet Otis Smith to Wallace Palmer, May 20, 1930, SSR/NYPL, box 28.

"I think he is just/If the books do not get under way": Harriet Otis Smith to Harriet Adams and Edna Stratemeyer, June 21, 1930, SSR/NYPL, box 28.

"The manuscript of 'The Mystery at Lilac Inn'": Harriet Otis Smith to Mildred Wirt, June 3, 1930, SSR/NYPL, box 28.

"My sister stopped by": Edna Stratemeyer to Harriet Otis Smith, June 4, 1930, SSR/NYPL, box 28.

"I really think that Mrs. Adams": Harriet Otis Smith to Edna Stratemeyer, June 16, 1930, SSR/NYPL, box 28.

"Before Mr. Stratemeyer's death": Harriet Otis Smith to Mildred Wirt, July 7, 1930, SSR/NYPL, box 28.

"They had wisely removed": Melanie Rehak interview with Rebekah Scott, Toledo, OH, June 10, 2003.

"A thrilling tale": Harriet Otis Smith to Edna Stratemeyer, July 11, 1930, SSR/NYPL, box 28.

"The books on the way": Edna Stratemeyer to Harriet Otis Smith, July 10, 1930, SSR/NYPL, box 28.

"Loved by me": *Lilac Inn* intro.

"My sister keeps me informed": Edna Stratemeyer to Harriet Otis Smith, June 13, 1930, SSR/NYPL, box 28.

"Personally I am very anxious": Edna Stratemeyer to Harriet Otis Smith, June 26, 1930, SSR/NYPL, box 46.

"In spite of ourselves": Edna Stratemeyer to Harriet Otis Smith, July 19, 1930, SSR/NYPL, box 46.

"Your sister went home armed": Harriet Otis Smith to Edna Stratemeyer, July 25, 1930, SSR/NYPL, box 28.

"A better idea": Edna Stratemeyer to Harriet Otis Smith, July 24, 1930, SSR/NYPL, box 46.

"Perhaps my sister has been": Edna Stratemeyer to Harriet Otis Smith, July 19, 1930, SSR/NYPL, box 46.

"I was 38": Dorothy H. Kelso, "Puzzle Solved," *Quincy (MA) Patriot Ledger*, March 8, 1978.

"More youthful": Edna Stratemeyer to Mildred Wirt, November 10, 1930, SSR/NYPL, box 28.

"While working on the mystery": Harriet Adams to Laura Harris, September 26, 1930, SSR/NYPL, box 28.

"We would advise": Harriet Adams to Mildred Wirt, September 26, 1930, SSR/NYPL, box 28.

"Satisfactorily": Harriet Adams to Barse & Co., August 29, 1930, SSR/NYPL, box 28.

"My dear Robert": Harriet Adams to Robert (no last name), October 14, 1930, SSR/NYPL, box 28.

"As you will see": Harriet Adams to Harriet Otis Smith, November 1, 1930, SSR/NYPL, box 28.

"I am sure you will be surprised": Edna Stratemeyer to unknown friend, August 15, 1932, SSR/NYPL, box 239.

"Getting courage": Linda Abrahams, "Mystery Writing a Family Tradition," *South Middlesex (NJ) Sunday News*, March 12, 1978.

CHAPTER EIGHT: AN UNFORTUNATE BREAK;
OR, THE CLEVELAND WRITER COMES INTO HER OWN

"It splattered": Mildred Benson, "More about Nancy," introduction to the facsimile edition of Carolyn Keene, *The Secret at Shadow Ranch* (Bedford, MA: Applewood Books, 1994) (hereafter cited as *Shadow Ranch* intro).

"An enticing invitation": All excerpts from *The Secret at Shadow Ranch* in this section come from Carolyn Keene, *The Secret at Shadow Ranch* (New York: Grosset & Dunlap, 1931).

"At the time": *Shadow Ranch* intro.

" 'Chats with Cleveland Writers' ": Ida M. Gurwell, "Chats with Cleveland Writers: Mildred Augustine Wirt," *Cleveland Plain Dealer*, n.d. (1931).

"The work for our syndicate": Edward Stratemeyer to Frank Hopley, August 1, 1929, SSR/NYPL, box 27.

"We have had an extremely busy year": Harriet Adams to Harriet Otis Smith, June 12, 1931, SSR/NYPL, box 28.

"Today it looked like Christmas": Harriet Adams to Edna Stratemeyer, May 5, 1931, SSR/NYPL, box 28.

"Was not surprised": Edna Stratemeyer to Harriet Adams, n.d. (July 1931), SSR/NYPL, box 46.

"Other high-lights": Harriet Adams to Edna Stratemeyer, n.d (July 1931), SSR/NYPL, box 46.

"We all dropped a penny": Edna Stratemeyer to Harriet Adams, n.d. (July 1931), SSR/NYPL, box 46.

"Dear Pardner": Agnes Pearson and Edna Stratemeyer to Harriet Adams, June 24, 1931, SSR/NYPL, box 28.

"Dear Miss Stratemeyer": Mildred Wirt to Edna Stratemeyer, May 11, 1931, SSR/NYPL, box 17.

"Dear Edna: Before I shut up shop": Harriet Adams to Edna Stratemeyer, May 15, 1931, SSR/NYPL, box 28.

"Well, we got to be": Edna Stratemeyer to Harriet Adams, May 15, 1931, SSR/NYPL, box 28.

"We are sorry that": Harriet Adams to Mildred Wirt, May 18, 1931, SSR/NYPL, box 28.

"Because of this": Harriet Adams to Mildred Wirt, September 10, 1931, SSR/NYPL, box 28.

"I...am sorry to learn": Mildred Wirt to Harriet Adams, September 14, 1931, SSR/NYPL, box 44.

"My books averaged about": Elizabeth Ward to Edna Stratemeyer, August 23, 1931, SSR/NYPL, box 17.

"I am sorry that I cannot": J. W. Duffield to Harriet Adams, August 12, 1931, SSR/NYPL, box 18.

"I realize what difficult times": Mildred Wirt to Harriet Adams, September 21, 1931, SSR/NYPL, box 17.

"Resume of the Management of Monies": memo from Edna Stratemeyer to Harriet Adams, n.d. (July 1931), SSR/NYPL, box 46.

"Dear Hat": Edna Stratemeyer to Harriet Adams, n.d. (September 1931), SSR/NYPL, box 17.

"You will notice": Harriet Adams to Walter Karig, October 1, 1931, SSR/NYPL, box 28.

"My dear Mrs. Wirt": Harriet Adams to Mildred Wirt, September 28, 1931, SSR/NYPL, box 28.

"Some places where": Harriet Adams to Walter Karig, October 29, 1931, SSR/NYPL, box 28.

"In any crowd": All excerpts from *The Clue in the Diary* in this section come from Carolyn Keene, *The Clue in the Diary* (New York: Grosset & Dunlap, 1932).

"Sales are not": Laura Harris to Harriet Adams, April 20, 1932, SSR/NYPL, box 18.

"One of the first hard facts": Edna Yost, "The Fifty-Cent Juveniles," *Publishers Weekly*, June 18, 1932.

"They have commissioned": Edna Yost to Harriet Adams, January 11, 1933, SSR/NYPL, box 17.

"Portraying the lives": Harriet Adams to Edna Yost, January 13, 1933, SSR/NYPL, box 28.

"Fan mail is indeed": Harriet Adams to Arthur Leon, April 18, 1932, SSR/NYPL, box 28.

"Another phrase": Harriet Adams to Laura Harris, January 13, 1933, SSR/NYPL, box 28.

"We have talked": Harriet Adams to Laura Harris, November 11, 1931, SSR/NYPL, box 28.

"In regard to": Harriet Adams to Henry Altemus, March 30, 1921, SSR/NYPL, box 28.

"We are wondering": Harriet Adams to Edna Stratemeyer, July 5, 1932, SSR/NYPL, box 28.

"Tomorrow I have": Harriet Adams to Edna Stratemeyer, September 7, 1933, SSR/NYPL, box 28.

"I am sorry I could not/However, I am": Harriet Adams to Laura Harris, September 7, 1933, SSR/NYPL, box 28.

"When I took over the Syndicate": *Secret of Nancy Drew*.

"I enjoyed my": Harriet Adams to Laura Harris, April 24, 1933, SSR/NYPL, box 28.

"This year, like every other writer": Leslie McFarlane to Edna Stratemeyer, June 18, 1932, SSR/NYPL, box 16.

"We have heard so much": Harriet Adams to J. W. Duffield, May 11, 1933, SSR/NYPL, box 28.

"Our price for": Edna Stratemeyer to Mildred Wirt, July 28, 1932, SSR/NYPL, box 28.

"In regard to writing": Mildred Wirt to Edna Stratemeyer, August 2, 1932, SSR/NYPL, box 17.

"From talking with": Harriet Adams to Arthur Leon, July 28, 1932, SSR/NYPL, box 28.

"Nancy Drew and the Hardy Boys": *GHB*, p. 198.

"Certain facts": Harriet Adams to *Publishers Weekly*, May 26, 1933, SSR/NYPL, box 28.

"My dear Mrs. Adams": Frederic G. Melcher to Harriet Adams, June 2, 1933, SSR/NYPL, box 16.

"Enclosed also is": Harriet Adams to Laura Harris, June 30, 1933, SSR/NYPL, box 28.

"We have received": Edna Stratemeyer to Grosset & Dunlap, July 20, 1933, SSR/NYPL, box 28.

"Your mildly implied": Walter Karig to Harriet Adams, September 21, 1931, SSR/NYPL, box 16.

"We wonder": Edna Stratemeyer to Mildred Wirt, March 24, 1934, SSR/NYPL, box 29.

"I have always been": Mildred Wirt to Edna Stratemeyer, March 26, 1934, SSR/NYPL, box 44.

CHAPTER NINE: MOTHERHOOD AND NANCY DREW

"'I'm Ned Nickerson'": All excerpts from *The Clue in the Diary* in this section come from Carolyn Keene, *The Clue in the Diary* (New York: Grosset & Dunlap, 1932).

"He does not appear": Edna Stratemeyer to Mildred Wirt, April 2, 1934, SSR/NYPL, box 29.

"Boys' books in which": Ayers Brinser to Harriet Adams, November 15, 1933, SSR/NYPL, box 18.

"It has few literary/the Stratemeyer daughters": "For It Was Indeed He," pp. 86, 87, 88, 204.

"The cat is out of the bag": Lucy M. Kinloch, "The Menace of the Series Book," *Elementary English Review* 12 (January 1935), pp. 10–11.

"The picture should have had": Harriet Adams to Laura Harris Grabbe, May 15, 1934, SSR/NYPL, box 29.

"Among the changes": Edna Stratemeyer to Mildred Wirt, April 28, 1934, SSR/NYPL, box 29.

"I am sorry you did not like": Mildred Wirt to Edna Stratemeyer, April 30, 1934, SSR/NYPL, box 18.

"We have tried to equalize/There is so much": Harriet Adams to Mildred Wirt, December 10, 1935, SSR/NYPL, box 29.

"I do think": Mildred Wirt to Harriet Adams, January 16, 1936, SSR/NYPL, box 44.

"My conference with": Harriet Adams to Edna Stratemeyer, September 17, 1934, SSR/NYPL, box 29.

"Yesterday Russell and I": Harriet Adams to Edna Stratemeyer, May 14, 1934, SRR/NYPL, box 29.

"Mrs. Adams and I": Edna Stratemeyer to Harriet Otis Smith, June 5, 1935, SSR/NYPL, box 29.

"Dear Miss Stratemeyer": Mildred Wirt to Edna Stratemeyer, June 15, 1935, SSR/NYPL, box 44.

"Fortune is publishing": Harriet Adams to Helen L. Mansfield, February 20, 1934, Harriet Stratemeyer Adams/Class of 1914 Collection, WCA.

"As soon as the children": Harriet Adams to "Rig," September 10, 1934, SSR/NYPL, box 29.

"Rai! Rai!/[The check] went out": Harriet Adams to Edna Stratemeyer, June 15, 1936, SSR/NYPL, box 19.

"Neatly dressed": All excerpts from *The Mystery of the Ivory Charm* in this section come from Carolyn Keene, *The Mystery of the Ivory Charm* (New York: Grosset & Dunlap, 1936).

"We have found": Edna Stratemeyer to Mildred Wirt, February 20, 1936, SSR/NYPL, box 44.

"Our only criticism": Edna Stratemeyer to Mildred Wirt, November 16, 1937, SSR/NYPL, box 30.

"The writing is well done": Harriet Adams to Mildred Wirt, May 25, 1938, SSR/NYPL, box 30.

"Enclosed is the outline": Harriet Adams to Mildred Wirt, June 10, 1938, SSR/NYPL, box 30.

"It never occurred to me": Mildred Wirt to Edna Stratemeyer, February 26, 1936, SSR/NYPL, box 44.

"I am just completing": Mildred Wirt to Edna Stratemeyer, January 10, 1937, SSR/NYPL, box 44.

"We hope you will": Edna Stratemeyer to Mildred Wirt, January 21, 1937, SSR/NYPL, box 44.

"The new baby's": Mildred Wirt to Edna Stratemeyer, January 23, 1937, SSR/NYPL, box 44.

"I am pleased to note": Mildred Wirt to Edna Stratemeyer, April 5, 1937, SSR/NYPL, box 44.

"Our vacation this year": Mildred Wirt to Edna Stratemeyer, October 18, 1937, SSR/NYPL, box 44.

"We are well settled": Mildred Wirt to Edna Stratemeyer, October 21, 1938, SSR/NYPL, box 44.

"At best...smoky": Mildred Wirt to Edna Stratemeyer, April 24, 1939, SSR/NYPL, box 44.

"Your son": Harriet Adams to Elizabeth Ward, September 8, 1936, SSR/NYPL, box 29.

"I must tell you/News from our house": Harriet Adams to Edna Stratemeyer, June 10, 1936, SSR/NYPL, box 19.

"We feel we should": Harriet Adams to Thomas Mitchell, January 18, 1939, SSR/NYPL, box 29.

"One agent": series of letters from Sarah Rollins to Harriet Adams, December 1938, SSR/NYPL, box 19.

"Advertisers would pay": Henry H. Hoople to Harriet Adams, July 29, 1941, SSR/NYPL, box 41.

"Your letter of": Harriet Adams to Jane Gavere, January 17, 1936, SSR/NYPL, box 19.

"How many times": Harriet Adams to Mildred Benson, May 23, 1950, SSR/NYPL, box 33.

"The matter now": Harriet Adams to Mary E. Black, May 4, 1939, SSR/NYPL, box 29.

"My lovely baby girl": Edna Squier to Grace North-Monfort, November 1, 1938, SSR/NYPL, box 29.

"The two sisters": "The Rover Boys Carry On," *East Orange (NJ) Record*, June 1939.

"Dear Patsy": Harriet Adams to Patricia Adams, July 18, 1939, SSR/NYPL, box 29.

"Dear Carolin Keene": Virginia Cook to Carolyn Keene, February 15, 1938, SSR/NYPL, box 19.

"For $6,000": Heiferman/Kismaric, p. 102.

"I think every intelligent woman": *Nancy Drew: Detective*, 66 mins., Warner Brothers, Hollywood, CA, 1938.

"The publicity for the films": All excerpts from publicity for Nancy Drew films in the section come from assorted publicity materials for *Nancy Drew: Detective*, 1938, SSR/NYPL, box 243.

"At the end of the movie": Elaine Tyler May, "Pushing the Limits: 1940–1961," in *No Small Courage: A History of Women in the United States*, ed. Nancy F. Cott (New York: Oxford University Press, 2000), p. 475 (hereafter cited as Tyler May).

"I enjoyed having you": Harriet Adams to Mildred Wirt, September 20, 1938, SSR/NYPL, box 30.

"I enjoyed my little chat with you": Mildred Wirt to Harriet Adams, September 22, 1938, SSR/NYPL, box 44.

"I am glad that you": Harriet Adams to Mildred Wirt, August 3, 1939, SSR/NYPL, box 30.

"Occasional holiday nights": "Nancy Drew: Reporter," *Variety*, March 1, 1939, p. 15.

"Yarn so implausible": "Nancy Drew: Detective," *Variety*, December 7, 1938, p. 12.

"Plot is so shaky": "Nancy Drew and the Hidden Staircase," *Variety*, November 8, 1939, p. 14.

"By the end of 1940": Harriet Adams to Henry H. Hoople, n.d. (1941), SSR/NYPL, box 239.

"Nancy Drew...has caused publishers": "The Rover Boys Carry On," *East Orange (NJ) Record*, June 1939.

CHAPTER TEN: "THEY ARE NANCY"

"When you receive": Harriet Adams to Mildred Wirt, October 6, 1939, SSR/NYPL, box 30.

"And while I am": Conrad Black, *Franklin Delano Roosevelt: Champion of Freedom* (New York: Public Affairs, 2003), p. 595.

"In a fireside chat": Mitchell, *The Complete Idiot's Guide to World War II* (Indianapolis, IN: Alpha Books, 2001), p. 100 (hereafter cited as Bard).

"In just one week": Bard, p. 97.

"Patriotic discomfort": Harriet Adams to Elizabeth Ward, December 12, 1941, SSR/NYPL, box 29.

"These are stirring times": Harriet Adams to Elizabeth Ward, December 17, 1941, SSR/NYPL, box 19.

"Wouldn't it be nice": Harriet Adams to Elizabeth Ward, January 24, 1941, SSR/NYPL, box 29.

"We are trying to play": Harriet Adams to Leslie McFarlane, March 9, 1943, SSR/NYPL, box 30.

"The average person": Bard, p. 167.

"In Norway": Hugh Juergens to Harriet Adams, January 8, 1947, SSR/NYPL, box 39.

"As you no doubt know": Harriet Adams to Mildred Wirt, May 31, 1944, SSR/NYPL, box 30.

"Be able to": Harriet Adams to Mildred Wirt, July 7, 1941, SSR/NYPL, box 30.

"Few books of that era": Geoffrey S. Lapin, "The Ghost of Nancy Drew," *Books at Iowa* 50 (April 1989).

"Until then, only about 5 percent": National Archives and Records Administration, "16th Amendment: U.S. Federal Income Tax" (Washington, DC: National Archives Trust Fund Board, 1995).

"Even the Syndicate": Harriet Adams to Edna Squier, September 1, 1942, SSR/NYPL, box 29.

"Our office has been closed": Edna Squier to Charles B. Fleming, January 19, 1942, SSR/NYPL, box 29.

"I appreciate very much": Harriet Adams to J. W. Duffield, July 3, 1942, SSR/NYPL, box 29.

"In commenting on": Harriet Adams to Mildred Wirt, December 8, 1942, SSR/NYPL, box 29.

"I had to write all the time": Vallongo.

"Thank you for getting": Harriet Adams to Mildred Wirt, September 2, 1942, SSR/NYPL, box 30.

"Two subjects": Harriet Adams to Mildred Wirt, April 8, 1943, SSR/NYPL, box 30.

"Romance has never been": Mildred Wirt to Harriet Adams, June 9, 1943, SSR/NYPL, box 44.

"We are somewhat disappointed": Harriet Adams to Mildred Wirt, May 28, 1943, SSR/NYPL, box 30.

"Maybe Ned has asked": All excerpts from *The Secret in the Old Attic* in this section come from Carolyn Keene, *The Secret in the Old Attic* (New York: Grosset & Dunlap, 1944).

"I believe we actually": Edna Squier to Harriet Adams, March 4, 1944, SSR/NYPL, box 46.

"I promised to tell you": Harriet Adams to Leslie McFarlane, March 31, 1944, SSR/NYPL, box 30.

"At all times": Authors Guild to Carolyn Keene, February 9, 1942, SSR/NYPL, box 19.

"We very much want": Calling All Girls to Carolyn Keene, January 23, 1942, SSR/NYPL, box 33.

"A poll of the magazine's readers": *Calling All Girls*, September 1942, SSR/NYPL, box 33.

"I did do": Marie Hammond to Harriet Adams, n.d. (January 1944), SSR/NYPL, box 19.

"As one girl": William M. Tuttle Jr., "The Homefront Children's Popular Culture," in *Small Worlds: Children and Adolescents in America, 1850–1950*, ed. Elliott West and Paula Petrik (Lawrence: University Press of Kansas, 1992), p. 242.

"In 1942": Bard, pp. 102–4.

"Over the course of the war": Collins, p. 383.

"At one point during the war/the Office of War Information": Tyler May, p. 476.

"At times it gets": Tyler May, pp. 477–79.

"'Once Wrote for Children'": Beatrice Borman, "Once Wrote for Children, Now Writes for Times," *Inside the Blade*, November 1944, p. 11.

"Taking a new position": Mildred Wirt to Harriet Adams, July 18, 1944, SSR/NYPL, box 44.

"Women made up": Susan M. Hartmann, *The Home Front and Beyond: American Women in the 1940s* (Boston: Twayne, 1982), p. 21.

"1000 Women's Airforce Service Pilots": Tyler May, p. 486.

"Too bad about": Edna Squier to Harriet Adams, July 30, 1944, SSR/NYPL, box 46.

"It was during the war": Mark Zaborney, "Thanks for the 50 Years, Millie," *Toledo Blade*, September 17, 1994.

"Alma goes to work": Tyler May, pp. 489–90.

"The war in general": Tyler May, pp. 484–85.

"I could always": Mark Zaborney, "Thanks for the 50 Years, Millie," *Toledo Blade*, September 17, 1994.

"Working the night shift": Vallongo.

"'City's Shops'": Mildred Wirt, "City's Shops on Verge of Bare Cases," *Toledo Times*, April 19, 1945.

"'Egg Black Market'": Mildred Wirt, "Egg Black Market Switch Reported," *Toledo Times*, April 24, 1945.

"The washing machines": Mildred Wirt, "Short of Hosiery and Housing, G.I. Brides Learn U.S. Ways," *Toledo Times*, March 21, 1946.

"I lived in": Mildred Wirt, "War-Torn Repatriate Families to 'Celebrate' Christmas Here," *Toledo Times*, n.d. (December 1946).

"I was a tired writer": Sally Vallongo, "Thoroughly Marvelous Millie," *Toledo Blade*, December 23, 2001.

"The salary is so excellent/I do feel": Mildred Wirt to Harriet Adams, October 15, 1944, SSR/NYPL, box 44.

"A synopsis": Harriet Adams to Mildred Wirt, October 13, 1944, SSR/NYPL, box 30.

"Mrs. Wirt certainly is": Edna Squier to Harriet Adams, October 23, 1944, SSR/NYPL, box 46.

"I think our plan": Harriet Adams to Mildred Wirt, December 5, 1944, SSR/NYPL box 30.

"A convincing/Before getting off the subject": Harriet Adams to Edna Squier, March 22, 1945, SSR/NYPL, box 46.

"Two hundred ninety-five thousand": Bard, p. 362.

"During the past": Mildred Wirt to Harriet Adams, September 8, 1945, private collection of Geoffrey S. Lapin.

"The MS": author unknown, memo, n.d. (July 1946), SSR/NYPL, box 46.

"Nancy does not seem": Harriet Adams to Mildred Wirt, July 18, 1946, SSR/NYPL, box 30.

"Right now we are": Harriet Adams to Edna Squier, July 18, 1946, SSR/NYPL, box 29.

"Drop her from the S.S.": Edna Squier to Harriet Adams, July 22, 1946, SSR/NYPL, box 46.

"Recently I have reflected": Harriet Adams to Gordon Allison, May 15, 1947, SSR/NYPL, box 33.

"I was rather amazed": Harriet Adams to Edna Squier, January 6, 1947, SSR/NYPL, box 29.

"Actually, the picture": Harriet Adams to Edna Squier, June 30, 1947, SSR/NYPL, box 46.

"On the day that": Mildred Wirt to Harriet Adams, June 9, 1947, SSR/NYPL, box 44.

"It was with surprise": Harriet Adams to Mildred Wirt, June 18, 1947, SSR/NYPL, box 30.

"You will notice": Harriet Adams to Mildred Wirt, July 30, 1947, SSR/NYPL, box 30.

"All one can do": Mildred Wirt to Harriet Adams, June 22, 1947, SSR/NYPL, box 44.

CHAPTER ELEVEN: THE KIDS ARE HEP

"We feel here": Hugh Juergens to Harriet Adams, February 28, 1944, SSR/NYPL, box 39.

"The ultimate symbol": Tyler May, p. 492.

"In 1946": Collins, p. 394.

"Writing in the *Atlantic Monthly*": Tyler May, pp. 492–93.

"And though 1947": Tyler May, p. 493.

"By the middle/they were afraid": Betty Friedan, *The Feminine Mystique* (1963; repr., New York: W. W. Norton, 2001), p. 16.

"She can be independent": Sara M. Evans, *Born for Liberty: A History of Women in America* (New York: Free Press, 1989), p. 261.

"We married what": Tyler May, pp. 496–97.

"Rosie the Riveter": Collins, p. 397.

"According to one study": Tyler May, p. 518.

"The tail is now": "Children Want Realism in Books, Authors Guild Told," *Publishers Weekly*, October 29, 1949, p. 1895.

"With life going along": Harriet Adams to Edna Squier, October 4, 1946, SSR/NYPL, box 29.

"I have had a feeling": Harriet Adams to Hugh Juergens, February 12, 1948, SSR/NYPL, box 39.

"Carry on your negotiations": Hugh Juergens to Harriet Adams, February 3, 1948, SSR/NYPL, box 39.

"No prospective": Harriet Adams to Edna Squier, November 17, 1948, SSR/NYPL, box 46.

"Interested in the church": Harriet Adams to Edna Squier, March 31, 1948, SSR/NYPL, box 46.

"Mr. Svenson plans": Harriet Adams to Edna Squier, April 20, 1948, SSR/NYPL, box 46.

"My long period of good health": Harriet Adams to Edna Squier, June 5, 1949, SSR/NYPL, box 46.

"I believe he eventually": Harriet Adams to Edna Squier, April 26, 1949, SSR/NYPL, box 46.

" 'Author of Children's Books' ": Ira Brock, "Author of Children's Book Works Out Endings First; Finds System Pays Off," *Toledo Blade*, August 8, 1949.

"The only confidential": Harriet Adams to Edna Squier, April 30, 1948, SSR/NYPL, box 46.

"Generally writers, eager for": Hannibal Towle, "The League for the Preservation of Prose," n.d. or newspaper name. George Benson file, *Toledo Blade* Library.

"He was a gregarious soul": "George Benson," *Toledo Times*, March 1, 1959.

"The new Dana book": Harriet Adams to Edna Squier, August 10, 1951, SSR/NYPL, box 46.

"Only ten feet": Melanie Rehak telephone interview with Bill Kennedy, August 4, 2003.

"I feel quite stale": Tyler May, p. 503.

"They expect us": Harriet Adams to Edna Squier, February 23, 1950, SSR/NYPL, box 46.

"Last fall": Harriet Adams to Edna Squier, February 7, 1951, SSR/NYPL, box 46.

"The attitude over at G&D": Harriet Adams to Edna Squier, February 28, 1951, SSR/NYPL, box 46.

"We have had so much trouble": Harriet Adams to Edna Squier, September 23, 1952, SSR/NYPL, box 46.

"Apparently you expect": Edna Squier to Harriet Adams, October 1, 1952, SSR/NYPL, box 46.

"Traveled to New York": Mildred Benson to Harriet Adams, March 8, 1952, SSR/NYPL, box 33.

"Reference sheets": n.d. (early 1950s), SSR/NYPL, box 239.

"Whether we do yarns about": "Tom, Jr.," *New Yorker*, March 20, 1954.

"By the end of the decade": Heiferman/Kismaric, p. 84.

"The publication that": Heiferman/Kismaric, p. 109.

"Even the proudest": "The Grinch & Co.," *Time*, December 23, 1957, p. 74.

"Translated and sold overseas": For the information in this section, I am indebted to Lea Shangraw Fox's comprehensive Web site about foreign editions of Nancy Drew, www.nancydrewworld.com.

"I am constantly": Harriet Adams to Edna Squier, October 8, 1957, SSR/NYPL, box 46.

"As I sat there": Hugh Juergens to Harriet Adams and Andrew Svenson, March 10, 1955, SSR/NYPL, box 46.

"Better watch the office": Edna Squier to Harriet Adams, March 7, 1951, SSR/NYPL, box 46.

"In your recent letter": Harriet Adams to Edna Squier, November 28, 1956, SSR/NYPL, box 46.

"Tried to buy her sister out": Stanley L. Gedney Jr. to Edna Squier, July 29, 1957, SSR/NYPL, box 46.

"Offhand I would say": John O'Connor to Harriet Adams, August 26, 1958, SSR/NYPL, box 39.

"The 'here and now'": "Dorothy the Librarian," *Life*, February 16, 1959.

"Very thoroughly, to see": Harriet Adams to Anne Hagan, April 19, 1948, SSR/NYPL, box 37.

"Thank you for your": Harriet Adams to Michael Chanalis, March 4, 1948, SSR/NYPL, box 19.

"The Syndicate is a challenge": Harriet Adams to Edna Squier, April 8, 1957, SSR/NYPL, box 46.

"It had never occurred to me": Jean Diefenbach to Grosset & Dunlap, February 15, 1961, SSR/NYPL, box 37.

"All of a sudden": Harriet Adams to Edna Squier, March 30, 1959, SSR/NYPL, box 46.

"The series will be about": Andrew Svenson to Edna Squier, September 29, 1965, SSR/NYPL, box 49.

"The publisher could find no": Andrew Svenson to Mary Kay Stark, January 14, 1978, SSR/NYPL box 49.

"The prolonged suspense": Heiferman/Kismaric, p. 111.

"The blue convertible": All excerpts from *The Secret of the Old Clock* in this section come from Carolyn Keene, *The Secret of the Old Clock* (New York: Grosset & Dunlap, 1959).

"I think an editor/You say Nancy": Harriet Adams to Anne Hagan, February 15, 1961, SSR/NYPL, box 37.

"We are expanding": Harriet Adams to Jim Lawrence, April 5, 1961, SSR/NYPL, box 41.

"Our company rarely accepts": Harriet Adams to unknown, August 18, 1969, SSR/NYPL, box 32.

"Harriet had her own": Deborah Felder, "Nancy Drew: Then and Now," *Publishers Weekly*, May 30, 1985.

"My idea is to have": Harriet Adams to Anne Hagan, August 11, 1966, SSR/NYPL, box 38.

"I wish you would dress": Harriet Adams to Martha Leder, July 13, 1966, SSR/NYPL, box 38.

"Though it is not": Harriet Adams to Martha Leder, February 17, 1966, SSR/NYPL, box 36.

"I do not like": Harriet Adams to Martha Leder, January 24, 1968, SSR/NYPL, box 36.

"I presently am": Mildred Benson to Frank Paluka, July 7, 1964, MAWB/IWA, box 1.

"Richard and Pat Nixon's visit": Mildred Benson, "Pat Worth Waiting for, Station Crowd Indicates," *Toledo Times*, n.d., memory book of Mildred Augustine, 1922–1928, MAWB/IWA, box 2.

"Radiation shelters": Mildred Benson, "Cooking in a Radiation Shelter Found Easy Once You've Mastered Tricks," *Toledo Times*, September 18, 1961.

"Much of my early work": Mildred Benson to Frank Paluka, July 7, 1964, MAWB/IWA, box 1.

CHAPTER TWELVE: NANCY IN THE AGE OF AQUARIUS

"In 1960": Betty Friedan, *The Feminine Mystique* (1963; repr., New York: W. W. Norton, 2001), pp. 22, 25.

"Though total sales": Manuel Siwek to Harriet Adams (telegram), March 25, 1963, SSR/NYPL, box 40.

"Sales of series in the United States": Manuel Siwek to Harriet Adams, March 23, 1965, SSR/NYPL, box 44.

"The pages of *Mademoiselle*": "The Lives and Times of Nancy Drew," *Mademoiselle*, July 1964, pp. 28–39.

"Again, may I say": Harriet Adams to Leo Lerman, May 12, 1964, and June 30, 1964, SSR/NYPL, box 42.

"It is my hope": "Harriet Stratemeyer (Mrs. Russell V. Adams)," *Wellesley College Record*, 1964.

"That ghostly dancer": All excerpts from *The Clue of the Dancing Puppet* in this section come from Carolyn Keene, *The Clue of the Dancing Puppet* (New York: Grosset & Dunlap, 1962).

"Perfectly ordinary looking": Tyler May, pp. 526–27.

"That same year/first acknowledgment/ardently determined": William H. Chafe, "The Road to Equality: 1962–Today," in *No Small Courage: A History of Women in the United States*, ed. Nancy F. Cott (New York: Oxford University Press, 2000), pp. 526–27, 535–37, 545 (hereafter cited as Chafe).

"In 1963 a poster": Betty Friedan book tour poster, October 29, 1962, reprinted in *No Small Courage: A History of Women in the United States*, ed. Nancy F. Cott (New York: Oxford University Press, 2000), p. 539.

"The percentage of married women": Chafe, p. 534.

"The final ingredient/macho radicalism": Chafe, pp. 551–52.

"Integration, not separation": Chafe, p. 555.

"*off our backs*": September 30, 1970, cover reprinted in *No Small Courage: A History of Women in the United States*, ed. Nancy F. Cott (New York: Oxford University Press, 2000), p. 560.

"When you have to top": Grosset & Dunlap sales flyer, SSR/NYPL, box 39.

"Titian-haired/Remember how": Nancy Moss, "Nancy Drew: Her Popularity with Young Readers Is No Mystery," *Chicago Tribune*, January 23, 1966.

"The dauntless, bewitching": Arthur Prager, "The Secret of Nancy Drew—Pushing Forty and Still Going Strong," *Saturday Review*, January 25, 1969 (hereafter cited as Prager).

"Your inference": Harriet Adams to Anne Hagan, October 19, 1960, SSR/NYPL, box 37.

"Mr. Karig never was": Harriet Adams to Bob Moore, January 7, 1965, SSR/NYPL, box 39.

"Needless to say": Harriet Adams to William Morris, December 8, 1966, SSR/NYPL, box 32.

"I am also enclosing": Harriet Adams to Frieda and Sam Tannenbaum, October 21, 1966, SSR/NYPL, box 33.

"It will give you an idea": Harriet Adams to Betty Marks, December 19, 1966, SSR/NYPL, box 39.

"Decided she was going to": Melanie Rehak interview with Nancy Axelrad, Indianapolis, IN, June 14, 2003.

"'This granny'": "This Granny Masterminds the Thrills and Spills," *Star Johannesburg* (South Africa), July 6, 1968.

"In a piece": Judy Klemesrud, "100 Books—and Not a Hippie in Them," *New York Times*, April 4, 1968.

"He owned": partnership agreement, January 1, 1961, SSP/Beinecke, box 1, folder 9.

"One secretary": Carlette Winslow, "Alias Carolyn Keene," *Suburban Life*, February 1968.

"Most of us have learned to read": Mike McGrady, "The East Orange Gold Mine Mystery," *New York Newsday*, June 29, 1968.

"The Bobbsey Twins in Sexville?": Advertisement for *Billy & Betty*, a novel by Twiggs Jameson, SSR/NYPL, box 43.

"Apparently there is a rock-ribbed": Prager.

"A pilot out barnstorming": Mildred Benson, "First Ride in a Jenny, Led My Way to Flight," *Toledo Blade*, December 30, 1970.

"Touch the throttle": Mildred Benson, "First Solo Flight—It's a Wonderful Feeling," *Toledo Times*, August 29, 1966.

"A three-day dugout canoe": Mildred Benson, "A Woman Dares the Jungle," *Cleveland Plain Dealer*, November 26, 1967.

"The quaint world/Carolyn Keene was alive and well": Geoffrey S. Lapin, "Carolyn Keene, pseud.," *Yellowback Library*, July/August 1983.

"The Artful Ways of Millie": James A. Treloar, "The Artful Ways of Millie," *Detroit News*, August 13, 1971.

"Acrobatic airplane": Mildred Benson, "Test Flight Reveals New Businessman Thrills," *Toledo Times*, June 16, 1969.

"Women these days": Mildred Benson, "Women Don Coveralls, Work on Planes," *Toledo Times*, March 23, 1968.

"Ms., the first national": Information about the creation and history of *Ms.* comes from www.msmagazine.com/about.asp and Chafe.

"By the mid-70s": Chafe, p. 563.

"I believe in freedom": Susan Stamberg interview with Mildred Benson, Weekend Edition, *All Things Considered*, National Public Radio, April 10, 1993.

" 'She's Studying to Be' ": Mildred Benson, "She's Studying to Be Aggressive," *Toledo Times*, July 26, 1969.

"Women of Toledo": Mildred Benson, "Are Toledo Gals Militant?" *Toledo Times*, August 24, 1970.

"For all her nay-saying": Mildred Benson, "Male Psyches Shaken, Millie Reports as She Lands New Broadside," *Toledo Times*, October 28, 1970.

"Are you hurting your daughter": Ann Aliasberg, "Are You Hurting Your Daughter without Knowing It?" *Family Circle*, February 1971.

"Psychologists say that": John T. Cunningham, "Where the Bobbseys Live," *Newark News*, March 23, 1973.

"She's an atypical": Julia Kagan, "Nancy Drew—18 Going on 50," *McCall's*, July 1973.

"Nancy Drew Circle": Caroline Drewes, "The Modern Vibes of Nancy Drew," *San Francisco Sunday Examiner and Chronicle*, February 11, 1973.

"Is it possible": Rose DeWolf, "The REAL Mystery Behind Nancy Drew," *Philadelphia Bulletin Sunday Magazine,* January 13, 1974.

"A DETECTIVE NEEDS ENERGY": Carolyn Keene, *The Nancy Drew Cookbook: Clues to Good Cooking* (New York: Grosset & Dunlap, 1977), p. 18.

"There are some books": Leo McConnell, "Book-Lookin'," n.d. (June or July 1973), newspaper unknown, SSR/NYPL, box 239.

"People are always asking me": Georgia Smith, "For Nancy Drew, Cooking Is No Mystery Now," *New York Daily News,* August 3, 1973.

"A first-person essay": Jane Ginsburg, "And Then There Is Good Old Nancy Drew," *Ms.,* January 1974.

"On cookies": memo from Andrew Svenson to Harriet Adams, November 18, 1970, SSR/NYPL, box 47.

"I think the NANCY DREW COOKBOOK": memo from Eric Svenson to the Stratemeyer Syndicate, April 30, 1973, SSR/NYPL, box 32.

"Every reader": Carolyn Keene, *The Nancy Drew Sleuth Book: Clues to Good Sleuthing* (New York: Grosset & Dunlap, 1979).

CHAPTER THIRTEEN: BECOMING THE GIRL DETECTIVE

"I feel you overstepped": Harriet Adams to Anne Hagan, January 27, 1972, SSR/NYPL, box 38.

"Anne, are your remarks": Harriet Adams to Anne Hagan, September 19, 1973, SSR/NYPL, box 38.

"I must tell you quite frankly": Harriet Adams to Anne Hagan, May 24, 1973, SSR/NYPL, box 38.

"National Lampoon": "The Case of the Missing Heiress," *National Lampoon,* June 1974, p. 66.

"A mock interview with an aged Nancy": Rosalyn Drexler, "The Real Nancy Drew," *New York Times Magazine,* October 19, 1975.

"Belittling and reversing/I did not tell all": "Missing the Mark," Letters, *New York Times Magazine,* November 23, 1975.

"Nobody's sure why/Their impact on me": Dick Pothier, "Nancy Drew Mystery: Her New Popularity," *Philadelphia Inquirer,* September 21, 1975.

"I can foresee": Rose DeWolf, "The REAL Mystery Behind Nancy Drew," *Philadelphia Bulletin Sunday Magazine,* January 13, 1974.

"Janis Ian": Bob Sarlin, "Janis Ian at 24," *Crawdaddy,* February 1976.

"Edna Squier passed away": diary of Harriet Adams, SSP/Beinecke, box 7.

"Harriet bought back": Harriet Adams to Marian Svenson, February 4, 1976, SSR/NYPL, box 72.

"Mrs. Adams originally agreed": Ed Zuckerman, "The Great Hardy Boys Whodunit," *Rolling Stone,* September 9, 1976.

"Two extremely bright": Cecil Smith, "Producers Bank on Mystery Series," *Bradenton (FL) Herald,* March 6, 1977.

"It has taken Nancy Drew": Winifred Elze, "Juvenile Mysteries Are in Vogue," *Newton Kansan*, July 29, 1977.

"For more than 45 years": Mildred Benson to Dixon Dern, November 12, 1975, private collection of Geoffrey S. Lapin.

"Dear Mr. Lapin": Mildred Benson to Geoff Lapin, April 24, 1978, private collection of Geoffrey S. Lapin.

"How could they take": Ruth Danckert, "Nancy TV," *Springfield (MA) Union*, February 23, 1977, SSR/NYPL, box 341.

"Ratings for Pamela Sue Martin's": *Laredo (TX) Citizen*, April 29, 1977, SSR/NYPL, box 341.

"At a younger age": Lana Russ, *Independence (OR) Enterprise-Herald*, April 27, 1977, SSR/NYPL, box 341.

"Pamela Sue Martin": *Modern People*, February 12, 1978, SSR/NYPL, box 349.

"I'm not gearing my career": "Pamela Sue Martin: Why I've Quit Nancy Drew," *National Enquirer*, February 28, 1978.

"In July 1978": "Nancy Drew Grows Up," *Playboy*, July 1978, pp. 86–92, 184.

"Fit to be tied": Melanie Rehak interview with Nancy Axelrad, Indianapolis, IN, June 14, 2003.

"Can the reputation": "Author Protects Nancy Drew: Sleuth Won't Enter the 70s," *Hackensack (NJ) Record*, November 30, 1978, SSR/NYPL, box 353.

"Confessed to having": "She Tells about Her Banning in Boston," *Shrewsbury (NJ) Daily Register*, September 22, 1978, SSR/NYPL, box 356.

CHAPTER FOURTEEN: WILL THE REAL CAROLYN KEENE
PLEASE STAND UP?

"We're extraordinarily happy about": Richard Haitch, "At 83, Her Pen Is Far from Dry," *New York Times*, March 27, 1977. (The *New York Times*, in fact, gave the wrong age for Harriet Adams; by the time of this article she would have been eighty-four.)

"It occurred to me recently": Harriet Adams to Manuel Siwek, June 16, 1969, SSR/NYPL, box 40.

"Harriet just absolutely held out": Melanie Rehak interview with Nancy Axelrad, Indianapolis, IN, June 14, 2003.

"$300 million": *Grosset & Dunlap v. Gulf & Western Corporation and Stratemeyer Syndicate*, 79 Civ 2242/79 Civ 3745 (1980), pre-trial memo, p. 3 (hereafter cited as *G&D v. SS*).

"Said he regretted": "Grosset Sues Simon & Schuster and Stratemeyer for $50 Million," *Publishers Weekly*, May 7, 1979.

"I think in some way": Melanie Rehak interview with Nancy Axelrad, Indianapolis, IN, June 14, 2003.

"In spite of": "Stratemeyer and S&S Call Grosset Suit Frivolous," *Publishers Weekly*, May 14, 1979.

"A model of": Joanne Kaufman, "The Adventures of Harriet Adams," *Good Housekeeping*, May 1980.

"She's read something like": Edward Wakin, "Solving the Nancy Drew Mystery," *American Way*, September 1979.

"I think my father": Jane See White, "Nancy Drew Is 18 Going on 50," *Chicago Tribune*, March 9, 1980.

"Making Nancy a bit more": Elizabeth Bumiller, "Nancy Drew: Squeaky Clean and Still Eighteen," *Washington Post*, April 17, 1980.

"I thought you might be interested": Susan Aukema to Frank Paluka, March 4, 1980, MAWB/IWA, box 1.

"Many thanks": Mildred Benson to Frank Paluka, March 11, 1980, MAWB/IWA, box 1.

"With honored guest": Program for Nancy Drew fiftieth anniversary party, SSR/NYPL, box 63.

"Some terribly serious contemporary writers": All the information on the Nancy Drew fiftieth anniversary party in this section comes from Elizabeth Bumiller, "Nancy Drew: Squeaky Clean and Still Eighteen," *Washington Post*, April 17, 1980.

"I thought you were dead": Geoffrey S. Lapin, "The Ghost of Nancy Drew," *Books at Iowa* 50 (April 1989).

"As you no doubt know": Mildred Benson to Nancy Hall, October 8, 1979, private collection of Geoffrey S. Lapin.

"In the early books": All excerpts from Harriet Adams's testimony come from *G&D v. SS*, pp. 342, 833.

"In the course": All excerpts from Mildred Benson's testimony in this section come from *G&D v. SS*, pp. 111, 176, 177, 189, 193, 225, 232.

"Even if I didn't": Mildred Benson to Geoffrey S. Lapin, October 23, 1980, private collection of Geoffrey S. Lapin.

"Skyrocketing Sales": Simon & Schuster press release, January 29, 1981, SSR/NYPL, box 54.

"On July 31": sales agreement, July 31, 1984, SSP/Beinecke, box 2.

"Juvenile publishing": Simon & Schuster press release, August 2, 1980, SSP/Beinecke, box 2.

"We have to breathe": Anne McGrath, "Eye on Publishing," *Wilson Library Bulletin*, December 1984.

"Nancy Drew will now": Lorelai Starck, "That Daring Detective Nancy Drew," *Milwaukee Reader* 44, no. 34 (August 25, 1986).

"Nancy studied herself": Carolyn Keene, *Secrets Can Kill* (New York: Archway Pocket Books, 1986), pp. 2–3.

"Extrapolated the new": Deborah Felder, "Nancy Drew: Then and Now," *Publishers Weekly*, May 30, 1986.

"All Nancy has to do": Carolyn Keene, *Two Points to Murder* (New York: Archway/Pocket Books, 1987).

"It is the 1980s": Robert Basler, "A New Image for Nancy Drew," *Philadelphia Inquirer*, June 29, 1986.

"We're trying to promote": Deborah Felder, "Nancy Drew: Then and Now," *Publishers Weekly*, May 30, 1986.

"The day the obituary": Jack A. Seamonds, "The Case of Nancy Drew's Creator," *Zanesville (OH) Times Record*, n.d. (May 1982).

"Before Geraldine Ferraro": "The Secret of the Ghost(writer) of Ladora," *Iowa Alumni Review* 38, no. 3 (May/June 1985).

"This should mark the end": Mildred Benson to Frank Paluka, December 14, 1982, MAWB/IWA, box 1.

"It seems to me": "The Secret of the Ghost(writer) of Ladora," *Iowa Alumni Review* 38, no. 3 (May/June 1985).

"If I am not able": Mildred Benson to Geoffrey S. Lapin, n.d. (September 1992), private collection of Geoffrey S. Lapin.

"The Great Purge": Cullen Murphy, "Starting Over," *Atlantic Monthly*, June 1991, pp. 18–21.

"Nancy is no longer": Jackie Vivelo, "The Mystery of Nancy Drew," *Ms.* 3, no. 2 (November/December 1992), p. 76.

"Mildred Wirt Benson": Mona Gable, "'The Real-Life Heroine Who Wrote Nancy Drew," *Los Angeles Times*, August 16, 1991.

"Bemused at this group of grown-ups": Cher Bibler, "Behind Nancy Drew: A Life of Mildred Benson," *Wasteland Review*, February 1993.

"Anything about Nancy Drew": Mildred Benson to Geoffrey S. Lapin, March 13, 1994, private collection of Geoffrey S. Lapin.

"Peter Jennings": *World News Tonight with Peter Jennings*, April 16, 1993.

"'The Crack in the Cannon'": Carolyn Stewart Dyer and Nancy Tillman Romalov, eds., *Rediscovering Nancy Drew* (Iowa City: University of Iowa Press, 1995).

"One woman...said": Jon Anderson, "Drew Still Draws," *Chicago Tribune*, April 26, 1993.

"I think she took": Mildred Benson press conference, University of Iowa Nancy Drew Conference, Iowa City, IA, April 17, 1993.

"Carrying a red leather": Patricia Leigh Brown, "A Ghostwriter and Her Sleuth: 63 Years of Smarts and Gumption," *New York Times*, May 9, 1993.

"Well, I'll see you later": Mike Tressler, "The Secret of the Ageless Scribe," *Editor & Publisher*, June 3, 2002.

"But how can": Carolyn Keene, *The Slumber Party Secret* (New York: Minstrel/Pocket Books, 1994), p. 1.

"It's 65 years later": Simon & Schuster press release, May 1995, SSR/NYPL, box 54.

"The classic Nancy Drew sleuth": The critic is Jennifer Fisher, president of the Nancy Drew Sleuths. Much more about Jenn and Nancy Drew can be found at www.nancydrewsleuth.com.

"You write about": Jim DeRogatis, "Tuscadero Applies Lessons Learned to Songs," *Chicago Sun-Times*, September 22, 1995.

"Like hamburgers": Judy Polumbaum, "The Case of the Girl Detective," *Boston Globe*, June 6, 1993.

"This quality": Reprinted in *Harper's Magazine*, November 1995.

"Nancy Drew, girl sleuth": Jennifer Frey, "A True Woman of Mystery," *Washington Post*, May 30, 2002.

"Nancy Drew demands have about": Mildred Benson to Geoffrey S. Lapin, n.d. (September 1992), private collection of Geoffrey S. Lapin.

"It reached the point": Roberta deBoer, "Millie's Gone, but She Didn't Go Meekly," *Toledo Blade*, May 30, 2002.

"It's hard to accept": Mary McNamara, "An Appreciation: Clued in to a Life of Adventure," *Los Angeles Times*, May 31, 2002.

"Long before Charlie's Angels/the cover design": Simon & Schuster promotional materials, January 2004, collection of the author.

"My friends always tell me": Carolyn Keene, *Without a Trace* (New York: Aladdin Books, 2004), pp. 1, 53.

"In 2002": Gary Strauss, "Nancy Drew Dusts Off 'Musty Appeal' for New Readers," *USA Today*, January 15, 2004.

BIBLIOGRAPHY

Bard, Mitchell G. *The Complete Idiot's Guide to World War II*. Indianapolis, IN: Alpha Books, 2004.

Billman, Carol. *The Secret of the Stratemeyer Syndicate: Nancy Drew, the Hardy Boys and the Million Dollar Fiction Factory*. New York: Ungar, 1986.

Black, Conrad. *Franklin Delano Roosevelt: Champion of Freedom*. New York: Public Affairs, 2003.

Butterfield, L. H., Marc Friedlander, and Mary-Jo Kline, eds. *The Book of Abigail and John: Selected Letters of the Adams Family, 1762–1784*. Cambridge, MA: Harvard University Press, 1975.

Capiro, Betsy. *The Mystery of Nancy Drew: Girl Sleuth on the Couch*. Trabuco Canyon, CA: Source Books, 1992.

Case, Victoria, and Robert Ormond Case. *We Called It Culture: The Story of Chautauqua*. Freeport, NY: Books for Libraries Press, 1948.

Collins, Gail. *America's Women: 400 Years of Dolls, Drudges, Helpmates, and Heroines*. New York: William Morrow, 2003.

Cott, Nancy F., ed. *No Small Courage: A History of Women in the United States*. New York: Oxford University Press, 2000.

Deane, Paul. *Mirrors of American Culture: Children's Fiction Series in the Twentieth Century*. Metuchen, NJ: Scarecrow Press, 1991.

Dyer, Carolyn Stewart, and Nancy Tillman Romalov, eds. *Rediscovering Nancy Drew*. Iowa City: University of Iowa Press, 1995.

Emerson, Alice B. *Ruth Fielding and Her Great Scenario; or, Striving for the Motion Picture Prize*. New York: Cupples & Leon, 1927.

Evans, Sara M. *Born for Liberty: A History of Women in America*. New York: Free Press, 1989.

Fass, Paula, and Mary Ann Mason. *Childhood in America*. New York: New York University Press, 2000.

Foner, Eric and John A. Garraty, eds. *The Reader's Companion to American History*. New York: Houghton Mifflin, 1991.

Friedan, Betty. *The Feminine Mystique*. Introduction by Anna Quindlen. 1963. Reprint, New York: W. W. Norton, 2001.

Garis, Roger. *My Father Was Uncle Wiggily: The Story of the Remarkable Garis Family*. New York: McGraw-Hill, 1966.

Geiger, Roger, ed. *The American College in the Nineteenth Century*. Nashville, TN: Vanderbilt University Press, 2000.

Glasscock, Jean, and Katherine C. Balderston, eds. *Wellesley College, 1875–1975: A Century of Women*. Wellesley, MA: Wellesley College, 1975.

Goddard, Stephen B. *Getting There: The Epic Struggle Between Road and Rail in the American Century*. New York: Basic Books, 1994.

Hackett, Alice Payne. *Wellesley: Part of the American Story*. New York: E. P. Dutton, 1949.

Harrison, John M. *The Blade of Toledo: The First 150 Years*. Toledo, OH: Toledo Blade Co., 1985.

Hartmann, Susan M. *The Home Front and Beyond: American Women in the 1940s*. Boston: Twayne, 1982.

Hawes, Joseph M., and N. Ray Hiner. *American Childhood: A Research Guide and Historical Handbook*. Westport, CT: Greenwood Press, 1985.

Heiferman, Marvin, and Carole Kismaric, *The Mysterious Case of Nancy Drew and the Hardy Boys*. New York: Simon & Schuster, 1998.

Heilbrun, Carolyn G. *Writing a Woman's Life*. New York: Ballantine, 1988.

Hope, Laura Lee. *The Bobbsey Twins; or, Merry Days Indoors and Out*. New York: Grosset & Dunlap, 1904.

Johnson, Deidre. *Edward Stratemeyer and the Stratemeyer Syndicate*. Twayne's United States Authors Series. New York: Twayne, 1993.

Keene, Carolyn. *The Bungalow Mystery*. New York: Grosset & Dunlap, 1930.

———. *The Clue in the Diary*. New York: Grosset & Dunlap, 1932.

———. *The Clue of the Dancing Puppet*. New York: Grosset & Dunlap, 1962.

———. *The Hidden Staircase*. Facsimile edition. Bedford, MA: Applewood Books, 1991.

———. *The Mystery at Lilac Inn*. Facsimile edition. Bedford, MA: Applewood Books, 1994.

———. *The Mystery of the Ivory Charm*. New York: Grosset & Dunlap, 1936.

———. *Mystery of the Tolling Bell*. New York: Grosset & Dunlap, 1976.

———. *The Nancy Drew Cookbook: Clues to Good Cooking*. New York: Grosset & Dunlap, 1977.

———. *The Nancy Drew Sleuth Book: Clues to Good Sleuthing*. New York: Grosset & Dunlap, 1979.

————. *The Secret at Shadow Ranch.* New York: Grosset & Dunlap, 1931.

————. *The Secret at Shadow Ranch.* Facsimile edition. Bedford, MA: Applewood Books, 1994.

————. *The Secret in the Old Attic.* New York: Grosset & Dunlap, 1944.

————. *The Secret of the Old Clock.* New York: Grosset & Dunlap, 1930.

————. *The Secret of the Old Clock.* New York: Grosset & Dunlap, 1959.

————.*The Secret of the Old Clock.* Facsimile edition. Bedford, MA: Applewood Books, 1992.

————. *Secrets Can Kill.* New York: Archway/Pocket Books, 1986.

————. *The Slumber Party Secret.* New York: Minstrel/Pocket Books, 1994.

————. *Two Points to Murder.* New York: Archway/Pocket Books, 1987.

————. *Without a Trace.* New York: Aladdin Books, 2004.

Lanes, Selma G. *Down the Rabbit Hole: Adventures and Misadventures in the Realm of Children's Literature.* New York: Atheneum Books, 1976.

Lurie, Alison. *Boys and Girls Forever: Children's Classics from Cinderella to Harry Potter.* New York: Penguin Books, 2003.

————. *Don't Tell the Grown-Ups: Subversive Children's Literature.* Boston: Little, Brown, 1990.

Marcus, Leonard S., ed. *Dear Genius: The Letters of Ursula Nordstrom.* New York: HarperCollins, 1998.

Mason, Bobbie Ann. *The Girl Sleuth: On the Trail of Nancy Drew, Judy Bolton, and Cherry Ames.* Athens: University of Georgia Press, 1995.

McFarlane, Leslie. *Ghost of the Hardy Boys.* New York: Methuen/Two Continents, 1976.

Meigs, Cornelia, et al., eds. *A Critical History of Children's Literature: A Survey of Children's Books in English from Earliest Times to the Present, Prepared in Four Parts Under the Editorship of Cornelia Meigs.* New York: Macmillan, 1953.

Milford, Nancy. *Savage Beauty: The Life of Edna St. Vincent Millay.* New York: Random House, 2001.

Orchard, Hugh. *Fifty Years of Chautauqua: Its Beginnings, Its Development, Its Message and Its Life.* Cedar Rapids, IA: Torch Press, 1923.

Palladino, Grace. *Teenagers: An American History.* New York: Basic Books, 1996.

Penrose, Margaret. *Dorothy Dale, A Girl of Today.* New York: Cupples & Leon, 1917.

————. *Dorothy Dale's Engagement.* New York: Cupples & Leon, 1917.

————. *The Motor Girls; or, A Mystery of the Road.* New York: Cupples & Leon, 1910.

Penzler, Otto, ed. *The Great Detectives: A Host of the World's Most Celebrated Sleuths Are Unmasked by Their Authors.* Boston: Little, Brown, 1978.

Plunkett-Powell, Karen. *The Nancy Drew Scrapbook: 60 Years of America's Favorite Teenage Sleuth.* New York: St. Martin's Press, 1993.

Prager, Arthur. *Rascals at Large; or, The Clue in the Old Nostalgia.* Garden City, NY: Doubleday, 1971.

Richmond, Rebecca. *Chautauqua: An American Place.* New York: Duell, Sloan and Pearce, 1943.

Rollin, Lucy. *Twentieth-Century Teen Culture by the Decades: A Reference Guide*. Westport, CT: Greenwood Press, 1999.

Rosenthal, Naomi. *Spinster Tales and Womanly Possibilities*. Albany: State University of New York Press, 2002.

Schrum, Kelly. *Some Wore Bobby Sox: The Emergence of Teenage Girls' Culture, 1920–1945*. New York: Palgrave Macmillan, 2004.

Shapiro, Laura. *Something from the Oven: Reinventing Dinner in 1950s America*. New York: Viking, 2004.

Stanton, Elizabeth Cady, et al., eds. *History of Woman Suffrage*. Vol. 1. New York: Fowler & Wells, 1881.

Steeples, Douglas, and David O. Whitten. *Democracy in Desperation: The Depression of 1893*. Westport, CT: Greenwood Press, 1998.

Stratemeyer, Edward. *Richard Dare's Venture; or, Striking Out for Himself*. Boston: Lee & Shepard, 1902.

Tarbox, Gwen Athene. *The Clubwomen's Daughters: Collectivist Impulses in Progressive Era Girls' Fiction, 1890–1940*. New York: Garland, 2000.

West, Elliott, and Paula Petrik, eds. *Small Worlds: Children and Adolescents in America, 1850–1950*. Lawrence: University Press of Kansas, 1992.

Woody, Thomas. *A History of Women's Education in the United States*. Lancaster, PA: Science Press, 1929.

Yellin, Emily. *Our Mothers' War: American Women at Home and at the Front During World War II*. New York: Free Press, 2004.

INDEX